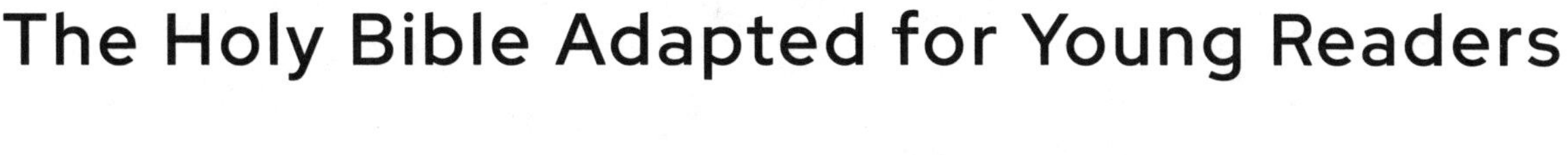

The Holy Bible Adapted for Young Readers

PRESENTED TO

____

FROM

____

ON

____

THE HOLY BIBLE ADAPTED FOR YOUNG READERS

SELECTED AND ARRANGED BY

Elsa Jane Werner and Charles Hartman

The Old Testament illustrated by

Feodor Rojankovsky

The New Testament illustrated by

Alice and Martin Provensen

SOPHIA INSTITUTE PRESS
Manchester, New Hampshire

Cover art created by LUCAS Art & Design from the original interior illustrations.

For the 1960 Edition:
Nihil obstat:
John A. Goodwine, J.C.D.
Censor Librorum

Imprimatur
Francis Cardinal Spellman
Archbishop of New York
March 29, 1960

Sophia Institute Press
Box 5284, Manchester, NH 03108
1-800-888-9344
www.SophiaInstitute.com

Sophia Institute Press is a registered trademark of Sophia Institute.

Hardcover ISBN 979-8-88911-276-1

ebook ISBN 979-8-88911-277-8

Library of Congress Control Number: 2024943831

First printing

THE OLD TESTAMENT

CONTENTS OF THE OLD TESTAMENT

CONTENTS OF THE OLD TESTAMENT

THE CREATION OF THE WORLD

THE FIRST DAY

IN THE beginning God created the heavens and the earth. But the earth was empty, and there was a great darkness everywhere. Then God said, "Let there be light," and there was light. He called the light Day and the darkness Night.

THE SECOND DAY

God said, "Let there be a sky to divide the waters below from the waters above." God made the sky and called it Heaven.

THE THIRD DAY

"Let the waters be gathered together and let dry land appear," said God. And so it was. God called the dry land Earth, and the waters He called Seas.

Then God said, "Let the earth bring forth grass, herbs, and fruit trees." And the earth brought them forth.

THE FOURTH DAY

God said, "Let there be lights in the sky to give light to the earth." He made two great lights, the greater to rule the day, and the lesser to rule the night, and He made the stars also.

THE FIFTH DAY

"Let the waters bring forth living, moving creatures, many of them, and let birds fly in the heavens," said God. Then He created great whales and every living creature of the waters, and every winged bird, and He blessed them all.

THE SIXTH DAY

God said, "Let the earth bring forth living creatures of all kinds, cattle and creeping things and beasts of the earth." He made the beasts of the earth, and the cattle, and everything that creeps upon the earth.

Then God said, "Let Us make man in Our image, and let him have power over the fish of the sea and over the birds of the air, and over the cattle, and over all the earth and everything that creeps upon the earth."

So God created man in His own image; male and female He created. And God blessed them and gave them dominion over the whole world.

Then God looked at everything He had made, and he saw that it was good.

THE SEVENTH DAY

Thus the heavens and the earth were finished and filled with life. And on the seventh day God rested from His work. God blessed the seventh day and made it holy because on that day He had rested.

THE CREATION OF ADAM AND EVE

HE LORD GOD formed man of the dust of the ground and into his nostrils He breathed the breath of life, and man became a living soul.

Then the Lord God planted a garden eastward in Eden, and there He put the man whom He had made. Out of the ground the Lord made to grow every tree that is pleasant to look at and good for food. The tree of life also grew in the midst of the garden, and the tree of knowledge of good and evil.

The Lord took the man, and put him into the garden of Eden to dress it and to keep it. And the Lord God commanded the man, saying, "Of every tree in the garden you may eat freely, but of the tree of the knowledge of good and evil do not eat. For in the day that you eat of it you will surely die."

The Lord God brought every beast of the field and every fowl of the air which He had made out of the earth to Adam to see what he would call them. Whatever Adam called each living creature became that creature's name. Adam gave names to all cattle, and to the birds of the air, and to every beast of the field, but for Adam himself there still was no helper.

The Lord God said, "It is not good that the man should be alone. I will make him a helper like himself."

Then the Lord God caused a deep sleep to fall upon Adam. As Adam slept, the Lord took one of his ribs, and filled its place with flesh. This rib the Lord God made into a woman, and He brought her to the man.

Adam said, "This is now bone of my bones and flesh of my flesh. She shall be called Woman because she was taken out of Man."

THE FALL OF ADAM AND EVE

NOW THE serpent was the most cunning beast which the Lord had made. He said to the woman, "Has not God told you that you may eat of every tree in the garden?"

"We may eat of the fruit of the trees of the garden," said the woman, "but of the fruit of the tree in the middle of the garden, God has said, 'You shall not eat of it nor touch it, lest you die.'"

"You would not die," said the serpent, "for God knows that the day you eat of that fruit your eyes will be opened, and you will be like God, knowing good from evil."

When the woman saw that the tree was good for food, and that it was pleasant to the eyes, and a tree to be desired because it could make one wise, she picked some of the fruit and ate it. She gave it to her husband, and he also ate it.

Then their eyes were opened, and they realized that they were naked, and they sewed fig leaves together to cover themselves.

They heard the voice of the Lord God walking in the garden in the cool of the day; and Adam and his wife hid themselves from the sight of the Lord among the trees of the garden.

The Lord God called to Adam, saying, "Where are you?"

"I heard your voice in the garden," said Adam, "and I was afraid because I was naked, and I hid myself."

"Who told you that you were naked?" asked the Lord God. "You have eaten of the tree whose fruit I commanded you not to eat." Adam said, "The woman whom you gave me to be with me, she gave me the fruit, and I ate." Then the Lord God said to the woman, "What is this you have done?"

And the woman said, "The serpent tempted me, and I ate."

Then the Lord God said to the serpent, "Because you have done this, you are cursed above all cattle and above every beast of the field. You shall crawl on your belly and eat dust all the days of your life. I shall cause war between you and the Woman, between your children and her Child. He shall crush your head and you shall bruise his heel."

To the woman, He said, "I will multiply your suffering. In sorrow you shall bring forth your children. You shall depend on your husband for happiness, and he shall rule over you."

To Adam, He said, "Because you listened to your wife and ate of the forbidden fruit, the ground shall be cursed for you; in sorrow you shall eat of it all the days of your life. Thorns and thistles it will bring forth for you, and you will have to eat wild grasses of the field. By the sweat of your brow you will earn your bread until you return to the earth."

The Lord God then made coats of skin for Adam and his wife, and dressed them.

And the Lord God said, "The man is like one of us now, knowing good and evil. Now if he were to put out his hand and eat also of the tree of life, he would live forever."

Therefore the Lord God sent Adam out of the garden of Eden, to till the ground from which he was made. He drove the man out, and placed at the east of the garden of Eden cherubims, and a flaming sword which turned in every direction to guard the path to the tree of life.

CAIN AND ABEL, SONS OF ADAM

DAM CALLED his wife Eve, because she was the mother of all. First she bore Cain and said, "I have made a man with the help of the Lord!" Later she bore Abel. Abel was a keeper of sheep, but Cain tilled the ground. And it came to pass one day that Cain brought the fruit of his harvest as an offering to the Lord. And Abel also brought some of the young of his flock, the best of them all. Now the Lord had respect for Abel and his offering, but for Cain and his offering He had no respect. Cain was very angry, and his face fell.

The Lord said to Cain, "Why are you angry? If you do well, shall you not be accepted?"

Cain said to Abel, his brother, "Let us go into the field." And it came to pass, when they were in the field, that Cain rose up against Abel his brother and killed him.

The Lord said to Cain, "Where is Abel, your brother?"

And he said, "How should I know? Am I my brother's keeper?"

"What have you done?" said the Lord. "The voice of your brother's blood cries to Me from the ground. And now you are cursed from the earth, which has received your brother's blood from your hand. Henceforth when you till the ground, it will not yield you its best. A fugitive and a vagabond you shall be on the earth."

Cain said to the Lord, "My punishment is greater than I can bear. Behold, You have driven me out this day from the face of the earth, and from Your face I shall be hid. I shall be a fugitive and a vagabond on the earth. Everyone who finds me will want to kill me."

The Lord said to him, "Whoever kills Cain shall be punished seven times over." And the Lord set a mark upon Cain, so that anyone finding him would not kill him.

Then Cain went out from the presence of the Lord, and dwelt in the Land of Nod, on the east of Eden.

NOAH AND THE GREAT FLOOD

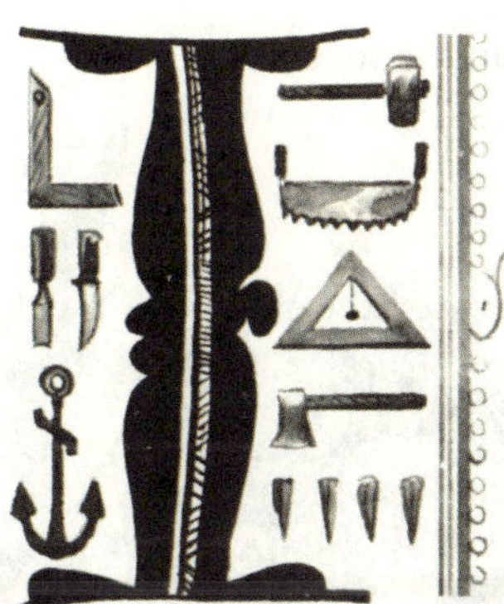

IT CAME to pass, when men began to multiply on the face of the earth, that God saw that the wickedness of man was great, and that every thought of his heart was evil. Then the Lord regretted that He had made man to live on the earth, and He grieved in His heart.

The Lord said, "I will destroy man, whom I have created, from the face of the earth, both man and beast and the creeping things and the birds of the air, for I am sorry I made them." Only Noah found approval in the eyes of the Lord.

Noah was a just man, the best of all the men of his time, and Noah lived by God's rule. He had three sons, named Shem, Ham, and Japheth.

God said to Noah, "I will destroy all living things on the earth, for the earth is filled with evil because of them.

"Make an ark of resin wood. Make rooms in the ark, and cover it with pitch within and without. And this is the shape which you shall make it: the length of the ark shall be four hundred fifty feet, the breadth of it seventy-five feet, and the height of it forty-five feet. You shall make a window in the ark. Put a door in the side of the ark, and make three stories in it.

"I will bring a flood of waters upon the earth to destroy all flesh under heaven that has the breath of life. And every thing that is on the earth shall die.

"But with you I will establish a covenant, and you shall come into the ark, and your sons, and your wife and your sons' wives with you.

"And of every living thing, two of each sort you shall bring into the ark to keep them alive with you. They shall be male and female. Birds of all kinds, and cattle of all kinds, creeping things of all kinds — two of every kind of creature shall come to you to keep them alive.

"Take up, too, some of every kind of food that is eaten, and gather it up. And it shall be food for you and for them."

All this Noah did, just as God commanded him.

Noah was six hundred years old when the flood of waters came upon the earth. He went into the ark, with his sons, and his wife, and his sons' wives, because of the waters of the flood. And two by two the beasts and birds and every thing that creeps upon the earth went into the ark, a male and female of each kind, as God had commanded Noah.

After seven days the fountains of the great deep were broken up, and the windows of heaven were opened. The rain fell upon the earth forty days and forty nights. The waters increased, and bore up the ark, and it rose above the earth. The waters spread out and increased still more, and the ark floated upon the face of the waters. The waters continued to rise all over the earth, and

all the high hills under heaven were covered. Forty-five feet more the waters rose, and the mountains were covered.

Every living creature that moved upon the earth was destroyed, all men and cattle, and the creeping things and the birds of the heavens.

Noah alone remained alive, and those who were with him in the ark. And the waters remained upon the earth a hundred and fifty days.

God remembered Noah and every living creature with him in the ark. God made a wind to pass over the earth, and the waters began to go down.

The fountains of the deep and the windows of heaven were stopped, and the rain from heaven was held back. The waters went down, day after day, for a hundred and fifty days.

In the seventh month, on the seventeenth day of the month, the ark rested upon the

mountain of Ararat. In the tenth month, on the first day, the tops of the mountains were seen.

Then Noah opened the window which he had made in the ark, and he sent out a dove to see if the waters had dried from the face of the earth. But the dove found no rest for the sole of her foot, and she returned to the ark, for the waters covered the face of the whole earth. Then Noah put out his hand and took her back into the ark.

He waited seven days, and once again he sent the dove out of the ark. In the evening the dove came in to him, and in her mouth was a green olive leaf. So Noah knew that the waters were lowered on the face of the earth.

Seven more days Noah waited, and then once again he sent out the dove. She did not return to the ark any more.

So it came about that the waters were dried up from the earth, and Noah removed the cover of the ark and looked out, and behold, the ground was dry.

God spoke to Noah, saying, "Go out of the ark and take every living creature that is with you, all the birds and animals and creeping things, that they may raise their young and multiply upon the earth."

Noah went out, and his sons and his wife and his sons' wives went with him. Every beast, every creeping thing, and every bird went out of the ark, too. And Noah built an altar to the Lord and offered up burnt offerings of every clean beast and every clean fowl.

The Lord smelled the sweet odor and said in His heart, "I will not curse the ground any more for man's sake; neither will I ever again strike down every living thing, as I have done. While the earth remains, seedtime and harvest, and cold and heat, summer and winter, and day and night shall not cease."

And God spoke to Noah, and to his sons with him, saying, "Behold, I establish my covenant with you, and with your children after you, and with every living creature that is with you, the birds, the cattle, and every beast of the earth, with all who come out of the ark. Never again will all flesh be cut off by the waters of a flood, nor will a flood destroy the earth.

"This is the token of the covenant which I make between Myself and you and every creature that is with you, through generations without end. I will set My rainbow in the cloud, and it shall be a token of the covenant between Me and the earth.

"And it shall come to pass, when I bring a cloud over the earth, that the rainbow shall be seen in the cloud. I will look upon it, and I will remember the everlasting covenant between God and every living creature upon the earth."

THE TOWER OF BABEL

Sons were born unto the sons of Noah after the flood and they went forth and were the fathers of the nations of the earth. The whole earth then was of one language and had one speech.

WHEN THE sons of Noah journeyed from the east they discovered a valley in the land of Sennaar, and they dwelt there.

Then they said one to another, "Come now, let us make bricks and bake them thoroughly." Soon they had brick for stone and slime for mortar.

Then they said, "Come now, let us build a city, and a tower whose top may reach up to heaven. Let us make a name for ourselves, lest we be scattered over the face of the whole earth."

The Lord came down to see the city and the tower which the children of men built. And the Lord said, "Behold, the people of the earth are one people and have one language, and this is just the beginning for them. Now nothing will be too much for them to attempt.

"Let Us go down, and there confuse their language so that they may not understand one another's speech."

And the Lord did as He promised, and scattered the people abroad over all the face of the earth, and they left off building the city. Therefore the name of

the place is called Babel, because it was there that the Lord made a confusion of all the languages of the earth, and it was from there that the Lord scattered the people over all the face of the earth.

GOD CALLS ABRAM TO FOLLOW HIM

ABRAM WAS a man who lived in Haran. One day the Lord said to Abram, "Leave your country and your kinfolk, and your father's house, and go to a land that I will show you. I will make of you a great nation, and I will bless you and make your name great. I will bless those who bless you, and curse whoever curses you, and through you shall all the families of the earth be blessed."

So Abram departed, as the Lord had told him. He took his wife, and Lot his brother's son, and all their goods, and the people they had gathered in Haran, and they went forth into the land of Canaan.

Abram passed through this land to Shechem, on the plain of Moreh.

There the Lord appeared to Abram and said, "To your children I will give this land." And Abram built an altar to the Lord. Then Abram moved on to a mountain on the east of Bethel, and pitched his tent, having Bethel on the west and Hai on the east, and there he built an altar to the Lord and called upon the name of the Lord. And Abram journeyed onward.

Abram was very rich in cattle and in silver and in gold.

Lot, who traveled with Abram, also had flocks and herds and tents, and the land was not able to support them all so that they could live together. There was trouble between the herdsmen of Abram's cattle and the herdsmen of Lot's cattle; and there were Canaanites and Perizzites, too, getting a living from the land.

Abram said to Lot, "Let us not have trouble, I beg of you, between me and you, nor between my herdsmen and your herdsmen, for we are brothers.

"Is not the whole land before us? Then let us separate, I beg you. If you will take the left hand, then I will go to the right. Or if you move to the right hand, then I will go to the left."

Lot lifted up his eyes, and looked out over all the plain of Jordan. He saw that it was well watered everywhere, like the garden of the Lord, and like the land of Egypt as you come to Zoar.

So Lot chose for himself all the plain of Jordan, and he journeyed east; and they separated one from the other.

So Abram lived in the land of Canaan, and Lot lived in the cities of the plain and pitched his tent near Sodom.

And the Lord said to Abram, after Lot had left him, "Lift up your eyes now, and look northward and southward, eastward and westward. For all the land which you see I will give to you and to your family forever. And I will make your children's children as the dust of the earth, so that if any man could count the dust of the earth, he would also be able to count your children.

"Arise, walk through the land, the length of it and the breadth of it, for I will give it unto you."

GENESIS 17–18, 21–22

GOD VISITS ABRAHAM

OW WHEN Abram was ninety-nine years old, the Lord appeared to him and said, "I am the Almighty God; walk in My ways and be perfect. I will make my covenant with you, and will make you the father of a great race. Your name shall be Abraham, the father of many, for I will make you the father of many nations." The Lord appeared to him again by the grove of Mamre as Abraham sat in the tent door in the heat of the day. And when Abraham lifted up his eyes, he saw three men standing some distance from him. He ran to meet them and bowed himself down to the ground.

"My Lords," he said, "if I have now found favor in your sight, do not pass away, I beg you, from your servant. Let a little water be fetched, and wash your feet, and rest yourselves under the tree. I will bring bread to refresh you, and then you may go on your way."

And they said, "Do as you have said." Abraham hastened into the tent where Sarah his wife was and said, "Make ready quickly three measures of fine meal, knead it, and make cakes upon the hearth."

Then he ran to the herd and fetched a calf, tender and good, and gave it to a servant who began to prepare it.

Abraham then took butter and milk, and the calf, and set the food before the men. And he stood by them under the tree while they ate. "Where is Sarah, your wife?" they asked him. And he said, "See there, in the tent."

One of the men said, "Lo, Sarah your wife shall have a son."

Sarah heard this, standing in the tent doorway behind him. Now Abraham and Sarah were old and well along in years and they were beyond the time for having children. Therefore Sarah laughed within herself.

Then the Lord said to Abraham, "Why did Sarah laugh, saying she is too old to have a child? Is anything too hard for the Lord? At the time appointed Sarah shall have a son." Then Sarah denied it, saying, "I did not laugh," for she was afraid.

But the Lord said, "No, you did laugh." Then the men rose up and looked off toward Sodom, and Abraham went with them to put them on the right path.

And the Lord did as he had promised, and Sarah bore Abraham a son in his old age. And Abraham called his son Isaac.

*ATER God tested Abraham by commanding him to offer Isaac in sacrifice. Abraham, strong in faith, obeyed. But at the last moment God stopped him and Isaac's life was spared.*

CHOOSING A WIFE FOR ISAAC

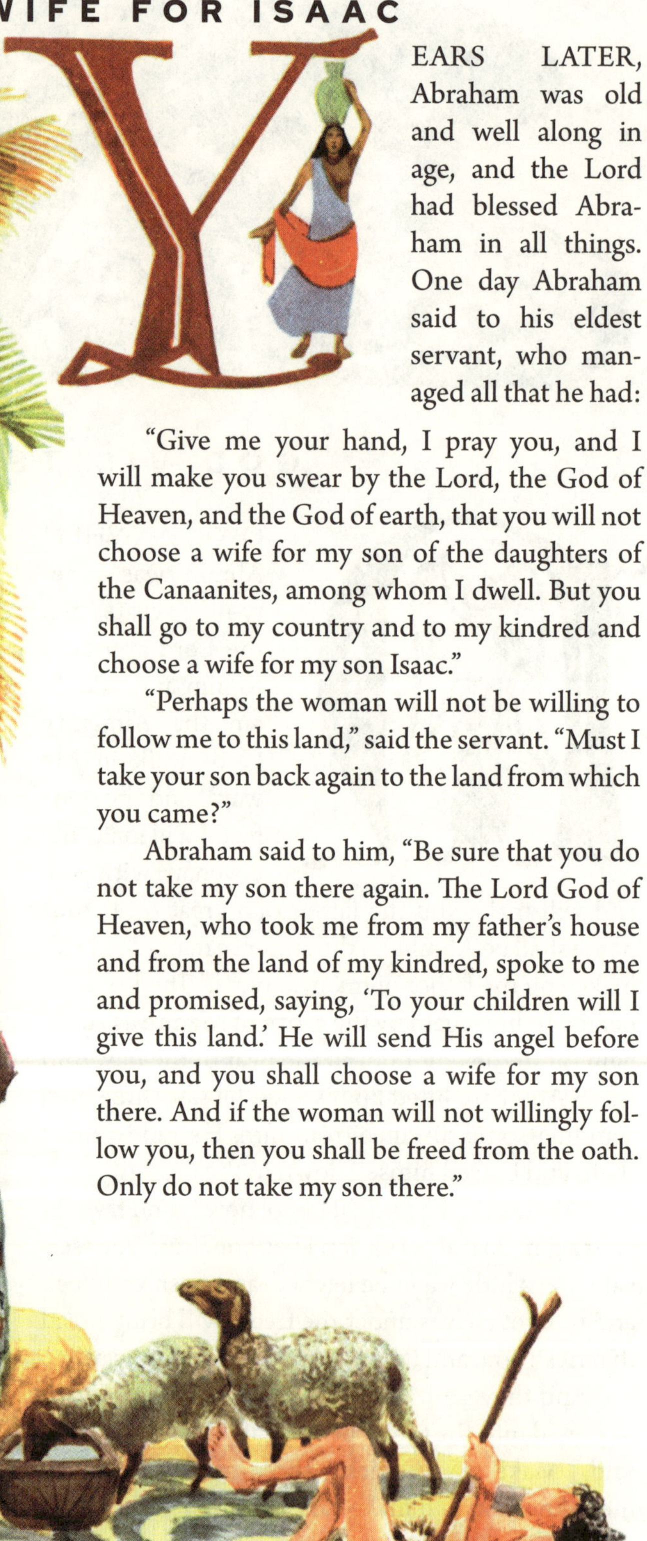

YEARS LATER, Abraham was old and well along in age, and the Lord had blessed Abraham in all things. One day Abraham said to his eldest servant, who managed all that he had:

"Give me your hand, I pray you, and I will make you swear by the Lord, the God of Heaven, and the God of earth, that you will not choose a wife for my son of the daughters of the Canaanites, among whom I dwell. But you shall go to my country and to my kindred and choose a wife for my son Isaac."

"Perhaps the woman will not be willing to follow me to this land," said the servant. "Must I take your son back again to the land from which you came?"

Abraham said to him, "Be sure that you do not take my son there again. The Lord God of Heaven, who took me from my father's house and from the land of my kindred, spoke to me and promised, saying, 'To your children will I give this land.' He will send His angel before you, and you shall choose a wife for my son there. And if the woman will not willingly follow you, then you shall be freed from the oath. Only do not take my son there."

So the servant gave his hand to Abraham, his master, and swore to him concerning this.

Then the servant took ten of his master's camels (for all the goods of his master were in his hands) and departed. He went up to Mesopotamia, to the city of Nahor.

There he made his camels kneel down outside the city, beside a well of water, at the time of the evening when the women go out to draw water.

Then he prayed, "O Lord God of my master Abraham, I pray you, send me good fortune today, and show kindness to my master Abraham. You see, I stand here by the well of water, and the daughters of the men of the city come out to draw water. To one girl I shall say, 'Let down your pitcher, I beg of you, that I may drink.' If she is the wife whom you have chosen for your servant Isaac, let her say, 'Drink, and I will give your camels a drink also.' By this I shall know that You have shown kindness to my master Abraham."

It came to pass, before he had finished speaking, that Rebekah, whose father was the son of Nahor, Abraham's brother, came out with her pitcher upon her shoulder. The girl was very fair to look upon, young and unmarried. She went down to the well, filled her pitcher, and came up.

Abraham's servant ran to meet her and said, "If you please, let me drink a little water from your pitcher."

And she said, "Drink, my lord," and quickly she lowered her pitcher upon her hand and gave him a drink. When she had finished giving him a drink, she said, "I will draw water for your camels, too, until they have finished drinking." She hurried and emptied her pitcher into the trough, and ran again to the well to draw water, and drew it for all his camels.

The man held his peace, wondering whether the Lord had made his journey successful or not. Then, as the camels finished drinking, he took out a golden earring of half a shekel weight and two bracelets for her hands, also of heavy gold.

"Whose daughter are you?" he asked. "Tell me, I beg of you, is there room in your father's house for me to spend the night there?"

She said to him, "I am the daughter of Bethuel, the son of Nahor. We have both straw and food enough, and room to lodge in."

Then the man bowed down his head and worshiped the Lord, saying, "Blessed be the Lord God of my master Abraham, who has not kept His mercy and His truth from my master, for, I being on the way, the Lord led me to the house of my master's brother."

The girl ran on to her mother's house and told these things.

Now Rebekah had a brother, and his name was Laban. When he saw the earring and the bracelets upon his sister's hands, and when he heard the words of Rebekah his sister, Laban ran out and found the servant of Abraham standing by the camels at the well.

Laban said, "Come in, you whom the Lord has blessed. Why do you stand outside? For I have prepared the house, as well as a place for the camels."

The man came into the house, and Laban unharnessed his camels and gave them straw and feed; and he brought water to wash the man's feet and the feet of the men who were with him. They set meat

before the man to eat, but he said, "I will not eat until I have told my errand." So Laban said, "Speak on."

The man began, "I am Abraham's servant. The Lord has blessed my master greatly, and he has become great. The Lord has given him flocks and herds, silver and gold, menservants and maidservants, and camels and asses. And Sarah, my master's wife, bore a son to my master when she was old, and to him Abraham has given all that he has."

Then the servant told how Abraham had sent him to find a wife for Isaac, and how the Lord had led him to Rebekah.

"And now if you will deal kindly and truly with my master, tell me, and if not, tell me, so that I may know which way to turn."

Then Laban and Bethuel answered and said, "The thing has been planned by the Lord. We cannot say anything to you, bad or good. Behold, Rebekah is here before you; take her and go, and let her be your master's son's wife, as the Lord has said."

When Abraham's servant heard their words, he worshiped the Lord, bowing himself to the earth. And he brought out jewels of silver and jewels of gold, and clothing, and gave them to Rebekah. To her brother and her mother also he gave precious things.

Then they ate and drank, he and the men that were with him, and they stayed all night. When they rose up in the morning, he said, "Send me back now to my master."

Rebecca's brother and her mother said, "Let the girl remain with us a few days, at least ten. After that she shall go with you."

But he said to them, "Do not hinder me, seeing the Lord has made my errand successful. Send me away, that I may go to my master."

"We will call the girl and ask her," they said. They called Rebekah and said to her, "Will you go with this man?"

And she said, "I will go."

So they sent away Rebekah their sister, and her nurse, and Abraham's servant, and his men. They blessed Rebekah, and she arose with her maidens, and they rode upon the camels and followed the man. And the servant took Rebekah and went his way.

JACOB AND ESAU AND THE BIRTHRIGHT

ATER WHEN Isaac was three score years old, Rebekah bore him twin sons. The firstborn they called Esau, and the other Jacob. The boys grew and Esau was a cunning hunter, a man of the out-of-doors, but Jacob was a plain man, dwelling in tents. Isaac loved Esau, because he liked to eat his venison, but Rebekah loved Jacob.

One day Jacob had boiled a thick soup, and Esau came in from the field, and he was faint with hunger.

"Feed me, I pray you, some of that good red soup," said Esau to Jacob, "for I am faint."

"Sell me this very day your birthright," said Jacob. For Esau, being the elder, was to inherit their father's goods.

"You can see," said Esau, "that I am at the point of death. What good then will this birthright do me?"

But Jacob said, "Swear to me this day."

So Esau swore to him, and he sold his birthright to Jacob. Then Jacob gave Esau bread and the lentil soup; and he ate and drank and rose up and went his way.

Thus Esau threw away his birthright.

JACOB TAKES THE BIRTHRIGHT

IT CAME to pass that when Isaac was old, and his eyes were dim, so that he could not see, he called Esau, his elder son, and said to him, "My son." And Esau said, "See, here I am."

Isaac said, "Look now, I am old, I do not know when I may die. Now therefore take your weapons, I pray you, your quiver and your bow, and go out to the field and get me some venison. Make me savory meat, such as I love, and bring it to me that I may eat, so that my soul may bless you before I die."

Now Rebekah heard when Isaac spoke to Esau his son. And Esau went to the field to hunt for venison and to bring it home.

Then Rebecca spoke to Jacob her son, saying, "Behold, I heard your father speak to Esau your brother, saying, 'Bring me venison and make me savory meat, that I may eat, and then I will bless you before the Lord, before my death.' Now, therefore, my son, obey my voice and do as I command you.

"Go now to the flock and fetch me from it two good kids of the goats, and I will make them into savory meat for your father, such as he loves. And you shall take it to your father, that he may eat, and that he may bless you before his death."

Jacob said to Rebekah his mother, "Behold, Esau my brother is a hairy man, and I am a smooth man. Perhaps my father will feel me, and I shall seem to him a deceiver, and I shall bring a curse upon myself, and not a blessing." But his mother said to him, "That curse would be upon me, my son. Only obey my voice and go fetch the kids to me."

So he went and fetched them to his mother; and his mother made savory meat, such as his father loved.

And Rebekah took good robes of her elder son Esau, which were in the house, and put them upon Jacob, her younger son. And she put the skins of the kids of the goats upon his hands and upon the smooth of his neck.

Then she put the savory meat, and the bread which she had prepared, into the hands of her son Jacob.

Jacob came to Isaac and said, "My father." And Isaac said, "Here I am. Who are you, my son?"

"I am Esau, your firstborn," Jacob said to his father. "I have done as you told me. Arise, I beg of you; sit up and eat of my venison, so that your soul may bless me."

But Isaac said to his son, "How have you found it so quickly, my son?"

"Because the Lord your God brought it to me," said Jacob.

Still Isaac said to Jacob, "Come near, I beg of you, so that I may feel you, my son, whether you are really my son Esau or not."

Jacob went near to Isaac his father, and Isaac felt him and said, "The voice is Jacob's voice, but the hands are the hands of Esau." He did not recognize him, because his hands were hairy like his brother Esau's hands, so he blessed him.

Once more Isaac said, "Are you really my son Esau?"

And Jacob said, "I am."

Then Isaac said, "Bring it near to me, and I will eat of my son's venison, that my soul may bless you."

Jacob brought the food close to him, and he ate; he brought him wine, and he drank.

Then his father Isaac said to him, "Come near now, and kiss me, my son."

And Jacob came near and kissed him, and Isaac smelled the smell of his robe and blessed him, saying:

"See, the smell of my son is as the smell of a field which the Lord has blessed. Therefore God give you of the dew of Heaven and the riches of the earth, and plenty of corn and wine.

"Let people serve you, and nations bow down to you. Be lord over your brothers, and let your mother's sons bow down to you. May everyone who wishes you evil be cursed, and may everyone who wishes you well be blessed."

Now it happened, as soon as Isaac had finished blessing Jacob, and when Jacob had scarcely left Isaac his father, that Esau his brother came in from his hunting. And he also made savory meat and brought it to his father and said, "My father, please rise up and eat of your son's venison, so that your soul may bless me."

Then Isaac his father said to him, "Who are you?"

And he said, "I am your son, your firstborn, Esau."

Then Issac trembled all over and said, "Who? Where is he who prepared venison and brought it to me, and I ate it before you came and have blessed him? Yes, and he shall be blessed." When Esau heard the words of his father, he cried out a very great and bitter cry, and said to his father, "Bless me, even me also, O my father!"

But Isaac said, "Your brother came with trickery and has taken away your blessing." Esau said, "Is he not rightly named Jacob? For he has taken my place now two times. He took away my birthright, and behold, now he has taken away my blessing." And he said, "Have you not saved a blessing for me?"

Isaac answered and said to Esau, "Behold, I have made him lord over you, and all his brothers I have given to him for servants. I have provided him with corn and wine; and what shall I do now for you, my son?"

But Esau said to his father, "Have you only one blessing, my father? Bless me, even me also, O my father!" And Esau lifted up his voice and wept.

Then Isaac his father answered and said to him, "Behold, your dwelling shall be the richness of the earth and the dews of Heaven above. You shall live by the sword and shall serve your brother, but the day will come when you will have power, and you will break his yoke from off your neck."

Still Esau hated Jacob because of the blessing with which his father had blessed him; and Esau said in his heart, "When the days of mourning for my father are over, I will kill my brother Jacob."

These words of Esau her elder son were told to Rebecca. She called Jacob her younger son to her. "Watch your brother Esau," she said to him. "He comforts himself concerning you by planning to kill you.

"Now, therefore, my son, obey my voice. Arise and go to Laban my brother, at Haran. Stay with him a while, until your brother's anger turns away from you and he forgets what you have done to him. Then I will send and fetch you home again. Why should I lose you both on the same day?"

JACOB'S VISION IN THE DESERT

JACOB SET out from Beer-sheeba and he started toward Haran. He came to a certain place and had to stay there all night, because the sun had set. He took some stones from the ground and he placed them for his pillow, and lay down to sleep.

Jacob dreamed, and he saw a ladder set up on the earth, the top of which reached to Heaven. And he saw angels of God going up and down on it.

The Lord stood above the ladder and said to him, "I am the Lord, the God of Abraham and the God of Isaac. The land on which you lie I will give to you and your children. And your children shall be as the dust of the earth; you will spread abroad to the west and to the east, to the north and to the south, and through you and your children all the families of the earth will be blessed.

"And, behold, I am with you, and I will guard you everywhere you go, and will bring you again to this place. For I will not leave you until I have done everything I have promised." Then Jacob waked out of his sleep, and he said, "Surely the Lord is in this place, and I did not know it." He was afraid and said, "How awesome this place is! This is surely the house of God, and this is the gate of Heaven."

Early in the morning Jacob rose up and took the stone that he had used for his pillow and set

it up for a pillar. Then he poured oil upon the top of it, and he called the name of that place Bethel. And Jacob vowed a vow, saying, "If God will be with me, and will guard me in the way that I go, and will give me bread to eat and clothes to wear, so that I may return again to my father's house in peace, then the Lord will be my God. And this stone, which I have set up for a pillar, will be God's house, and of all that you give to me, O God, I will give a tenth to you."

JACOB AND RACHEL

ONTINUING ON his journey, Jacob came into the land of the people of the east. He looked about and saw a well in the field and three flocks of sheep lying by it, for out of that well all the flocks round about were watered.

Jacob said to the shepherds, "My brothers, where are you from?"

They replied, "We are from Haran."

"Do you know Laban, the son of Nahor?" he asked them.

And they said, "We know him."

"Is he well?" Jacob asked.

"He is well," replied the shepherds, "and see there, Rachel his daughter is coming with the flock of sheep."

While they were still talking, Rachel came with her father's sheep, for she looked after them. When Jacob saw Rachel, the daughter of Laban, his mother's brother, and Laban's sheep, he rolled away the stone which covered the well's mouth and watered the flock. Then Jacob kissed Rachel and lifted up his voice and wept.

When Jacob told Rachel that he was her father's kin, and Rebekah's son, she ran and told her father, Laban. He hastened out to meet Jacob, and embraced him and kissed him, and brought him to his house.

Jacob told Laban all the things that had happened to him, and Laban said to him, "Surely you are my bone and flesh."

Jacob stayed with him for a month. Then Laban said to him, "Because you are my kin, should you work for me for nothing? Tell me, what shall your wages be?"

Now Laban had two daughters. The name of the elder was Leah, and the name of the younger was Rachel. Leah was tender-eyed, but Rachel was beautiful and pleasing to look upon. Jacob loved Rachel, so he said to Laban, "I will work for you seven years for Rachel, your younger daughter."

Then Laban answered, "It is better for me to give her to you than to any other man; stay with me."

So Jacob worked seven years for Rachel, and they seemed to him but a few days, because he loved her.

FTER many years with Laban, Jacob had prospered exceedingly. He had much cattle, and maidservants and menservants, and camels and asses. And it came to pass that Jacob said to Laban, "Send me away, so that I may go to a place of my own, and to my own country. Give me my wife and my children, for whom I have served you, and let me go." Laban did not like to have Jacob leave, but at last he made a covenant with Jacob and said, "The Lord watch between me and thee, when we are absent one from the other."

Then Jacob went on his way, and the angels of the Lord met him. Jacob wrestled by night with an angel of the Lord, and at daybreak the angel said, "Your name shall no longer be called Jacob, but Israel, for you have the power of a prince with God." And ever after, Jacob's children and his children's children were called "the children of Israel."

When Jacob heard that Esau his brother was coming to meet him with four hundred men, he was frightened, thinking that Esau still wanted to kill him. But when Esau came near, he ran to meet Jacob, and embraced him and kissed him, and they wept. So Jacob came home to his own country.

JOSEPH IS SOLD INTO SLAVERY

NOW CANAAN, the land in which his father had been a stranger, became home to Jacob.

Joseph, his son, being seventeen years old, daily fed the flocks with all his brothers, the sons of his father's wives. And Joseph brought his father an evil report of them.

Now Jacob loved Joseph more than all his other children, because he was the son of his old age, so he made him a coat of many colors.

When his brothers saw that their father loved Joseph more than all his brothers, they hated Joseph and could not speak peaceably to him.

Once Joseph dreamed a dream, and he told it to his brothers, and they hated him still more. He said to them:

"Hear, I pray you, this dream which I have dreamed. We were all binding sheaves in the field, and lo, my sheaf arose and stood upright,

and your sheaves stood round about and bowed down to my sheaf."

Then his brothers said to him, "Shall you indeed be king over us? Shall you really rule over us?" And they hated him still more for his dreams, and for his words.

He dreamed another dream, and told it to his brothers, saying, "Behold, I have dreamed another dream, and the sun, and the moon, and the eleven stars bowed down to me."

He told it to his father and to his brothers, and his father rebuked him, saying, "What is this dream you have dreamed? Shall your mother and I and your brothers really come to bow ourselves down to the earth before you?" His brothers envied him, but his father remembered the words.

Now his brothers went to feed their father's flock in Shechem. One day Jacob said to Joseph, "Are your brothers not feeding the flock in Shechem? Come, I will send you to them." "Here I am," said Joseph.

"Go, then," said Jacob, "and see whether all is well with your brothers and the flocks, and bring me word."

So he sent Joseph out of the valley of Hebron, and the boy arrived at Shechem. There a man found him wandering in the field, and the man asked him, "What are you looking for?"

"I am looking for my brothers," he said. "Can you tell me where they are feeding the flocks?"

And the man said, "They went on from here. I heard them say, 'Let us go to Dothan.'" So Joseph went on after his brothers and found them in Dothan.

When they saw him far off, even before he came close to them, they plotted against him, to slay him.

"Behold, here comes this Dreamer!" they said to one another. "Let us kill him for that and throw him into some pit. We can say some evil beast has devoured him, and then we shall see what becomes of his dreams!"

But Reuben heard this, and he said, "Let us not kill him. Shed no blood, but throw him into this pit here in the wilderness, and do not lay hands on him." He planned to save Joseph from their hands and to take him to his father again.

So it happened that when Joseph came up to his brothers, they stripped his coat from him, his coat of many colors which he was wearing, and they took him and threw him into a pit. It was an empty pit, with no water in it.

Then they sat down to eat bread; but when they lifted up their eyes and looked, there they saw a company of Ishmaelites coming from Gilead, with camels loaded with gum and balm and myrrh, which they were carrying down to Egypt.

Then Judah said to his brothers, "What will we gain if we kill our brother and hide the deed? Come, let us sell him to the Ishmaelites, and let us not lay hands on him, for he is our brother and our flesh."

This satisfied the brothers.

So they lifted Joseph up out of the pit and sold him to the Ishmaelites for twenty pieces of silver; and the merchants took him to Egypt.

Reuben was sad. He said to his brothers: "The child is not here, and I, where shall I go?"

But the brothers took Joseph's coat, and killed a young goat and dipped the coat in the blood. Then they took the coat of many colors and brought it to their father, and said, "We found this. Do you know whether or not it is your son's coat?"

He recognized it and said, "It is my son's coat. An evil beast has eaten him. Joseph is without doubt torn in pieces!"

Then Jacob tore his clothes and put on sackcloth, and mourned for his son many days. All his sons and all his daughters tried to comfort him, but he refused to be comforted. "I will go down to the grave," he said, "mourning for Joseph, my son."

JOSEPH IN THE LAND OF EGYPT

OWN INTO Egypt Joseph was brought, and Potiphar, who was an officer of Pharaoh and captain of the guard, bought him from the Ishmaelites.

The Lord was with Joseph, and he became a favored servant, living in the house of his master the Egyptian. His master saw that the Lord was with him, and that the Lord made all that he did prosper in his hands. So the master approved of Joseph, and he made him overseer in his house.

The Lord blessed the Egyptian's house for Joseph's sake. So Potiphar left all that he had in Joseph's hands, and he did not even know what he owned, except the bread he ate.

Now Joseph was a handsome young man. It happened, after a while, that his master's wife loved Joseph, and when he would not love her she told her husband lies about him, and her husband was angry.

Joseph's master put him into prison where the king's prisoners were kept, and there he stayed.

But the Lord was with Joseph and showed him mercy, and made the keeper of the prison think well of him. So the keeper of the prison put all the prisoners that were in the prison into Joseph's hands, and he was in charge of them.

The keeper of the prison paid no attention to anything that went on, because the Lord was with Joseph, and whatever he did, the Lord made it prosper.

It happened, some time later, that the butler of the king of Egypt and his baker offended their lord Pharaoh, and he put them in the same prison where Joseph was kept.

The captain of the guard turned them over to Joseph and he looked after them, and they stayed on in prison for some time.

Now one night each of them dreamed a dream, and each of them a different dream, the butler and

"Only think of me when it is going well with you, and be kind to me, I beg of you, and mention me to Pharaoh, and get me out of this place. For I was really stolen away from the land of the Hebrews, and I have done nothing here that makes me deserve this dungeon." When the chief baker saw that the interpretation was good, he said to Joseph, "I also had a dream, and in it I had three white baskets on my head. In the topmost basket were all kinds of baked goods for Pharaoh, and the birds ate them out of the basket upon my head."

Joseph answered him and said, "This is the meaning of it: The three baskets are three days. Within three days Pharao will call you up and hang you on a tree, and the birds will eat your flesh."

It happened that on the third day, which was Pharaoh's birthday, he made a feast for all his servants, and he called up the chief butler and the chief baker among his servants. He returned the chief butler to his butlership again, and the butler gave the cup to Pharaoh; but Pharaoh hanged the chief baker, as Joseph had said.

the baker of the king of Egypt. And when Joseph came in to them in the morning and looked at them, he saw that they were sad. He asked, "Why do you look so sad today?" "We have dreamed a dream," they said to him, "and there is no one to interpret it for us." Joseph said, "Do not interpretations come from God? Tell me the dreams."

So the chief butler told his dream to Joseph, saying, "In my dream I saw a vine before me, and on the vine were three branches. It seemed as though it budded and the blossoms shot forth, and the clusters grew into ripe grapes. Pharaoh's cup was in my hand, and I took the grapes and pressed them into Pharaoh's cup, and I put the cup into Pharaoh's hands."

Joseph said to him, "This is the interpretation of it: The three branches are three days. Within three days Pharaoh will restore you to your place, and you will put Pharaoh's cup into his hands, as you used to when you were his butler.

Yet the chief butler did not remember Joseph but forgot him.

Two whole years went by, and then it happened one night that Pharaoh dreamed. He stood by the river, and there came up out of the river seven handsome, fat cows, and they fed in a meadow. Then seven other cows came up after them out of the river, scrawny and thin, and stood by the other cows upon the brink of the river. And the scrawny and thin cows ate up the seven fat and handsome cows. Then Pharaoh awoke.

He slept again and dreamed the second time. He saw seven ears of corn come up on one stalk, hardy and good. Then seven thin ears, blasted by the east wind, sprang up after them, and the seven thin ears devoured the seven hardy and full ears.

Pharaoh awoke and knew it was a dream, but in the morning his spirit was troubled. He sent for all the magicians of Egypt, and all the wise men of the land. Pharaoh told them his dream, but there was no one who could interpret it to Pharaoh.

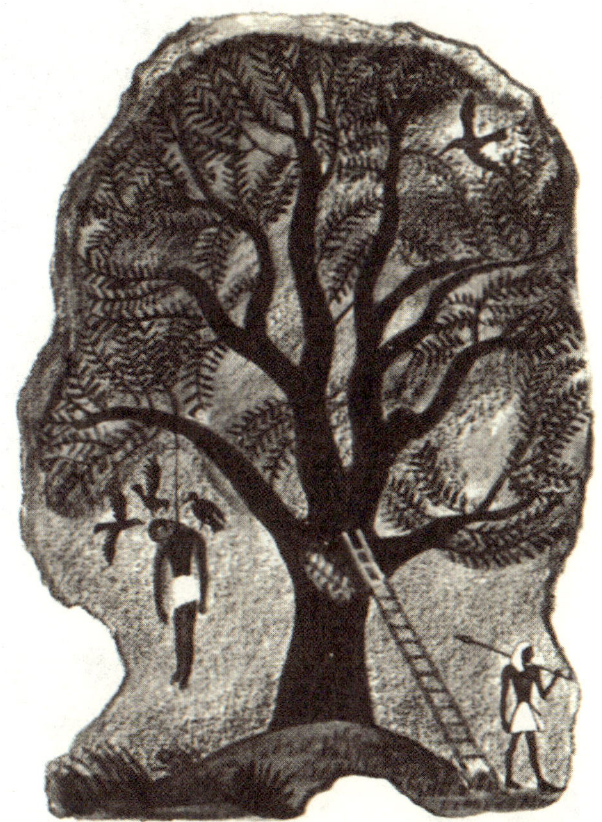

Then the chief butler spoke to Pharaoh and said, "Today I remember my faults. Pharaoh was angry with his servants and put the chief baker and me in the prison of the captain of the guard. We each dreamed a dream one night, he and I, and there was in prison with us a young man, a Hebrew, servant to the captain of the guard. We told him our dreams, and he interpreted them to us; to each man he gave the meaning of his dream. And everything happened just as he told us: I was restored to my office, and the baker was hanged."

Then Pharaoh sent for Joseph, and they brought him hastily out of the dungeon. He shaved himself and changed his clothing and came in to Pharaoh.

Pharaoh said to Joseph, "I have dreamed a dream, and no one can interpret it. I have heard it said that you can understand a dream and tell its meaning."

Joseph answered Pharaoh, saying, "It is not my power. God shall give Pharaoh an answer." Then Pharaoh told Joseph his dreams, and Joseph said

to Pharaoh, "The two dreams of Pharaoh are one. God has shown Pharaoh what He is about to do.

"The seven good cows are seven years, and the seven good ears are seven years; the dream is the same. The seven thin and scrawny cows that came up after them are seven years, and the seven empty ears, blasted with the east wind, will be seven years of famine. What God is about to do He is showing Pharaoh.

"There will be seven years of great plenty throughout the whole land of Egypt. And after them will come seven years of famine, and all the plenty will be forgotten in the land of Egypt, and the famine will consume the land.

"For this reason the dream was sent to Pharaoh twice; the thing has been planned by God, and He will make it happen soon.

"Now, therefore, let Pharaoh search for a man discreet and wise, and set him over the land of Egypt. Let Pharaoh do this, and let him appoint officers to control the land, and gather up a fifth of the harvest of the land of Egypt in the seven years of plenty.

"Let them gather up the food of those good years that come, and store up grain under the order of Pharaoh, and let them keep food in the cities. And that food shall be for the land to draw on during the seven years of famine, which shall come in the land of Egypt, so that the land may not perish through the famine." This plan seemed good to Pharaoh, and to all his advisers. But Pharaoh said to his servants, "Can we find another man like this in whom is the spirit of God?"

Then Pharaoh said to Joseph, "Inasmuch as God has shown you all this, there is no one as discreet and wise as you. You shall be in charge of my house, and according to your word all my people will be ruled. Only on the throne itself will I be greater than you." And he said, "See, I have set you over all the land of Egypt." Then Pharaoh took off his ring from his hand and put it upon Joseph's hand, and dressed him in robes of fine linen and put a gold chain about his neck. And he made him ride in the second royal chariot, and people cried before him, "Bow the knee!" So Pharaoh made him ruler over all the land of Egypt.

Then Pharaoh gave Joseph an Egyptian name, and an Egyptian wife, and Joseph was known throughout all the land of Egypt. Joseph was then thirty years old.

Joseph traveled all over the land of Egypt. In the seven years of plenty the earth yielded grain in abundance. And Joseph gathered up food in those seven years in the land of Egypt, and stored up the food in the cities; in each city he stored the harvest of the fields which were around it.

Joseph gathered grain as the sand of the sea, so much that he stopped counting, for it was without number.

Two sons were born to Joseph before the years of famine came, and he called the firstborn Manasseh, and the second Ephraim.

Then the seven years of plenty in the land of Egypt were ended, and the seven years of poverty began, just as Joseph had said. The famine was in all countries, but in the land of Egypt there was food.

When all the land of Egypt was hungry, the people cried to Pharaoh for bread, and Pharaoh said to all the Egyptians, "Go to Joseph, and do as he tells you."

As the famine spread over the face of the earth, Joseph opened all the storehouses and sold food to the Egyptians, for the famine was severe in Egypt, too. And from all countries people came to Egypt to Joseph to buy grain, because the famine was so severe in all lands.

JOSEPH'S BROTHERS IN EGYPT

AS SOON as Jacob heard that there was grain in Egypt, he said to his sons, "Why do you sit and look at one another? I have heard that in Egypt there is grain for sale. Go down and buy some for us there, so that we may live and not die."

So ten of Joseph's brothers set out to buy grain in Egypt. Benjamin, Joseph's youngest brother, did not go with them. "For harm might befall him," said Jacob.

So, among the crowds that came to buy grain, came the sons of Jacob, for the famine was in the land of Canaan, too.

Now Joseph was the governor of the land, and it was he who sold to all the people of the land, and Joseph's brothers came and bowed themselves before him with their faces to the earth.

When Joseph saw his brothers, he recognized them, but he acted like a stranger toward them, and he spoke roughly to them.

Where did you come from?" he said.

"From the land of Canaan to buy food," they answered.

Joseph's brothers did not know him. He remembered the dreams he had dreamed of them, and he said to them, "You are spies; you have come to see the nakedness of the land."

"We are twelve brothers," they said, "the sons of one man in the land of Canaan. The youngest one is with our father now, and one is no more."

But Joseph said again, "It is just as I told you: you are spies. This shall be the proof; by the life of Pharaoh, you shall not go out of here unless your youngest brother comes to this place. Send one of you and let him fetch your brother, and you shall be kept in prison so that it may be proved whether there is any truth in your words. Otherwise, by the life of Pharaoh, surely you are spies!"

And he put them all under guard for three days.

The third day Joseph said to them, "Do this and save your lives, for I am a God-fearing man. If you are honest men, let one of your brothers stay bound in prison. The rest of you take grain to feed the hungry in your houses. But bring your youngest brother to me; this will prove your words are true, and you shall not die." They decided to do this, saying to one another, "Truly we are guilty about our brother, for we saw the suffering of his soul, when he pleaded with us, and we would not listen; that is why this distress has come to us."

And Reuben answered them, saying, "Did I not speak to you, saying, 'Do not sin against the child,' and you would not listen? Because of that we must settle now for his blood." Now they did not know that Joseph understood them, for he spoke to them through an interpreter, but he turned away from them and wept. Turning back again, he spoke to them and took Simeon from them and bound him before their eyes.

Then Joseph commanded servants to fill their sacks with grain, and to put every man's money back into his sack, and to give them provisions for the journey. That was how he treated them.

They loaded their asses with the corn, and started home.

When one of them opened his sack to feed his ass at an inn where they stopped, he spied his money, for it was in the mouth of his sack. And the others also found money in their sacks. Then their hearts failed them and they were afraid, and said to one another, "What is this that God has done to us?"

They came home to Jacob their father in the land of Canaan and told him all that had happened to them.

Jacob said to them, "You have taken away my children from me. Joseph is no more, and Simeon is no more, and you want to take Benjamin away. All these things are hard." Then Reuben spoke to his father, saying, "You may kill my two sons if I do not bring Benjamin back to you. Put him into my hands, and I will bring him to you again."

But Jacob said, "My son shall not go down with you, for his brother is dead, and he alone is left. If harm should come to him on the journey, you would bring down my gray hairs with sorrow to the grave."

BENJAMIN GOES TO EGYPT

HE FAMINE continued in the land. And the time came when Jacob and his sons had eaten up the grain which the sons had brought up from Egypt, and their father said them, "Go again, buy us some food in the land of Egypt."

But Judah told him, "If you will send our brother with us, we will go down and buy you food, but if you will not send him, we will not go down, for the man said to us, 'You shall not see my face unless your brother is with you.' "

"Why did you deal so badly with me as to tell the man you had another brother?" asked Jacob.

And they explained, "The man asked us strictly about ourselves and our family, saying, 'Is your father still alive?' Have you another brother?' And we answered his questions. How could we know that he would say, 'Bring your brother down'?"

Judah said to his father Jacob, "Send the lad with me, and we shall get up and go, so that we may live and not die, we and you yourself, and all our little ones.

"I will be responsible for him, and you may demand him of me. If I do not bring him to you and set him before you, then let me bear the blame forever. If we had not lingered so long, surely we would already have been back a second time."

Then their father said to them, "If it must be so now, do this: take some of the best fruits of the land in your containers, and carry down to the man a present, a little balm, and a little honey, spices, and myrrh, nuts and almonds. Also carry double the

money with you, and take back again the money that you brought home in the mouths of your sacks, for perhaps it was an oversight.

"Take your brothers, too, and go again to the man. May God Almighty grant you mercy from the man, so that he may send home Simeon and Benjamin. For if I must grieve for my children, it is bitter grief indeed."

And the men took presents, and double the money and Benjamin, and started off and went down to Egypt, and came before Joseph.

When Joseph saw Benjamin with them, he said to the manager of his house, "Take these men home, and kill some meat, and make it ready, for these men will dine with me at noon." The servant did as Joseph told him, and brought the brothers to Joseph's house. But the men were afraid because they were taken to Joseph's house, and they said, "Because of the money that was returned in our sacks the first time, we are being brought in here, so that he may find some fault with us, and fall upon us, and take us for slaves, and seize our asses, too." So they approached the steward of Joseph's house, and they spoke to him at the doorway.

"O sir," they said, "we came down the first time just to buy food, but it happened that when we came to the inn and opened our sacks, behold, every man's money was in the mouth of his sack, our money in full amount, so we have brought it back with us.

"We have brought other money down, too, to buy food. We do not know who put the money in our sacks."

"Peace be to you!" said the steward. "Fear not. Your God, the God of your father, gave you the treasure in your sacks. I had your money."

Then he brought Simeon out to them.

The man took the brothers into Joseph's house and gave them water, and they washed their feet, and he gave their asses food. Meanwhile they prepared the present to give to Joseph when he came in at noon, for they had been told that they were to eat there.

When Joseph came home, they gave him the present which they had brought into the house, and they bowed themselves down to the earth before him.

He asked them how they were and said, "Is your father well, the old man of whom you spoke? Is he still alive?"

"Your servant our father is in good health," they answered. "He is still alive." And they bowed down their heads respectfully.

Lifting up his eyes, Joseph saw his brother Benjamin, his own mother's son, and he said, "Is this your youngest brother, of whom you told me?" And he added, "God be gracious to you, my son."

Then Joseph hurried away, for his heart yearned for his brother, and he sought a place to weep. He went into his room and wept there. Then he washed his face and calmed himself and went out and said, "Serve the food."

The servants served him separately, and themselves separately, and Joseph's brothers also by themselves. The Egyptians could not eat a meal with the Hebrews, for that was against their laws.

The brothers sat before Joseph in order, from the firstborn with his birthright down to the youngest in his youth, and the men marveled at one another.

Joseph sent servings to them from his table, but Benjamin's serving was five times as much as any of the others. And they drank and were merry with him.

He gave orders to the steward of his house, saying, "Fill the men's sacks with food, as much as they can carry, and put every man's money in his sack's mouth. And put my cup, the silver cup, in the sack's mouth of the youngest with his grain money."

The steward did everything just as Joseph told him.

As soon as the morning was light, the men were sent away, they and their asses. And when they had left the city, but were not yet far off, Joseph said to his steward, "Up, follow the men! And when you have overtaken them, say to them, 'Why have you returned evil for good? Why have you stolen the very cup from which my lord drinks? He will surely guess where it is. You have done evil!' "

The steward set out at once and overtook the brothers. He spoke to them in the very same words. But they said to him, "Why does my lord say these things; God forbid that your servants should do anything like this. Look, the money which we found in our sacks' mouths we brought back to you from the land of Canaan; would we then steal silver or gold out of your lord's house?

"Let whoever is found to have it die, and the rest of us will be your lord's slaves."

He said, "Now let it be just as you say, but he who is found to have it shall be my servant, and the rest of you shall go free."

Then each man speedily put down his sack on the ground, and each man opened his sack. The steward searched, beginning with the eldest and finishing with the youngest, and the cup was found in Benjamin's sack.

Then Joseph's brothers tore their clothes, and each man loaded his ass, and they returned to the city. When they came to Joseph's house, they fell down before him on the ground.

Joseph said to them, "What is this that you have done? Do you not know that a man like me can see through these things?"

And Judah said, "What shall we say to my lord? How shall we speak? Or how shall we clear ourselves? God has found out the wickedness of your servants. Behold, we are my lord's servants, all of us as well as he in whose sack the cup was found."

"God forbid that I should demand that," he said, "but the man in whose hand the cup was found, he shall be my servant. As for the rest of you, go in peace up to your father."

Then Judah came closer to him and said, "Oh, my lord, let your servant, I beg of you, speak a word in my lord's ear, and do not let your anger burn against your servant, for you are as powerful as Pharaoh.

"My lord asked his servants, 'Have you a father or a brother?' And we said, 'We have a father, an old man, and a child of his old age, a little boy, whose brother is dead and he alone is left of his mother, and his father loves him.' "And you said to your servants, 'Bring him down to me, that I may have a look at him.' And we said to my lord, 'The lad cannot leave his father, for if he should leave his father, his father would die.' And you said, 'Unless your youngest brother comes down with you, you will not see my face again.'

"So when we came up to your servant our father, we told him your words. When our father said, 'Go again, and buy us a little food,' we said, 'We cannot go down; only if our youngest brother is with us can we go, for we may not see the man's face unless our youngest brother is with us.'

"And your servant our father said to us, 'You know that my wife bore me two sons, and one of them I lost and surely he is torn to pieces; I have not seen him since. If you take this one from me, too, and any harm befalls him, you will bring down my gray hairs with sorrow to the grave.'

"Now, therefore, when I come to your servant our father and the lad is not with us, seeing that his life is bound up with the lad's life, he shall surely die; and your servants will have brought down their father to the grave with sorrow.

"For your servant took responsibility for the lad to my father, saying, 'If I do not bring him back to you, then I shall bear the blame forever.'

"Now, therefore, I beg of you, let your servant stay instead of the lad, a slave to my lord, and let the lad go home with his brothers. For how can I go home to my father if the lad is not with me, and see the evil that would come to my father?"

Then Joseph could not control himself before the Egyptians around him, and he cried, "Let everyone leave me!" So the Egyptians departed and Joseph made himself known to his brothers. But he wept aloud, and the Egyptians and Pharao's household heard it.

Joseph said to his brothers, "I am Joseph. Is my father still alive?"

And his brothers could not answer him, for they were all overcome with wonderment.

Then Joseph said to his brothers, "Come close to me, I beg you." They came near, and he said, "I am Joseph, your brother, whom you sold into Egypt. Now do not grieve nor be angry with yourselves

because you sold me here, for God sent me here ahead of you, to save your lives.

"For two years now the famine has been in the land, and there are five years to come in which there shall be neither tilling nor harvest. God sent me before you to preserve your families on the earth and to save your lives. So it was not really you that sent me here, but God; and He has made me an adviser to Pharaoh, and lord of his household, and a ruler throughout the land of Egypt.

"Hurry now, and go up to my father and say to him, 'Your son Joseph says, "God has made me lord of all Egypt; come down to me without delay. You shall dwell in the land of Goshen, and you shall be near me, you and your children and your children's children, and your flocks and your herds, and all you own. And I will nourish you here, for there are still five years of famine to come and you and your household would otherwise know poverty." '

"Now your eyes and Benjamin's can see that it is really I who speak to you. And you are to tell my father of all my honors in Egypt, and of all you have seen. Go and hurry, and bring my father down here."

Then he embraced Benjamin and wept, and Benjamin wept.

Joseph kissed all his brothers, and wept with them, and after that his brothers talked with him.

News of the reunion was heard in Pharaoh's house. "Joseph's brothers have come," it was said. And Pharaoh and his servants were pleased.

Pharaoh said to Joseph, "Say to your brothers, 'Load your beasts, and go, hurry up to the land of Canaan. Get your father and your households and come to me, and I will give you the best of the land of Egypt, and you shall eat of the fat of the land. These are your orders: Take wagons up from Egypt for your little ones and your wives, and bring your father and come back. Do not bring with you your goods, for the best of all the land of Egypt shall be yours.' " Therefore Joseph gave his brothers wagons and gave them provisions for the journey. To each of them he gave changes of clothes, but to Benjamin he gave three hundred pieces of silver and five changes of clothes. And to his father he sent these gifts: ten asses loaded with the good things of Egypt, and ten she asses loaded with corn and bread and meat for his provisions on the journey.

So he sent his brothers away, and they left. And he said to them, "See that you do not quarrel on the way."

They went up out of Egypt and came to the land of Canaan, to Jacob their father. They told him everything, saying, "Joseph is still alive, and he is governor over all the land of Egypt." Jacob's heart grew faint, for he could not believe it.

They told him every word Joseph had said to them, and when he saw the wagons which Joseph had sent to carry him, their father Jacob at last believed.

"It is enough," Jacob said. "Joseph my son is still alive. I will go and see him before I die."

THE FINDING OF MOSES

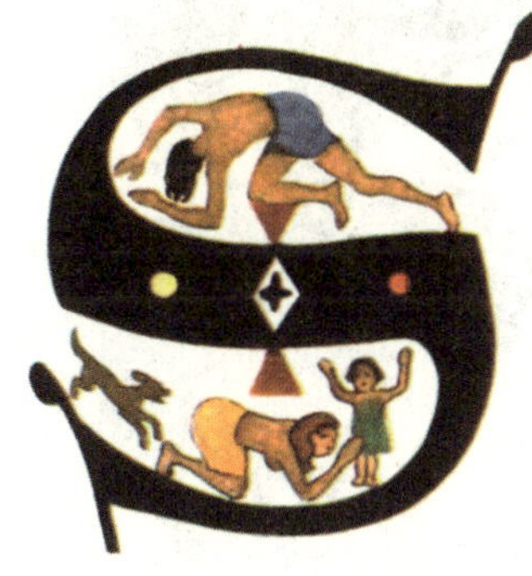

OME YEARS later Joseph died, and a new Pharaoh was king over Egypt. He said to his people, “The people of Israel are more numerous and mightier than we are. Come, let us deal wisely with them, lest they should outnumber us and, in case of war, should join our enemies and fight against us. We must get them out of the land, lest they take it from us.”

Therefore the Egyptians set over the Israelites taskmasters to make them work very hard. And they built for Pharaoh treasure cities, Pithom and Rameses. But the more the Egyptians mistreated them, the more they grew in strength and increased in numbers. And the Egyptians were worried because of the children of Israel.

So Pharaoh commanded all his people with these words: “Every son that is born to the Israelites you shall cast into the river, and every daughter you shall save alive.”

Now a man of the house of Levi married a daughter of the house of Levi, and the woman bore a son. When she saw that he was a sturdy child, she hid him for three months and when she could not hide him any longer, she took a covered basket of reeds, daubed it with pitch, and laid the baby in it. Then she put it among the reeds by the river's bank. The baby's sister stood at a distance to see what would happen to him.

The daughter of Pharaoh came down to wash herself at the river, and her maids walked along by the riverside. When she saw the basket among the reeds, she sent her maid to fetch it. And she opened it, and saw the child, and the baby began to cry. She took pity on him, and said, "This is one of the Hebrews' children."

Then the baby's sister said to Pharaoh's daughter, "Shall I go and bring you a nurse of the Hebrew women, so that she may nurse the child for you?"

"Go," said Pharaoh's daughter, and the girl went and called the child's mother.

Pharaoh's daughter said to her, "Take this child away and nurse it for me, and I will give you your wages." So the woman took her own child and nursed him.

When the child grew older, she took him to Pharaoh's daughter, and he became her son. She called him Moses, "because," she said, "I drew him out of the water."

MOSES IN EXILE

IT HAPPENED in those days, when Moses was grown, that he went out among his kinsmen and saw how heavily burdened they were; and he saw an Egyptian striking a Hebrew, one of his kinsmen. He looked this way and that way, and when he saw that there was no one near, he killed the Egyptian and hid him in the sand.

When he went out the next day, he saw two of the Hebrew men fighting each other, and he said to the one who was in the wrong, "Why did you strike this man?"

The man said, "Who made you a prince and a judge over us? Do you intend to kill me as you killed the Egyptian?"

Then Moses was afraid, for he thought, "Surely my misdeed is known."

When Pharaoh heard this story, he tried to kill Moses, but Moses fled from Pharaoh's presence and lived in the land of Midian.

There one day he sat down beside a well. Now the priest of Midian had seven daughters, and they came and drew water, and filled the troughs to water their father's flock. Shepherds came and drove them away, but Moses stood up and helped them and watered their flock.

When they came home to Reuel their father, he said, "How is it that you have returned so early today?"

And they said, "An Egyptian defended us from the shepherds, and also drew water enough for us and watered the flock."

"Well, where is he?" he said to his daughters. "Why did you leave the man? Ask him to come and eat with us."

Later Moses decided to live with this man, and the man gave Moses his daughter Zipporah for a wife. She bore him a son, and Moses called him Gershom, for he said, "I have been a stranger in a strange land."

MOSES AND THE BURNING BUSH

UNDER HARSH masters the children of Israel sighed against their slavery, and they cried out, and their cry came up unto God. God heard their groaning and remembered his covenant with Abraham, with Isaac, and with Jacob. And God looked down upon the children of Israel, and had pity upon them.

At this time Moses was keeping the flock of Jethro (or Reuel), his father-in-law, the priest of Midian, and he led the flock to the far side of the desert and came to the mountain of God, to Horeb. And the angel of the Lord appeared to him in a flame of fire from the middle of a bush. He looked, and saw that the bush burned with fire, but it was not destroyed.

Then Moses said, "I will turn aside now and see this great sight, and learn why the bush is not burnt."

When the Lord saw that he turned aside to see, God called to him out of the middle of the bush: "Moses, Moses."

He answered, "Here am I."

"Do not come near," God said. "Take your shoes off your feet, for the place where you are standing is holy ground." And He said also, "I am the God of your father, the God of Abraham, the God of Isaac, and the God of Jacob." Then Moses hid his face, for he was afraid to look upon God.

The Lord said, "I have certainly seen the hardships of my people who are in Egypt, and have heard their cries because of their taskmasters. Because I know their sorrows, I have come down to deliver them from the grasp of the Egyptians and to bring them out of that land to a land good and large, a land flowing with milk and honey. Now you can see that the cry of the children of Israel has come to me, and I have also seen the hardships with which the Egyptians bow them down.

"Come now, therefore, and I will send you to Pharaoh, so that you may lead forth my people, the children of Israel, out of Egypt." But Moses said to God, "Who am I, that I should go to Pharaoh, and that I should lead out the children of Israel from Egypt;"

The Lord said, "Certainly I will be with you, and this shall be a token to you that it is I who have sent you: When you lead forth the people out of Egypt, you shall worship God upon this very mountain."

Moreover God said to Moses, "Go and gather the elders of Israel together, and say to them, 'The Lord God of your fathers, the God of Abraham, of Isaac, and of Jacob, appeared to me,' and tell them all I have said to you." Moses answered and said, "But they will not believe me nor listen to my voice; for they will say, 'The Lord has not appeared to you.'" Then the Lord said to him, "What is that in your hand?"

And he said, "A rod."

"Cast it on the ground," he said. And he cast it on the ground, and it became a serpent, and Moses ran away from it.

The Lord said to Moses, "Put out your hand and take it by the tail." So he put out his hand and caught the serpent, and it became a rod in his hand. "That is so they may believe that the Lord God of their fathers, the God of Abraham, the God of Isaac, and the God of Jacob, has appeared to you."

Furthermore the Lord said to him, "Put your hand against your breast now."

He put his hand against his breast, and when he took it away, he saw that his hand was white as snow and diseased.

The Lord said, "Put your hand against your breast again," and he put his hand against his breast again, and when he took it away, behold, it had turned again like his other flesh.

"It shall come to pass, if they will not believe you nor be impressed by the first sign, that they will believe the second sign. But if they will not believe either of these two signs, nor listen to your voice, you shall take water from the river and pour it on the dry land. And the water which you take out of the river will become blood on the dry land."

Still Moses said to the Lord, "If you please, my Lord, I am not a good speaker; I was not before, and I am not since you have spoken to your servant; but I am slow of speech, and have a slow tongue."

The Lord said to him, "Who has made man's mouth? Who makes the dumb, the deaf, the seeing, or the blind? Have not I, the Lord, done it? You go now, and I will be with your mouth and will teach you what to say."

He said, "O my Lord, send, I beg you, whom you will send."

Then the Lord became angry with Moses, and he said, "Is not Aaron the Levite your brother; I know that he can speak well. Also I see that he is coming out to meet you, and when he sees you, he will be glad at heart. You shall speak to him and put words in his mouth. And I will be with your mouth and with his, and will teach you what you shall do. He shall be your spokesman to the people; he shall take the place of a mouth to you, and you shall be

to him like God. Also you shall take this rod in your hand, to do signs with it."

Then Moses went home, back to his father-in-law Jethro, and said to him, "Let me go, I beg of you, and let me return to my kinfolk who are in Egypt, and see if they are still alive." Jethro said to Moses, "Go in peace."

Then the Lord said to Moses in Midian, "Go, return to Egypt, for all the men are dead who sought your life."

So Moses took his wife and his sons, and set them upon an ass, and started back to the land of Egypt.

And the Lord said to Aaron, "Go into the wilderness to meet Moses."

And Aaron went and met Moses at the mountain of God, and kissed him. And Moses told Aaron all that the Lord had told him, and the signs he had taught him.

So Moses and Aaron gathered together all the elders of the children of Israel, and Aaron spoke all the words which the Lord had told Moses, and they did all the signs for the people to see.

Then the people believed, and when they heard that the Lord had visited the children of Israel, and that He had seen their hardships, they bowed their heads and worshiped.

THE PLAGUES OF EGYPT

OSES AND Aaron went in to Pharaoh and told him, "These are the words of the Lord God of Israel: 'Let my people go, so that they may hold a feast to me in the wilderness.'" Pharaoh said, "Who is the Lord that I should obey His voice and let Israel go? I do not know the Lord; neither will I let Israel go."

The same day Pharaoh commanded the taskmasters of the people, and their officers, saying, "You shall not give the people straw to make bricks any more, as you have done. Let them go and gather straw for themselves. And the number of bricks which they made before, you are still to demand of them. You shall not lessen it at all, for they are idle. That is why they cry out, saying, 'Let us go and offer sacrifice to our God.'"

The taskmasters went out and told the people, "Pharaoh says, 'I will not give you straw. Go out and get straw where you can find it, but do not let your work fall behind.'"

Then the people met Moses and Aaron, who stood in the road as they came out from Pharaoh, and they said to them, "May the Lord look upon you and judge you because you have made us have a bad reputation in Pharaoh's eyes and in the eyes of his servants, so that they want to kill us."

Then Moses turned back to the Lord and said, "Lord, why have you treated these people so badly? Why have you sent me? For since I came to Pharaoh to speak in your name, he has been wicked to these people, and you have not done anything to save them."

The Lord said to Moses, "You shall say all that I will tell you, and Aaron your brother will tell it to Pharaoh, so that he may send the children of Israel out of his land. But I will harden Pharaoh's heart and perform many signs and miracles in the land of Egypt. Still Pharaoh will not listen to you, so that I may lay my hand on Egypt and bring forth my armies and my people, the children of Israel, out of Egypt by my great power. And the Egyptians shall know that I am the

Lord, when I stretch forth my hand upon Egypt and bring the children of Israel out from among them."

Moses and Aaron did whatever the Lord commanded them. Moses was eighty years old and Aaron was eighty-three years old when they spoke to Pharaoh.

The Lord spoke to Moses and to Aaron, saying, "When Pharaoh asks you to show him a miracle, then you say to Aaron, 'Take your rod and throw it down before Pharaoh,' and it will become a serpent."

So Moses and Aaron went in to Pharaoh, and they did as the Lord commanded them, and Aaron cast down the rod before Pharaoh and his servants, and it became a serpent.

Then Pharaoh called all the wise men and the sorcerers and the magicians of Egypt. In the same manner each man cast down his rod, and they became serpents. But Aaron's rod swallowed up their rods.

Then the Lord hardened Pharaoh's heart, so that he did not pay any attention to them, as the Lord had said.

The Lord said to Moses, "Pharaoh's heart is hardened. He refuses to let the people go. Go to Pharaoh again in the morning. He is going out to the river; so you stand by the river bank until he comes, and take the rod which turned to a serpent in your hand.

"You shall say to him, 'The Lord God of the Hebrews has sent me to you, saying, "Let my people go, that they may worship me in the wilderness," and still up to this time you would not listen. Now these are the words of the Lord: "In this way you shall know that I am the Lord." See, I will strike the rod that is in my hand upon the water in the river, and it shall be turned to blood. And the fish in the river will die, and the river will smell foul, and the Egyptians will not be able to drink the water of the river.'"

Then the Lord said further to Moses, "Say to Aaron, 'Take your rod and stretch out your hand upon the waters of Egypt, upon her streams, upon her rivers, and her ponds and all her pools of water, so that they may become blood, so that there may be blood throughout all the land of Egypt, in all the pails of wood and jars of stone.'"

Moses and Aaron did all this just as the Lord commanded; Aaron lifted up the rod and struck the

water in the river, in the sight of Pharaoh and his servants, and all the water in the river was turned to blood. And the fish in the river died, and the river smelled foul, so that the Egyptians could not drink the water of the river.

But the magicians of Egypt could do that with their enchantments, so Pharaoh's heart was hardened, and he did not pay any attention to Moses and Aaron, as the Lord had said.

Then Pharaoh turned and went into his house, his heart unmoved by this. And all the Egyptians dug round about the river for water to drink, for they could not drink of the water of the river for seven days after the Lord had smitten the waters.

Then the Lord said to Moses, "Go to Pharaoh, and say to him, 'These are the words of the Lord: "Let my people go, so that they may worship me. If you refuse to let them go, I warn you that I will punish your whole country with frogs. The river will bring forth quantities of frogs, which will come into your house and into your bedroom and onto your bed, and into the houses of your servants, and upon your people, and into your ovens and into your kitchens. The frogs will swarm over you and your people and your servants."

Then the Lord said further to Moses, "Tell Aaron to stretch out his hand with your rod over the streams, over the rivers and the ponds, and make frogs swarm over the land of Egypt." And Aaron stretched out his hand over the waters of Egypt, and the frogs came up and covered the land.

But the magicians also could do this, and they brought up frogs over Egypt.

Pharaoh called for Moses and Aaron, and said, "Speak to your Lord and ask him to take away the frogs from me and from my people, and I will let the people go to make sacrifices to their Lord."

Then Moses said to Pharaoh, "O glorious king, when shall I ask, for you and for your servants and for your people, to have the frogs taken away from you and your houses, so that they may remain only in the river?"

He said, "Tomorrow."

And Moses said, "It shall be just as you say, so that you may know that there is no one like the Lord our God. The frogs shall be taken from you and from your houses, and from your servants and from your people. They shall remain in the river alone."

Moses and Aaron left Pharaoh, and Moses spoke to the Lord about the frogs which he had brought down upon Pharaoh. The Lord did as Moses asked: the frogs died out of the houses, out of the villages, and out of the fields. And they were gathered up in heaps, and the whole land smelled of them.

When Pharaoh saw that there was relief from them, he hardened his heart and would not listen to Moses and Aaron, just as the Lord had said.

THEN the Lord sent dust which turned to gnats on all the men and beasts; he sent swarms of flies, and a plague upon the cattle, and a siege of festering boils upon the men; but still the Lord hardened Pharaoh's heart and he would not listen to Moses and Aaron.

The Lord sent thunder and hail, and fire ran along the ground; and the Lord rained hail upon the land of Egypt. And the hail struck down every growing thing in the fields and broke every tree of the fields. Only in the land of Goshen, where the children of Israel were, was there no hail.

But still the heart of Pharaoh was hard, and he would not let the children of Israel go.

The Lord sent a plague of locusts, and he sent a great darkness which hung over all the land of Egypt for three days, a darkness so thick that it could be felt. Each time Pharaoh promised to let the children of Israel go, but each time the Lord hardened his heart so that he would not.

Then the Lord gave Moses directions for the last and most terrible plague, and he said, "Afterward he will surely let you go."

THE NIGHT OF THE PASSOVER

Then Moses called for all the elders of Israel, and told them what the Lord had told him:

CHOOSE A lamb according to the size of your families, and kill it. Take a bunch of hyssop and dip it in the blood that is in the basin, and sprinkle with the blood the top piece and the two side posts of the door of your house; and none of you shall go out the door until morning.

"For the Lord will pass through to strike the Egyptians, and when he sees the blood upon the lintel and on the two side posts, the Lord will pass over the door, and will not allow death to come into your houses to strike you.

"And you shall observe this thing as an order from God to you and your sons forever. It shall come to pass when you come to the land which the Lord will give you, according to His promise that you shall keep this service. And when your children say, 'What do you mean by this service?' you shall say, 'It is the sacrifice of the Lord's Passover, for He passed over the houses of the children of Israel in Egypt when He struck down the Egyptians, and He saved our families.'" The people bowed their heads and worshiped. Then the children of Israel went away and did as the Lord had commanded Moses and Aaron.

And it came to pass that at midnight the Lord struck down all the firstborn in the land of Egypt, from the firstborn child of Pharaoh on his throne to the firstborn of the captive in the dungeon, and all the firstborn of cattle.

Pharaoh rose up in the night, he and all his servants, and all the Egyptians, and there was a great cry in Egypt, for there was not a house where there was not one dead.

Pharaoh called for Moses and Aaron at night, and said, "Rise up and get out from among my people, you and all the children of Israel with you. Go and worship your Lord, as you have been saying."

The Egyptians were urging the people, trying to send them out of the land in haste, for they said, "We are all dead men."

So the people took their dough before it was raised, and bound their kneading boards up in their clothing bundles on their shoulders. And the people of Israel departed and journeyed from Rameses to Succoth.

CROSSING THE RED SEA

ONTINUING THEIR journey from Succoth, they camped at Etham, at the edge of the wilderness. And the Lord went before them by day in a pillar of cloud to show them the way, and by night in a pillar of fire to give them light, so they could travel by day and night. He did not take away the pillar of cloud by day nor the pillar of fire by night, from the people.

It was told to the king of Egypt that the people had fled, and the hearts of Pharaoh and his servants were turned against the people, and they said, "Why have we done this, and let Israel free from serving us?"

Then Pharaoh made ready his chariot and took his people with him. He took six hundred chosen chariots, of all the chariots of Egypt, and put warriors in all of them.

The Lord hardened the heart of Pharaoh, king of Egypt, and Pharaoh pursued the children of Israel, for the children of Israel had marched away proudly.

The Egyptians came after them, all the horses and chariots of Pharaoh, his charioteers and his army, and overtook them camping beside the sea, near Pi-hahiroth in front of Baal-zephon.

When Pharaoh came near, the children of Israel looked up, and, seeing the Egyptians marching after them, they were badly frightened. Then the children of Israel cried out to the Lord, and they said to Moses, "Were there no graves in Egypt? Have you brought us away to die in the wilderness? Why did you treat us so? Why did you bring us out of Egypt? Did we not tell you in Egypt, 'Let us alone, so that we can serve the Egyptians'? For it would have been far better for us to serve the Egyptians than to die in the wilderness."

"Do not be afraid," Moses said to the people. "Stand still and see the power of the Lord to save you, as He will show it to you today; for the Egyptians whom you have seen today you will never see again, forever. The Lord will fight for you, if you will have patience."

The Lord said to Moses, "Why are you crying to me? Tell the children of Israel to go forward. Just lift up your rod and stretch out your hand over the sea, and it will divide, and the children of Israel will go on dry ground through the middle of the sea.

"And you will see that I will harden the hearts of the Egyptians, and they will follow you; then I will

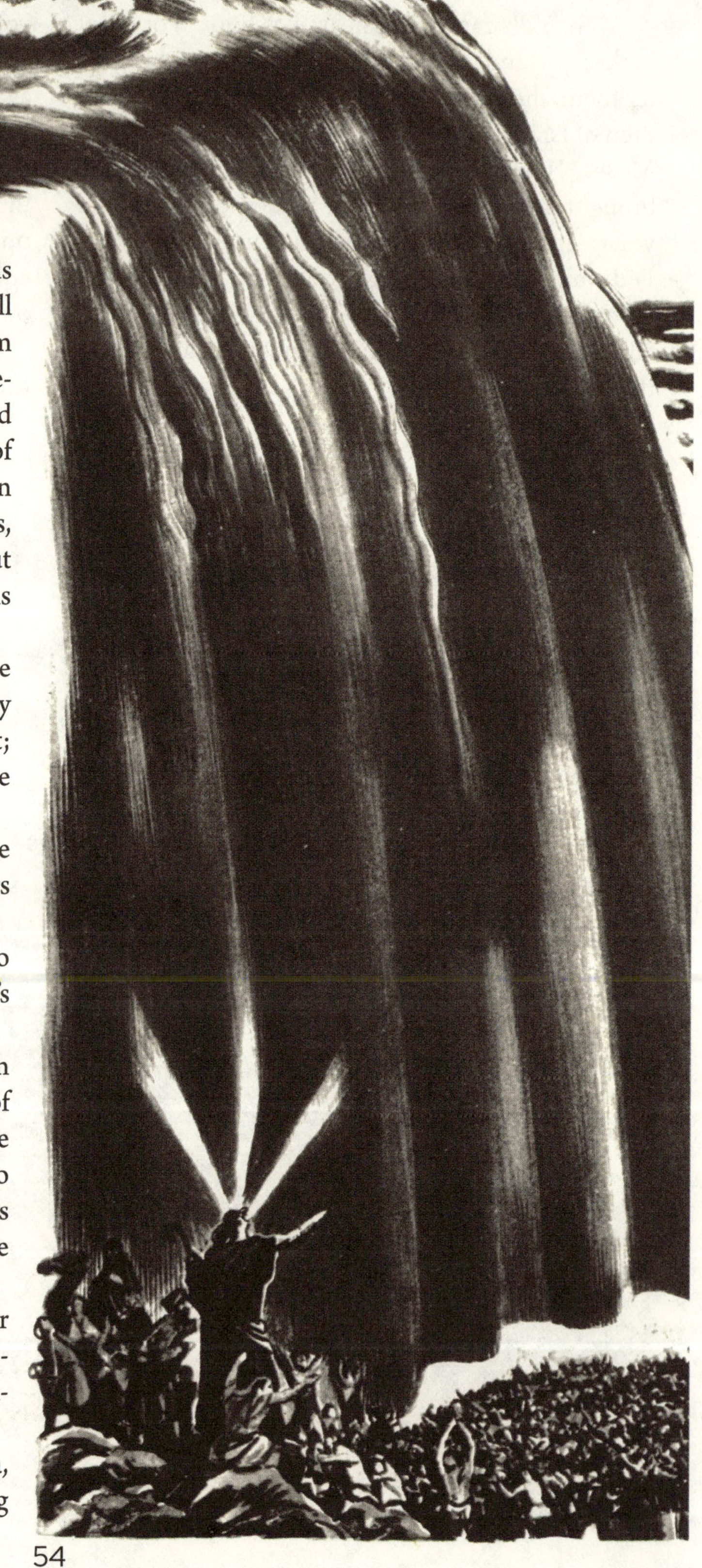

show my power to Pharaoh and all his host and his chariots and his horsemen. And the Egyptians will know that I am the Lord, when I have shown them my power." Then the angel of God which went before the camp of Israel moved and went behind them; the pillar of cloud moved from in front of them and rose up behind them. It came between the camp of Israel and the camp of the Egyptians, and was a cloud of darkness to the Egyptians, but it gave light by night to Israel, so that the Egyptians did not come near Israel all night.

Then Moses stretched out his hand over the sea, and the Lord caused the sea to go back by making a strong east wind to blow all that night; it made the sea dry land, and the waters were divided.

The children of Israel walked into the middle of the sea upon the dry ground, and the waters were a wall on their right hand and on their left.

The Egyptians pursued them and went into the middle of the sea after them, all Pharaoh's horses, his chariots, and his horsemen.

When morning came, the Lord looked down on the host of the Egyptians through the pillar of fire and the cloud, and troubled the forces of the Egyptians, and he clogged their chariot wheels so that they could hardly drive, and the Egyptians said, "Let us flee from the children of Israel, for the Lord is fighting for them against the Egyptians."

Then the Lord said to Moses, "Stretch out your hand over the sea, so that the waters may come together again and cover the Egyptians, their chariots, and their horsemen."

Moses stretched out his hand over the sea, and the sea returned to its bed when morning

appeared. The Egyptians fled before it, but the Lord overthrew the Egyptians in the middle of the sea. The waters returned and covered the chariots and the charioteers and all the forces of Pharaoh that had followed him into the sea. Not one of them survived.

But the children of Israel had walked on dry ground in the middle of the sea, and the waters were a wall on their right hand and on their left. Thus the Lord saved Israel that day from the clutch of the Egyptians, and the Israelites saw the Egyptians dead upon the seashore.

When Israel saw the great work the Lord did against the Egyptians, the people stood in awe of the Lord, and believed in Him and in His servant Moses.

Then Moses and the children of Israel sang this song to the Lord:

> "I will sing to the Lord, for He has triumphed gloriously;
> Horse and chariot He has thrown into the sea.
> The Lord is my strength and my courage,
> and He has been my Savior;
> He is my God, and I will praise Him.
> He is my father's God, and I will extol Him."

And Miriam the prophetess, the sister of Aaron, took a tambourine in her hand, and all the women went out after her with tambourines and danced. And Miriam replied to them in song:

> "Sing to the Lord, for He has triumphed gloriously;
> Horse and chariot He has thrown into the sea."

THE BITTER WATERS OF MARAH

SO MOSES led the Israelites from the Red Sea into the wilderness of Shur; and they traveled three days in the wilderness and found no water.

When at last they came unto Marah, they could not drink the water there, for it was bitter; that was why the name of the place was Marah. The people murmured against Moses, saying, "What shall we drink?"

He cried to the Lord, and the Lord showed him a tree which, when he cast it into the waters, made the waters sweet. And there the Lord also laid down a law for them. He said, "If you will listen carefully to the voice of the Lord your God, and will do what is right in His sight, and will give an ear to His commandments, and keep all His laws, I will not bring upon you any of those diseases which I brought upon the Egyptians, for I am the Lord who heals and protects you."

Then they came to Elim, where there were twelve wells of water and a grove of seventy palm trees, and they camped beside the waters.

BREAD FROM HEAVEN

ONWARD FROM Elim they journeyed, and all the company of the children of Israel came to the wilderness of Sin, which is between Elim and Sinai, on the fifteenth day of the second month after their departure from Egypt. And the children of Israel were murmuring against Moses and Aaron in the wilderness.

"It would have been better for us to perish by the hand of the Lord in the land of Egypt, when we sat down to bowls of meat and ate our fill of bread. For you have brought us out into this wilderness to kill the whole band of us with hunger."

Then the Lord said to Moses, "You will see, I will rain down bread from Heaven for you. The people shall go out and gather a certain amount every day, so that I may test them, to see whether they will obey my laws or not. And it will be arranged so that on the sixth day they shall prepare what they bring in, which will be twice as much as they gather on other days." Moses and Aaron said to all the children of Israel, "When evening comes, you will know that it is the Lord who has brought you out of the land of Egypt. And when morning comes, you will see the glory of the Lord. For He has heard your murmurings against Him; your murmurings are not against us — for what are we? — but against the Lord."

And while Aaron was speaking to the congregation of the children of Israel, they looked out over the wilderness, and there they saw the glory of the Lord appear in the clouds.

Then the Lord spoke to Moses, saying, "I have heard the murmuring of the children of Israel. Speak to them and say: 'At evening you will eat meat, and in the morning you will have your fill of bread, and so you will know that I am the Lord your God.' "

And it came to pass that in the evening quails flew up all over the camp; and in the morning dew lay all around the people. And when the dew had disappeared, they saw lying on the face of the wilderness small round things, as small as hoarfrost, on the ground.

Moses said to them, "That is the bread which the Lord has sent for you to eat. And this is the commandment of the Lord: You are to gather a omer [about a tenth of a bushel] for each man, depending on how many you have to feed; each man is to gather for those in his tents." So the children of Israel went out and gathered it. Some took more and some took less, but when they measured it with a omer, those who had gathered a great deal had nothing over, and those who had gathered little had no less; each man had enough to feed his people.

Moses said to them, "Let no one keep any until morning."

Nevertheless they did not listen to Moses, and some of them left it until the next morning; and it bred worms and smelled foul. Then Moses was angry with them.

So they gathered it every morning, each man according to those he had to feed; and when the sun grew hot, it melted.

When the sixth day came, they gathered twice as much food, two omers for each man; and all

the leaders of the community came to Moses for directions.

He said to them, "This is what the Lord has said: 'Tomorrow is the day of rest, the Lord's Sabbath; bake what you want to bake today, and boil what you want to boil, and what is left you may save, to keep for tomorrow.'"

So they laid it away until morning as Moses told them to, and it did not smell bad, nor was there a single worm in it.

Moses said, "Eat that today, for today is the Lord's Sabbath; today you will not find manna in the field. Six days you are to gather it, but on the seventh day, which is the Sabbath, there will not be any."

And so it was: for some of the people went out on the seventh day to gather, and they found none.

Now the house of Israel called the name of the food manna; and it was white like coriander seeds, and the taste of it was like wafers made with honey.

And the children of Israel ate manna forty years, until they came to the borders of the land of Canaan.

THE TEN COMMANDMENTS

T WAS in the third month after the children of Israel left Egypt that they came into the wilderness of Sinai. They pitched their tents in the wilderness and they camped together there before the mountain. Moses went up to talk to God, and the Lord called to him from the mountain, saying: "Tell this to the children of Israel; 'You have seen what I did to the Egyptians, and how I lifted you up on eagles' wings and brought you to myself. Now, if you will obey my voice and keep your agreement with me, then you will be a special treasure to me, more than any other people. You will be a kingdom of priests to me, and a holy nation.' This is what you are to tell the children of Israel." Moses came down and called the elders of the people together, and laid before them all the words of the Lord. And the people answered together and said, "All that the Lord has said, we will do."

Then Moses told the Lord what the people had said.

Then the Lord said to Moses, "Lo, I will come to you in a thick cloud, so that the people may hear when I speak to you and believe forever.

"Now go to the people, and purify them today and tomorrow, and have them wash their clothes and be ready for the third day. For the third day the Lord will come down in the sight of all the people upon Mount Sinai. Set bounds for the people, and warn them to take care not to go up on the mountain or touch the base of it, for whoever touches the mountain shall surely be put to death. Anyone who does touch it shall be stoned or shot, whether it be man or beast. But when the trumpet sounds a long blast, they shall come up to the mountain."

Then Moses went down from the mountain to the people, and he purified them, and they washed their clothes. And he said to the people, "Be ready for the third day."

The third day came at last, and in the morning there was thunder and lightning, and a thick cloud lay upon the mountain. Then the voice of the trumpet sounded so loud that all the people in the camp trembled.

Then Moses led the people out of the camp to meet with God, and they stood at the foot of the mountain.

Mount Sinai was covered with smoke, because the Lord descended on it in fire; the smoke rose up like the smoke of a furnace, and the whole mountain trembled and shook.

When the voice of the trumpet sounded long blasts, and grew louder and louder, Moses spoke and God answered him in a voice. Then the Lord came down upon the top of Mount Sinai, and He called Moses up to the top of the mount, and Moses went up.

And God spoke all these words:

"I am the Lord your God, who has brought you out of the land of Egypt, out of the house of slavery. You shall not have strange gods before me. You shall not carve idols for yourselves resembling anything in the sky above, or on the earth below, or in the waters under the earth. You shall not bow down to them or worship them.

"You shall not take the name of the Lord your God in vain.

"Remember to keep holy the Sabbath Day. Six days you shall work, but the seventh is the Sabbath of the Lord your God; on it you must not do any work.

"Honor your father and your mother.

"You shall not kill.

"You shall not commit adultery.

"You shall not steal.

"You shall not bear false witness against your neighbor.

"You shall not covet your neighbor's wife.

"You shall not covet your neighbor's goods."

All the people saw the thunder and lightning and heard the noise of the trumpet and saw the mountain smoke; and they were frightened and moved away, and waited at a distance.

They said to Moses, "You speak to us and we will listen; but do not let God speak to us, lest we die."

And Moses said to the people, "Do not fear, for God has come to test you, so that you may learn to have respect for Him, so that you will not do wrong."

Then the people stood far off, while Moses drew near to the thick darkness where God was. And the Lord spoke to Moses and gave him laws to govern the tribes of Israel in all their acts.

Moses came down and told the people all the words of the Lord and all His laws, and the people answered and said, "Everything the Lord has said, we will do." Moses wrote down all the words of

the Lord, and he arose early in the morning and built an altar to the Lord, with twelve pillars for the twelve tribes of Israel, and he sacrificed to the Lord.

Then, as the Lord had commanded, Moses took Aaron and seventy of the elders up on to the mountain.

But only Moses went up into the cloud which covered the top of the mountain, and he stayed forty days and forty nights, while the Lord gave him all the rules for the temple and the priests. And when the Lord had finished talking with him upon Mount Sinai, the Lord gave Moses two tablets of stone, bearing the laws written with the finger of God. These tablets were to be kept in a special box (known later as the Ark of the Covenant).

AARON MAKES THE GOLDEN CALF

HEN THE people saw that Moses was not coming down from the mountain at once, they gathered around Aaron and said to him, "Make us a god that will lead us, for as for this Moses, the man who brought us up out of the land of Egypt, we do not know what has become of him."

Aaron said to them, "Break off the golden earrings which your wives and sons and daughters wear in their ears, and bring them to me." So all the people broke off the golden earrings in their ears and brought them to Aaron. He took the offerings from their hands and melted the gold and fashioned it with a tool into a golden calf.

"Let this be your god, O Israel, which brought you up out of the land of Egypt," they said.

When Aaron saw this, he built an altar before the calf; then he made a proclamation and said, "Tomorrow is a feast to the Lord."

They rose up early the next morning and offered burnt offerings and brought peace offerings, and the people sat down to eat and to drink and rose up to play.

Then the Lord said to Moses, "Go down there, for your people, whom you have brought out of the land of Egypt, have wandered from the right path; they have turned aside from the way I commanded them to go, and they have made themselves a golden calf and worshiped it. They have made sacrifices to it and said, 'This is your god, O Israel, which brought you out of the land of Egypt.' " And the Lord said, "I have watched this people, and they are a stubborn people. Now leave me alone, for my anger has grown hot against them and I will destroy them and make a great nation of you alone." Then Moses pleaded with the Lord his God, saying, "Lord, why are you angry against this people you have brought out of the land of Egypt by Your great power and with Your mighty hand? Do You want the Egyptians to be able to say, 'He led them out as a trick to slay them in the mountains and destroy them from the face of the earth'? Remember Abraham, Isaac, and Israel, Your servants, to whom You swore by Your own name that You would multiply their race as the stars of the Heaven and give all this land You have spoken of to their children, so that they would inherit it forever."

So the Lord withdrew the threat which He had made against His people.

Then Moses turned and went down from the mountain, with the two tablets of laws in his hand; the tablets were filled with writing on both sides and were the work of God, and the writing was the writing of God engraved upon the tablets.

There was a man with Moses named Joshua. When he heard the noise of the people as they shouted, he said to Moses, "There is noise of war in the camp."

But Moses said, "It is not the voice of those who shout for victory, nor those who cry out in defeat; the sounds that I hear are the voices of those who sing."

As soon as he came close to the camp, he saw the calf and the dancing. With that, Moses' anger grew hot, and he hurled down the tablets from his hands, and they broke at the foot of the mountain.

He took the calf which they had made and burned it in the fire and ground it to powder and strewed it upon the water and made the children of Israel drink of it.

And Moses said to Aaron, "What did the people do to you that made you lead them into such great wrongdoing?"

Aaron said, "Do not be so angry, my lord; you know the people, and how they turn to mischief. They said to me, 'Make us a god to lead us, for we do not know what has become of Moses who led us out of the land of Egypt.' " Moses returned again to the Lord and said, "Oh, this people have done a great

wrong, and have made an idol of gold; yet, if You can, I ask You to forgive them; if not, I beg You to blot me entirely out of Your book."

The Lord said to Moses, "Go down and get on your way again, you and the people you have led up out of the land of Egypt, to the land which I promised to Abraham, to Isaac, and to Jacob for their children. I will send an angel before you to the land flowing with milk and honey, for I will not go with you myself, because you are a stubborn people."

When the people heard these words they mourned, and not a man of them wore his ornaments.

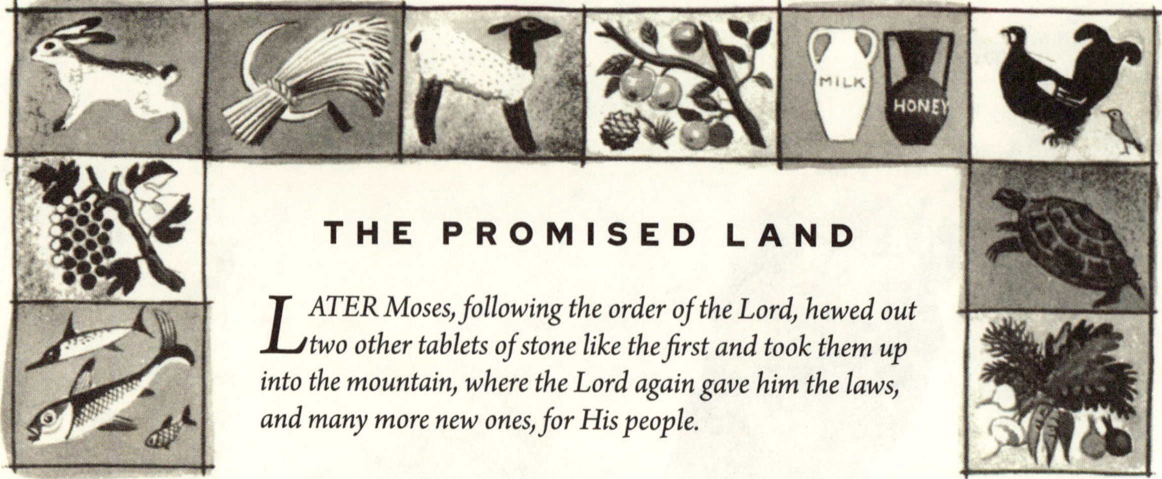

THE PROMISED LAND

LATER Moses, following the order of the Lord, hewed out two other tablets of stone like the first and took them up into the mountain, where the Lord again gave him the laws, and many more new ones, for His people.

"SEND OUT men to look over the land of Canaan, which I am giving to the children of Israel," said the Lord, speaking to Moses. "Send a man from every tribe, and let each one be a leader among his people." Moses chose the men and sent them to spy out the land of Canaan, and said to them, "Start off to the south, and go up into the mountains, and see the land. See what it is like, and whether the people who dwell there are strong or weak, few or many. See what the land itself is like that they dwell in, whether it is good or bad, and what their cities are like, whether they live in tents or in strongholds. See whether the country is rich or poor, whether or not it has wood, and bring back some of the fruit of the land."

Now it was time for the first ripe grapes. When the men went up and searched the land, they came to the brook of Eshcol, and there they cut down a branch with one cluster of grapes and carried it between two of them upon a long staff because of its size; and they brought some pomegranates and some figs.

After forty days they returned from searching through the land; they came back to Moses and Aaron and all the congregation of the children of Israel at Kadesh in the wilderness of Paran, and brought word to them and showed them the fruit of the land.

"We came to the land you sent us to," they told Moses, "and it is indeed flowing with milk and honey, and this is the fruit of it. Nevertheless, the people are strong who dwell in the land, and the cities are walled and very large." Caleb, one of the searchers, silenced the people and said, "Let us go up at once and take possession of the land, for certainly we are strong enough to do so."

But the other men who had gone up with him said, "We are not able to fight those people, for they are stronger than we." And they gave an evil report to the children of Israel on the land they had searched out, saying, "The land which we went up to look over is a land that eats up its inhabitants. And all the people we saw in it are men of great height. And in that land we saw giants, the sons of Enoch who was descended from giants; and we looked to ourselves like grasshoppers and were like grasshoppers in their sight."

Then all the congregation lifted up their voice and cried, and all the people wept that night.

The children of Israel murmured against Moses and Aaron, and the whole congregation said, to them, "Would to God that we had died in the land of

Egypt, or that we had died in the wilderness! Why has the Lord brought us to this land to fall by the sword, so that our wives and children will be captured? Would it not be better for us to return to Egypt?"

They said to one another, "Let us choose a captain and return to Egypt."

MOSES and Aaron, and Joshua and Caleb, two of the men who had gone to see the promised land, spoke to the people saying, "The land is an exceedingly good land. If the Lord is pleased with us, then He will bring us into this land and give it to us." But the people threatened to stone them.

Then the Lord was angry and wanted to disinherit the children of Israel, because they would not believe in Him. Moses begged the Lord to forgive His people, and at last He did; but the Lord decreed that the children of Israel should wander in the desert for forty years before they could enter the promised land.

MOSES COMPLETES HIS WORK

WHEN the forty years of wandering, with hardships and fighting, were over, Moses gathered the children of Israel together and reminded them of all the laws God had laid down for them and of their covenant with the Lord.

Moses knew that when he was no longer there to lead them, the people would forget their duty to God and disobey His laws, so he wrote them a song, and taught it to them, to remind them of the Lord's love for them.

He gave a special blessing to each of the tribes of Israel, and he finished with these words:

"THERE IS none like the God of Israel, who rides the highest heavens in His power, and in His majesty rides upon the sky. The eternal God is your refuge, and beneath you are His everlasting arms. He shall push away the enemy from before you and shall say, 'Destroy them.' Then Israel shall dwell alone in safety; the fountain of Jacob shall be upon a land of corn and wine, and His Heaven shall drop down dew.

"How happy you are, O Israel! Who is like you, O people saved by the Lord, the shield of your weakness and the sword of your power! You will find out the faults of your enemies and walk in the courts of their power."

Then Moses went up from the plain of Moab to the mountain of Nebo, to the peak of Pisgah over toward Jericho. The Lord showed him all the land He was giving to each of the tribes of Israel. He looked off to the farthest sea, and southward over the plain of the valley of Jericho, the city of palm trees, to Zoar.

And the Lord said to him, "This is the land which I promised to Abraham, to Isaac, and to Jacob; I have let you see it with your own eyes, but you shall not go over there."

So Moses, the servant of the Lord, died there in the land of Moab. They buried him in a valley in the land of Moab, near Beth-Peor, but no man knows to this day where his grave lies. And Moses was a hundred and twenty years old when he died; but his eyes were not dimmed, and his strength had not failed him.

The children of Israel wept for Moses in the plains of Moab thirty days. Then the days of weeping and mourning for Moses were over.

Now Joshua, the son of Nun, was full of the spirit of wisdom, for Moses had blessed him, and the children of Israel listened to his words and did as the Lord commanded. But never again in all Israel was there a prophet like Moses, whom the Lord knew face to face.

JOSHUA SENDS SPIES INTO CHANAAN

AFTER THE death of Moses, the Lord put Joshua in command of the children of Israel. "You must be strong and of good courage," said the Lord. "Do not be afraid, and do not be dismayed; for the Lord your God is with you wherever you go."

Joshua commanded the officers of the people: "Go among the people and tell them to prepare food, for within three days we shall pass over the Jordan river to enter the land which the Lord our God has given us."

Then Joshua sent out two men to spy secretly, saying, "Go look over the land and Jericho." They went, and came to the house of a woman named Rahab and took a room there.

Then the king of Jericho was told, "Men came here in the night from the children of Israel, to look over our country."

The king of Jericho sent word to Rahab: "Bring out the men who came to you and are now in your house, for they have come to spy in our country."

The woman took the two men and hid them and said, "There were two men who came here, but I did not know where they had come from. And about the time of the shutting of the gate, when it was getting dark, the men went out. Where they were going I do not know, but if you pursue them quickly you will overtake them."

But really she had brought them up to the roof of the house and hidden them under stalks of flax which she had laid out on the roof.

Meanwhile the king's men searched for them all the way to the fords of the Jordan.

Before the men on the roof had settled themselves, Rahab came up and said, "I know that the Lord has given you the land, and that your terror hangs over us, and all the inhabitants of the land faint because of you. For we have heard how the Lord dried up the water of the Red Sea for you when you came out of Egypt, and as soon as we heard that, our hearts melted, and not a man had any courage left, all because of you. For the Lord your God is God in Heaven above and in the earth beneath."

WHEN Rahab asked them to spare her family's lives in return for her helping them escape, the men agreed. They said to her:

"When the children of Israel come into the land, you tie a bit of scarlet cord in the window, and bring your father and mother and your brothers and all your father's household into your house. Then if anyone goes out from your house into the street, whatever happens to him will be his own fault, and we shall not be guilty; but we will be responsible for whoever stays with you in the house, to see that no one touches him. But if you say a word about our business here, then we will no longer keep our promise."

"It shall be just as you say," she said. Then she sent them away, and after they had left she tied the bit of scarlet in the window.

The two men went back down the mountain and crossed the river and came back to Joshua, the son of Nun, and told him all the things that had happened. And they said to Joshua, "Truly the Lord has delivered all the country into our hands, for all the people of the land faint with fear of us."

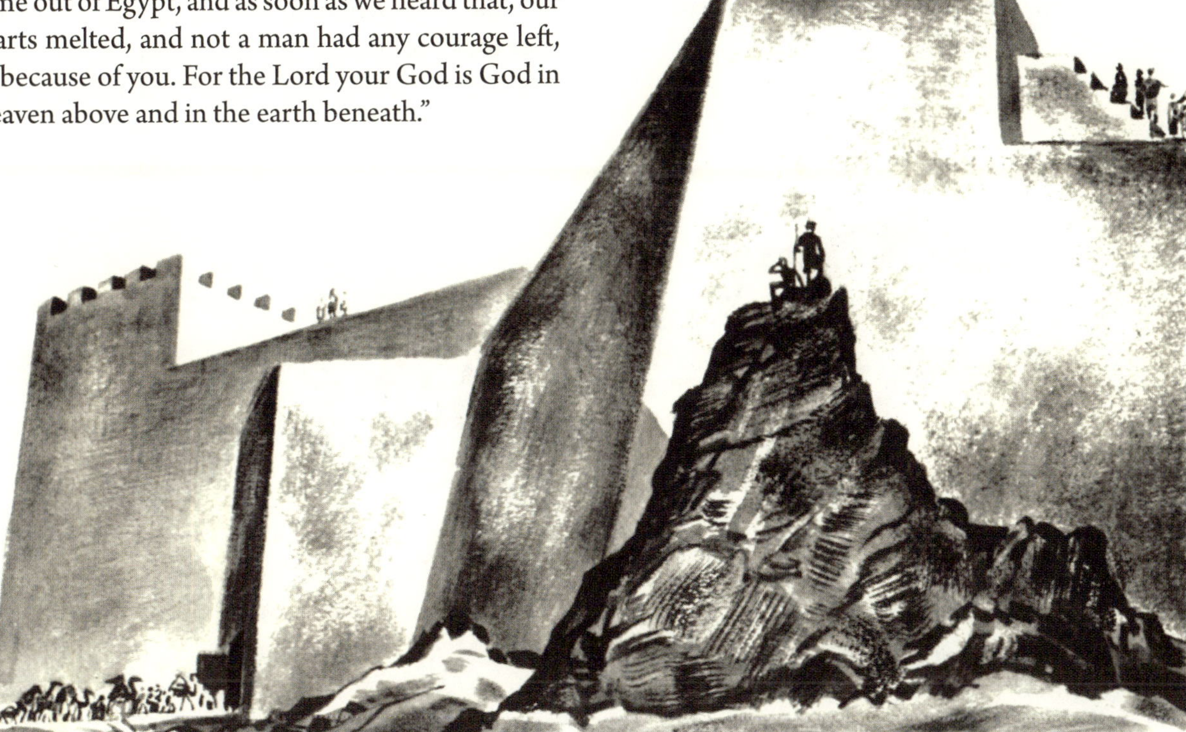

THE FALL OF JERICHO

JERICHO, THAT great city, was tightly shut up, because of the children of Israel; no one went out of the city, and no one came in.

Then the Lord told Joshua how he and the children of Israel could capture the city, and Joshua called the priests and the people and gave them their orders.

It came to pass, when Joshua had spoken to the people, that seven priests bearing seven trumpets made of rams' horns went forward before the ark of the Lord and blew on the trumpets, and the ark followed them. The armed men went before the priests blowing on trumpets, and the rear guard came after the ark.

Now Joshua had commanded the people, "You shall not shout nor make any noise with your voices, nor shall any word come out of your mouths until the day when I bid you to shout. Then you shall shout."

So the ark of the Lord circled the city, going about it once. Then they came back to the camp and stayed there.

Next day Joshua rose up early in the morning, and the priests took up the ark of the Lord. Again seven priests, bearing seven trumpets of rams' horns before the ark of the Lord, went steadily ahead, blowing on the trumpets; and the armed guard went before them; but the rear guard came after the ark of the Lord.

The second day they circled the city once and returned to the camp; this they did for six days.

It came to pass on the seventh day that they rose early, about the dawning of the day, and circled the city in the same way seven times. On that one day they circled the city seven times.

At the seventh time, while the priests blew on their trumpets, Joshua said to the people, "Shout, for the Lord has given you the city."

So the people shouted while the priests blew on their trumpets; and when the people heard the sound of the trumpet and shouted with a great shout, the wall fell down flat, so that the people went into the city, each man walking straight ahead, and they took the city.

Afterward Joshua took the whole land, according to all that the Lord had said to Moses, and Joshua gave it for an inheritance to Israel, according to their division by tribes. Then the land rested from war.

GIDEON AND THE MIDIANITES

BECAUSE THE children of Israel did evil in the sight of the Lord, the Lord delivered them into the power of the Midianites for seven years.

When the seven years were up, there came an angel of the Lord and sat under a certain oak in Ophrah, which belonged to Joash the Abiezrite. His son Gideon was threshing wheat in the winepress, to hide it from the Midianites.

The angel of the Lord appeared to him and said to him, "The Lord is with you, you mighty man of valor."

Gideon said to him, "Oh, my lord, if the Lord is with us, why has all this happened to us? Where are all His miracles, of which our fathers told us? The Lord has forsaken us now and has given us up to the Midianites."

Then the angel looked at him and said, "Go out in your strength, and you shall save Israel from the Midianites. Have I not sent you?"

"If I have found favor in your sight," Gideon said to him, "show me a sign that it is you who are talking with me. Stay here until I come back and bring a present and set it before you."

"I will wait here until you come again," the angel said.

So Gideon went in and prepared a kid and unleavened cakes of a measure of flour. The meat he put in a basket, and he put the broth in a pot and brought it out to the angel under the oak, and presented it.

The angel of God said to him, "Take the meat and the unleavened cakes and lay them upon this rock and pour out the broth." Gideon did so.

Then the angel of the Lord stretched out the end of the staff that was in his hand and touched the meat and the unleavened cakes, and fire rose up out of the rock and consumed the meat and the unleavened cakes. And the angel of the Lord disappeared from sight.

When Gideon saw that this was indeed an angel of the Lord, he said, "Alas, O Lord God! I am frightened because I have seen an angel of the Lord face to face."

The Lord said to him, "Be at peace, and do not be afraid; you shall not die."

Then Gideon built an altar there to the Lord, and called it Yahweh-Shalom, which interpreted means, "The Lord is peace."

THE TRUMPETS AND THE LAMPS

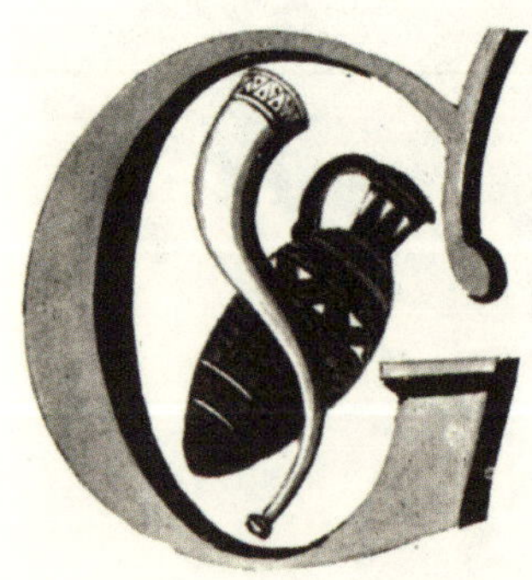

GIDEON ASSEMBLED an army of the men of Israel behind him. They pitched their tents beside the well of Harod, so that the ranks of the Midianites were off to the north of them by the hill of Moreh, in the valley.

The Lord said to Gideon, "The people with you are too many for me to give them a victory over the Midianites, for then Israel might boast of its own power, saying, 'Our own hands have saved us.' Go to the people, therefore, and tell everyone who is fearful and afraid to go back, and leave Mount Gilead."

Twenty-two thousand of the people returned, and ten thousand stayed.

Then the Lord said to Gideon, "There are still too many people. Bring them down to the water, and I will test them for you. If I say, 'This one shall go with you,' he shall go with you, and if I say, 'This one shall not go with you,' he shall not go."

So Gideon brought the people down to the water, and the Lord said to Gideon, "Set apart those who lap the water with their tongues, as a dog laps, and those who kneel down to drink." The number of those who lapped, putting their hands to their mouths, was three hundred men; but all the rest of the people bowed down upon their knees to drink water carelessly.

Then the Lord said to Gideon, "By the three hundred alert men who lapped I will save you and will deliver the Midianites into your hands; let all the other people go to their homes." So the chosen people took food in their hands, and their trumpets, and Gideon sent all the rest of the Israelites to their tents and kept only those three hundred men. And the army of Midian was beneath, in the valley.

That same night the Lord said to Gideon, "Arise, go down to the camp, for I have given it into your hands. But if you are afraid to go down, take your servant Purah down with you; you will hear what they are saying, and afterward your hands will be strengthened for the battle."

Then Gideon went down with Purah his servant to the outermost of the armed men that were in the camp. There the Midianites and the Amalekites and all the children of the east lay along the valley like grasshoppers in their numbers, and their camels were countless, as many as the sands by the seaside.

When Gideon came near, a man was telling a dream to his companion; and he said, "I just dreamed a dream, and in it a cake of barley bread tumbled into the camp of Midian. It came to a tent and struck it so that it fell and overturned, so that the tent lay flat on the ground."

His companion answered and said, "This is nothing else than the sword of Gideon, the son of Joash, a man of Israel. For God is giving him a victory over Midian and all the army." When Gideon heard the telling of the dream and the interpretation of it, he worshiped God; then he returned to the army of Israel and said, "Arise, for the Lord has given into your hands the army of Midian."

He divided the three hundred men into three companies, and he put a trumpet into every man's hand, and gave them empty pitchers with lights inside them.

"Watch me and do likewise," he said to them; "and see that when I come to the outskirts of the camp, you do just what I do. When I blow on a trumpet, I and those who are with me, then you blow on the trumpet too, on every side of the whole camp, and shout, 'The sword of the Lord and of Gideon!' "

So Gideon and the hundred men who were with him came to the outskirts of the camp in the beginning of the middle watch, when a new watch had just been posted. Then they blew on their trumpets and broke the pitchers that were in their hands. And the three companies all blew on their trumpets and broke the pitchers and held the lights in their left hands and the trumpets in their right hands. And they cried, "The sword of the Lord and of Gideon!"

They stood, every man in his place, round about the camp, and all the army of Midian cried out and fled.

The three hundred blew on their trumpets and through the whole army of the Midianites the Lord made men turn their swords against one another and they fled in confusion. The men of Israel pursued them beyond the Jordan, killing their leaders Oreb and Zeeb.

THE PARABLE OF THE TREES

GIDEON died, leaving seventy sons. One son, Abimelech, killed all his brothers but the youngest, Jotham, who hid himself. Then Abimelech made himself king.

JOTHAM HEARD of this and he went and stood on the top of Mount Gerizim, and lifted up his voice. And he cried, "Listen to me, you men of Shechem, that God may listen to you. "The trees went forth once upon a time to choose a king, and they said to the olive tree, 'Rule over us.'

"But the olive tree said to them, 'Should I leave my rich oil, by means of which both men and gods are honored, and go to be king over the trees?'

"Then the trees said to the fig tree, 'You come and rule over us.'

"But the fig tree said to them, 'Should I forsake my sweetness, and my good fruit, and go to be king over the trees?'

"Then the trees said to the vine, 'You come and rule over us.'

"And the vine said to them, 'Should I leave my wine, which cheers gods and men, and go to be king over the trees?'

"Then all the trees said to the worthless bramble, 'You come and rule over us.'

"And the bramble said to the trees, 'If you really appoint me king over you, then come and put your trust in me, and if not, let fire come out of the bramble and devour the cedars of Lebanon.' "

(Things happened just as Jotham's story suggested. Abimelech did turn upon and destroy the men who had made him king.)

SAMSON AND HIS MIGHTY STRENGTH

NOW Samson was the son of Manoah, of the family of the Danites. Before he was born, an angel of the Lord appeared to his parents to tell them that he was to be consecrated to God, and was never to drink wine or cut his hair. Samson grew up to be a powerful young man who killed a lion with his bare hands, and with the jawbone of an ox slew a thousand of the Philistines, who were enemies of the Israelites.

AMSON LOVED a woman in the valley of Sorek whose name was Delilah. The leaders of the Philistines came to her and said to her, "Coax him and learn what gives him his great strength, and by what means we may triumph over him, so that we may bind him and humble him; for this we will give you, every one of us, eleven hundred pieces of silver." So Delilah said to Samson, "Tell me, I beg you, what gives you your great strength, and how you could be bound to be made helpless."

"If anyone bound me with seven fresh bowstrings that have never been dried, I should be as weak as any other man," Samson said to her.

Then the leaders of the Philistines brought to her seven fresh bowstrings which had not been dried, and she bound him with them.

Now there were men lying in wait, waiting with her in the chamber. And Delilah said to Samson, "The Philistines are upon you, Samson.

Then he broke the strings as a strand of hemp is broken when it touches the fire; so the secret of his strength was not known.

Delilah said to Samson, "See, you have mocked me and told me lies. Now tell me, I beg you, with what could you be securely bound?"

And he said to her, "If they bind me fast with new ropes that have never been used, then I shall be weak and just like any other man." Delilah therefore took new ropes and bound him with them and said to him, "The Philistines are upon you, Samson!"

For again there were men lying in wait in the chamber. But Samson broke the ropes from his arms like a thread.

Delilah said again to Samson, "Up to now you have mocked me and told me lies. Tell me now with what you could really be bound." And he said, "Weave the seven locks of my hair with the web of cloth on your loom, and I shall be as weak as any other man."

She did so while he slept, and fastened it with the pin of the loom. Then she said to him, "The Philistines are upon you, Samson!"

But he waked out of his sleep and carried away the pin of the loom and the web of cloth.

Then she said to him, "How can you say 'I love you,' when you do not trust me in your heart.' Three times now you have mocked me and have not told me what the secret of your great strength is."

She kept on entreating him every day with her words, and when she had urged him, so that he was annoyed to desperation, he told her all that was in his heart.

"A razor has never touched my head," he said to her, "for I have been consecrated to God, a Nazirite, since before I was born. If I were shaved, my strength would go from me, and I would become weak and be like any other man."

When Delilah saw that he had told her the secret of his heart, she sent out a call for the lords of the Philistines, saying, "Come up once more for he has told me the secret of his heart." Then the lords of the Philistines came up to her, bringing the money in their hands.

Meanwhile she made Samson go to sleep on her knees; then she called for a man and had him shave off the seven locks of Samson's hair. By that she humbled him, for his strength went from him.

Then she said, "The Philistines are upon you, Samson!"

He awoke from his sleep, and said, "I will go out, as I did the other times, and shake myself." For he did not know that the power of the Lord was gone from him.

But quickly the Philistines took him, and put out his eyes, and took him down to Gaza. There they bound him with fetters of brass and made him grind in the prison house.

Gradually the hair of his head began to grow again. But the Philistines did not notice. They gathered together to offer a great sacrifice to Dagon, their god, and to rejoice; for they said, "Our god has delivered Samson our enemy into our hands."

It happened that, while the hearts of the people were merry, they said, "Call Samson out, so that he can entertain us." So they brought Samson up out of the prison house and made fun of him.

Seeing Samson, the people praised their god and said, "Our god has delivered into our hands our enemy and the destroyer of our country, who has slain many of us."

When they stood Samson between two pillars, he said to the boy who held him by the hand, "Let me touch the pillars which support the house, so that I may lean upon them." Now the house was full of men and women, and all the leaders of the Philistines were there; and there were about three thousand men and women on the roof, watching while Samson was made fun of.

Then Samson called out to the Lord and said, "O Lord God, remember me, I pray You, and strengthen me, I pray You, only this once, O God, that I may take revenge on the Philistines for my two eyes."

Then Samson took hold of the two middle pillars upon which the house stood, and which held it up; he held one with his right hand, and the other with his left.

Samson said, "Let me die with the Philistines." And he bowed himself with all his might, and the house fell upon all the people who were inside; so the number he killed at his death was greater than he had killed in his life.

Then his brothers, and all the household of his father, came down and took his body. And they took him home, and buried him between Zorah and Eshtaol, in the burying place of Manoah his father.

RUTH, THE FAITHFUL DAUGHTER-IN-LAW

IT HAPPENED, in the old days when the judges ruled Israel, that there was a famine in the land. And a certain man from Bethlehem went to stay in the country of Moab, he and his wife and his two sons. The name of the man was Elimelech, and the name of his wife was Naomi, and his two sons were Mahlon and Chilion. They came into the country of Moab and stayed there.

Elimelech, Naomi's husband, died, and she was left with her two sons. They took wives of the women of Moab; the name of the one was Orpah, and the name of the other Ruth. They lived there about ten years.

Then Mahlon and Chilion both died, and their mother was left without husband or sons. She arose, with her daughters-in-law, to return home from the country of Moab, for she had heard in the country of Moab how the Lord had visited His people and given them food again. Therefore she left the place where she was, with her two daughters-in-law, and they started to go back to the land of Judah.

But Naomi said to her two daughters-in-law, "Go, return each of you to her mother's house. May the Lord be as kind to you as you have been to the dead and to me."

They lifted up their voices and wept; and Orpah kissed her mother-in-law, but Ruth clung to her.

And Naomi said to Ruth, "See, your sister-in-law has gone back to her people and to her god. You go after your sister-in-law."

But Ruth said, "Do not ask me to leave you or to go back instead of following after you; for where you go, I will go; and where you stop, I will stop; your people shall be my people, and your God my God. Where you die I will die, and there I will be buried. The Lord punish me and more, if anything but death part me from you!"

When Naomi saw that Ruth was determined to go with her, she agreed. So the two traveled on together until they came to Bethlehem. They reached Bethlehem at the beginning of the barley harvest.

Now Naomi had a kinsman of her husband's, a mighty man of great wealth, of the family of Elimelech; and his name was Boaz.

Ruth the Moabite said to Naomi, "Let me go now to the fields and glean ears of grain after whoever gives me his approval to do so." And Naomi said to her, "Go, my daughter." So Ruth came to the field and gleaned after the reapers; and it was her luck to light on a part of the field belonging to Boaz, who was the kin of Elimelech.

It happened that Boaz came from Bethlehem and said to the reapers, "The Lord be with you."

And they answered him, "The Lord bless you."

Then Boaz said to the servant who was in charge of the reapers, "Whose girl is that?" The servant in charge of the reapers answered and said, "It is the Moabite girl who came back with Naomi from the country of Moab. She asked permission to glean and gather after the reapers among the sheaves, so she came and has worked since morning, until just now when she rested a little in the shelter."

Then Boaz said to Ruth, "Do you hear me, my daughter? Do not go to glean in another field, nor go away from here, but stay close by my maidservants. Watch the field where they reap and follow them. I have ordered the servants not to touch you. And when you are thirsty, go to the water jars and drink from the water which the young men have drawn." Then she fell on her face and bowed herself to the ground and said to him, "Why have I found favor in your eyes, that you should take notice of me, seeing that I am a stranger?"

Boaz answered and said to her, "I have heard all that you have done for your mother-in-law since the death of your husband, and how you have left your father and mother and the land of your birth, and have come to a people you had never known before. May the Lord repay your good deeds, and may a full reward be given you by the Lord God of Israel, under whose wings you have come to rest."

Then she said, "Let me find favor in your sight, my lord; for you have comforted me by speaking friendly words to your handmaid, though I am not really one of your handmaids." And Boaz said to her, "At mealtime come here and eat of the bread, and dip your piece into the sauce."

So she sat beside the reapers, and he passed her roasted grain, and she ate until she had had enough, and then left.

When she arose to glean again, Boaz gave orders to his young men, saying, "Let her glean even among the sheaves, and do not reproach her. And also let fall some handfuls on purpose for her, and leave them so that she may glean them, and do not stop her."

So she gleaned in the field until evening, and threshed out what she had gleaned, and it was about an ephah of barley.

She gathered it up and went into the city and showed her mother-in-law what she had gleaned.

Her mother-in-law said to her, "Where did you glean today? Where did you work? Blessed be he that took notice of you."

She told her mother-in-law with whom she had worked, saying, "The man's name with whom I worked today is Boaz."

Then Naomi said to her daughter-in-law, "May the Lord bless him, for the Lord has not stopped

showing kindness to the living and the dead." And she added, "The man is near of kin to us, one of our next kinsmen."

Ruth the Moabite said, "He told me, too, to stay near his young men until they have finished his harvest."

And Naomi said to Ruth her daughter-in-law, "It is good that you go out with his maidservants, so that you do not go into any other field."

So she stayed close by the maidens of Boaz to glean until the end of the barley harvest and of the wheat harvest; and she lived with her mother-in-law.

Ruth the Moabite pleased Boaz very much. When the harvest was over he went to the gate where the elders of the city sat, and, according to the custom of the Israelites, he announced that he wanted to marry Ruth. All the people who were at the gate wished them well, and gave them a blessing. So they were married, and Ruth bore a son. Then Naomi was happy again, and she became the child's nurse. They called the child Obed, and he became the father of Jesse, who was the father of David.

SAMUEL, CHILD OF THE LORD

NCE THERE was a woman named Hannah who was bitter in her soul because she had no sons or daughters. She prayed to the Lord and shed many tears. And she vowed a vow:

> "O Lord of hosts, if you will look down
> upon the sadness of your handmaiden
> and remember me, and will give to your
> handmaiden a manchild, then I will give
> him to the Lord all the days of his life, and
> no razor shall touch his head."

It came to pass in due time that Hannah bore a son, and she called him Samuel, "because," she said, "I asked him of the Lord."

Her husband Elkanah, and all his household, went up to offer to the Lord the yearly sacrifice. But Hannah did not go, for she said to her husband, "I will not go up until the child is weaned, and then I will take him so that he may appear before the Lord and stay there forever."

Elkanah her husband said to her, "Do what seems best to you; wait until you have weaned him; only keep your word to the Lord." So the woman stayed home and nursed her son until he was old enough to wean.

When she had weaned him, she took him up with her, with three calves and one measure of flour and a bottle of wine, and brought him to the house of the Lord in Shiloh, when the child was still very young.

They slew a calf and brought the child to Eli the priest. And Hannah said, "O my lord, I am the woman who stood in the temple here, praying to the Lord. I prayed for this child, and the Lord has given me what I asked of Him. Therefore I have lent him to the Lord. As long as he lives, he shall be lent to the Lord."

Then they worshiped the Lord there. And when Elkanah and his household went home, Samuel stayed, and was taught by Eli the priest.

Each year Samuel's mother made him a little coat and brought it to him when she came up with her husband to offer the yearly sacrifice.

And the child Samuel grew, and was in favor both with the Lord and with men. And he ministered to the Lord before Eli.

Eli's eyes began to grow dim, so that he could not see. Once when Eli was lying down in his place, before the lamp of God was put out in the temple where the ark of the Lord was kept, and before Samuel had lain down to sleep, the Lord called Samuel.

Samuel answered, "Here I am." He ran to Eli and said, "Here I am; you called me." Eli said, "I did not call. Lie down and sleep." He went and lay down, and again the Lord called, "Samuel."

Samuel arose and went to Eli and said, "Here I am, for you called me."

And Eli answered, "I did not call, my son; lie down again."

Now Samuel did not yet recognize the Lord, nor had the voice of the Lord been made known to him.

The Lord called Samuel again the third time, and he arose and went to Eli and said, "Here I am, for you called me."

Then Eli understood that the Lord had called the child. So Eli said to Samuel, "Go and lie down, and if He calls you, you are to say, 'Speak, Lord, for your servant is listening.' " So Samuel went and lay down in his place. The Lord came, and stood there, and called as at the other times, "Samuel, Samuel."

Then Samuel answered, "Speak, for your servant is listening."

And the Lord said to Samuel, "Behold, I am going to do something in Israel at which the ears of every one who hears it shall tingle. On an appointed day I will perform against Eli all the things I have spoken of concerning his household" (for Eli's sons were very wicked); "and when I begin I shall finish it. For I have told him that I will judge his house forever for the wickedness of which he knows, because his sons made themselves evil, and he did not stop them. Therefore I have sworn to the house of Eli that their wickedness shall not be cleansed with sacrifices nor offerings forever."

Samuel lay until morning; then he opened the doors of the house of the Lord, but he feared to tell Eli of the vision. Then Eli called Samuel and said, "Samuel, my son."

And he answered, "Here I am."

And he said, "What was it that the Lord said to you? I beg you not to hide it from me. May God punish you, and more, if you hide anything from me of the things that He said to you."

So Samuel told him everything, and hid nothing from him.

Eli said, "It is the Lord; let Him do whatever seems good to Him."

Samuel grew, and the Lord was with him. And all Israel, from Dan to Beer-sheba, knew that Samuel was a true and faithful prophet of the Lord.

DAVID, THE LORD'S CHOSEN ONE

FOR many years the tribes of Israel had been ruled by judges, but now the elders of the children of Israel gathered themselves together and asked Samuel to choose a king to rule over them. Samuel did not approve, for he felt the people would be poorer under a king and would come to regret it.

Nevertheless the people refused to obey the advice of Samuel, and they said, "Still we want a king over us."

So Samuel went out among the people of Israel and chose young Saul, a Benjamite, who was out with his servant hunting for his father's asses which were lost. Samuel took a vial of oil and poured it upon Saul's head and kissed him, and said, "The Lord has chosen you to be the captain of his people."

Saul was a handsome young man, head and shoulders taller than any of his fellows, and he became the first king over the children of Israel, and led them into many battles against their enemies, the Philistines.

But after a while, Saul disobeyed the laws of the Lord, so that the Lord took Saul's kingship from him.

THE LORD said to Samuel, "How long will you mourn for Saul, seeing I have rejected him from reigning over Israel? Fill your horn with oil and go; I will send you to Jesse of Bethlehem, for I have chosen a king from among his sons." Samuel did as the Lord told him and came to Bethlehem; and the elders of the town trembled at his coming and they said to him, "Do you come peaceably?"

"Peaceably," he said. "I have come to sacrifice to the Lord. Make yourselves ready and come with me to the sacrifice."

He blessed Jesse and his sons and called them to the sacrifice.

When they came, Samuel looked at Eliab and said, "Surely the Lord's chosen one is before him now."

But the Lord said to Samuel, "Do not look at his face or the height of him, because I have refused him. For the Lord does not see as man sees; man looks on the outward appearance, but the Lord looks at the heart."

Then Jesse called Abinadab and made him pass before Samuel; but Samuel said, "The Lord has not chosen this one either."

Then Jesse made Shammah pass by, and Samuel said, "Neither has the Lord chosen this one.

One after the other, Jesse made seven of his sons pass before Samuel. And Samuel said to Jesse, "The Lord has not chosen these." Then he asked, "Are all your children here?"

And Jesse said, "There is still the youngest, David. He is keeping the sheep."

Samuel said to Jesse, "Send and fetch him here, for we will not sit down until he comes." David was sent for, and soon appeared. He was a rosy, healthy boy, and handsome.

The Lord said to Samuel, "Arise, anoint him, for this is he."

Then Samuel took the horn of oil and anointed David in the midst of his brothers. And the Spirit of the Lord was with David from that day on.

DAVID MEETS SAUL, THE KING

ND THE Spirit of the Lord departed from Saul, and an evil spirit troubled him.

Then the servants of Saul said to him, "You see, an evil spirit from God is sent to trouble you. Now if you will command your servants, who are here before you, to find a man who is a cunning player on a harp, then when the evil spirit comes from God, he will play upon the strings, and you will be well."

"Find me a man who can play well," said Saul to his servants, "and bring him to me." Then one of the servants answered and said, "I have seen a son of Jesse the Bethlehemite, who is clever at playing and a mighty, courageous man, a man of war, sensible about business, a handsome person, and the Lord is with him." Therefore Saul sent messengers to Jesse, and said, "Send me your son David, who is out with the sheep."

Jesse took an ass loaded with food, and a bottle of wine, and a kid, and sent them by David his son to Saul. And David came to Saul and stood before him, and served him.

David became very fond of Saul and was made the king's armorbearer. Then Saul sent word to Jesse, saying, "Let David stay with me, for he pleases me very much."

And it was true that when the evil spirit from God came upon Saul, David took a harp and played upon the strings, and Saul was refreshed and felt well again, and the evil spirit departed from him.

DAVID AND GOLIATH

OW THE Philistines gathered their forces for battle. They gathered at Socoh, and they camped between Socoh and Azekah.

Saul and the men of Israel were gathered together and camped in the valley of Elah, lined up in battle array against the Philistines.

The Philistines stood on a mountain on one side, and Israel stood on a mountain on the other side, and there was a valley between them.

Out from the camp of the Philistines came a champion named Goliath of Gath, whose height was nine feet and nine inches. He had a helmet of brass upon his head, and he was armed with a coat of mail, and the weight of the coat was five thousand shekels of brass. He had plates of brass upon his legs, and a shield of brass covered his shoulders. The staff of his spear was like a weaver's beam, and his spear's head weighed six hundred shekels of iron. A shield bearer walked before him.

Goliath stood and cried out to the armies of Israel, "Why have you come out to set up your armies in battle array? Am I not a Philistine, and you servants of Saul? Choose a man to represent you, and let him come down to me. If he can fight me and kill me, then we will be your servants, but if I win over him and kill him, then you shall be our servants and serve us." And the Philistine said, "I defy the armies of Israel this day: send me a man, that we may fight together!"

When Saul and all the Israelites heard those words of the Philistine, they were dismayed and very much frightened. And every morning and evening for forty days, the Philistine drew near and challenged the Israelites.

David meanwhile had left the court of Saul to go home and feed his father's sheep at Bethlehem. His three eldest brothers were in the army of Saul.

Now Jesse said to David his son, "Take a measure of this roasted grain and these ten loaves for your brothers and run to your brother's camp. Carry these ten cheeses to the captain of their group, and see how your brothers are getting along."

David rose up early in the morning and left the sheep with a keeper, and started off as Jesse had commanded him. He came to the battle line just as the army was going out to the fight, shouting their battle cry. For Israel and the Philistines had put the army in battle array, army against army.

David left his baggage in the hands of the keeper of the baggage and ran among the army; he came up to his brothers and saluted them.

As he talked with them, up came the champion, Goliath of Gath, out of the armies of the Philistines, and he spoke his usual words, and David heard them.

All the men of Israel, when they saw the man, fled from him and were terribly afraid. "Have you seen this man who came up?" the men of Israel said. "He has come up to challenge Israel, and to the man who can kill him, the king will give great riches, and he will give him his daughter in marriage, and will make his father's house tax-free in Israel."

And David spoke to the men standing near him saying, "Who is this heathen Philistine, that he should challenge the armies of the living God?"

Eliab, his oldest brother, heard him speak to the men, and Eliab's anger was kindled against David, and he said, "Why did you come down here? With whom did you leave those few sheep in the wilderness? I know your pride, and the wickedness of your heart, for you have come down just so that you might see the battle." And David said, "What have I done now? Is there not a reason?" He turned from him toward another man and spoke to him in the same way, and the people answered him again just as before.

And when people heard the words which David spoke, they repeated them before Saul, and he sent for the boy.

But David said to Saul, "Let no man's heart be troubled because of Goliath. I, your servant, will go and fight this Philistine."

Saul said, "You are not able to go out to fight with this Philistine, for you are but a boy, and he has been a man of war since his youth." David said to Saul, "Your servant kept his father's sheep, and a lion came, or a bear, and took a lamb out of the flock. I went after him, and struck him down, and rescued it out of his mouth, and when he arose against me, I caught him by his beard and struck him and killed him. Your servant has killed both a lion and a bear, and this heathen Philistine will be as one of them, seeing that he has challenged the armies of the living God."

Moreover, David said, "The Lord who saved me from the paw of the lion and from the paw of the bear, he will save me from the hand of this Philistine."

Then Saul said to David, "Go, and the Lord be with you."

Saul armed David with his armor, and he put a helmet of brass upon his head, and clothed him in a coat of mail. David fastened Saul's sword upon his armor and tried to walk, for he had not yet tried it. Then David said to Saul, "I cannot fight with these, for I am not used to them." And he took them off.

He took his staff in his hand, and chose five smooth stones out of the brook, and put them in a shepherd's bag which he had, and with his sling in his hand he drew near to the Philistine.

The Philistine came on and drew near to David, and the shield bearer went before him. But when the

Philistine looked and saw David he scorned him, for he was but a boy, rosy and fair of face.

The Philistine said to David, "Am I a dog, that you come to fight me with sticks?" And the Philistine cursed David by his gods.

Then David said to the Philistine, "You come to me with a sword and with a spear and with a shield, but I come to you in the name of the Lord of hosts, the God of the army of Israel, whom you have challenged. This day the Lord will put you into my hands, and I will strike you down and take your head from you, and I will give the bodies of the army of the Philistines to the birds of the air and to the wild beasts of the earth, so that all the earth may know that there is a God in Israel. And everyone gathered here will know that the Lord saves not with sword and spear, but the battle is the Lord's and He will give you into our hands." Then, as the Philistine rose up and came nearer to meet David, David hurried and ran toward the army to meet the Philistine. And he put his hand in his bag and took out a stone, and slung it, and hit the Philistine in his forehead, so that the stone sank into his forehead and he fell upon his face on the earth.

So David triumphed over the Philistine with a sling and with a stone, and struck down the Philistine and killed him; but there was no sword in David's hand. Therefore David ran and stood over the Philistine and took his sword and drew it out of its sheath, and killed him and cut off his head with it.

When the Philistines saw that their champion was dead, they fled. And the men of Israel arose, shouting, and pursued the Philistines all the way to the valley, to the gates of Ekron.

THE FRIENDSHIP OF DAVID AND JONATHAN

SAUL took David home that day and would not let him go back to his father's house any more, and David and Jonathan, the son of Saul, became the best of friends.

But it happened as they came along, when David was returning from killing of the Philistine, that the women came out with joy from all the cities of Israel, singing and dancing, to meet King Saul, with tambourines and other musical instruments. And the women sang to one another as they played, and said, "Saul has killed his thousands and David his ten thousands." That displeased Saul, and he eyed David with suspicion from that day forward. Saul was afraid of David because the Lord was with him and had departed from Saul.

Twice, when the evil spirit was upon Saul, he tried to kill David, but still Jonathan loved David and protected him with his loyalty.

At last it was necessary for David to flee from the court, to be safe from Saul's anger, but still David and Jonathan swore to be friends forever.

ONE DAY Jonathan said to David, "Tomorrow is the feast of the new moon, and you will be missed, because your seat will be empty. When you have stayed away three days, come down quickly and wait by the stone Ezel.

"I will shoot three arrows beside the stone, as if I were shooting at a target. And watch, I will send a boy, saying, 'Go, find the arrows.' If I expressly say to the boy, 'See, the arrows are on this side of you, pick them up,' then you come out, for there will be peace, and no harm will be done to you, as the Lord lives.

"But if I say to the young man, 'See, the arrows are beyond you,' go your way, for the Lord will have sent you away.

"And about the matter of which we have spoken, may the Lord be between you and me forever."

So David hid himself in the field.

When the new moon had come, the king sat down to the feast. The king sat upon his seat, which, as always, was a seat along the wall, and Jonathan arose, and Abner sat beside Saul, but David's place was empty.

Still Saul did not say anything that day.

But it happened on the next day, which was the second day of the month, that David's place was empty again, and Saul said to Jonathan his son, "Why did the son of Jesse not come to dinner either yesterday or today?"

And Jonathan answered, "David earnestly asked permission of me to go to Bethlehem, for he said his family was to have a sacrifice there and his brother had bidden him to come, and he was eager to see all his brothers. That is why he did not come to the king's table." Then Saul's anger was kindled against Jonathan, and he said to him, "You son of a perverse, rebellious woman, do I not know that you have chosen the son of Jesse to your own downfall? For as long as he lives, you shall not be established in the kingdom. Now send and fetch him to me, for he must die."

But Jonathan answered Saul his father, and said to him, "Why should he be slain? What has he done?"

Then Saul threw a javelin at him to strike him, and by that Jonathan knew that his father was determined to kill David. So Jonathan arose from the table in fierce anger and ate no dinner the second day of the month, for he was grieving for David.

In the morning Jonathan went out into the field at the time he had set with David, taking a little boy with him.

He said to the lad, "Run and hunt for the arrows which I am going to shoot." And, as the lad ran, he shot an arrow beyond him.

When the lad had come to the place where the arrow fell, Jonathan cried out to the lad and said,

"Is the arrow not beyond you?" And again he cried, "Make speed, hasten, do not delay!" Jonathan's lad took up the fallen arrow and came to his master, but the lad did not understand the thing: only Jonathan and David knew of the matter.

Then Jonathan gave his weapons to the lad and said to him, "Go, and carry them to the city." And as soon as the lad was gone, David rose up from a place toward the south and fell on his face on the ground, and bowed himself three times.

They kissed one another and wept with one another, and Jonathan said to David, "Go in peace, for we have both sworn in the name of the Lord, saying, 'May the Lord be between you and me, and between your children and my children for ever.' "

David arose and departed, and Jonathan went back into the city.

DAVID SPARES SAUL'S LIFE

AVID AROSE one night and came to where Saul had pitched his tent, and David saw the place where Saul lay, and Abner, the son of Ner, the captain of his army, beside him. Saul lay in the middle of the camp, and his men were encamped around him.

So David took the spear and the jug of water from beside Saul's pillow, and stole away, and no man saw him or knew he was there or waked up, for they were all asleep; a deep sleep from the Lord had fallen upon them.

Then David went over to the other side and stood on the top of a hill far off, a long distance from the camp.

David cried to the people, and to Abner, the son of Ner, saying, "Are you not a courageous man? Who is like you in Israel? Why then have you not guarded the lord your king? For one of the people came in to destroy the king your lord. Look now for the king's spear and the jug of water that was at his pillow."

Then Saul knew David's voice and said, "Is that your voice, my son David?"

And David said, "It is my voice, O King." And he added, "Why does my lord pursue his servant this way? What have I done?"

Then Saul said, "I have sinned; return, my son David, for I will never more do you any harm, because my life was precious to you this day. I see now that I have been very wrong." Then David went on his way, and Saul returned to his palace.

ATER, Saul and Jonathan were both killed in battle. David then became king of Judah, and ruled for many years. After he died, his son Solomon became king.

THE PSALMS OF DAVID

PSALM 22

THE LORD is my shepherd; I shall not want.
He gives me rest in green pastures;
He leads me beside still waters.
He refreshes my soul.
He guides me in the right paths
for His name's sake.
Even though I walk in the dark valley
I will fear no evil, for You are with me.
Your rod and Your staff:
they give me courage.
You prepare a table before me
in the sight of my enemies;
You anoint my head with oil;
my cup runs over.
Only goodness and mercy shall follow me
all the days of my life.
And I will dwell in the house of the Lord
forever.

PSALM 26

The Lord is my light and my salvation;
whom should I fear?
The Lord is the protector of my life;
of whom should I be afraid?
When evildoers come at me
to destroy me completely.
My foes and my enemies
themselves stumble and fall.
Though an army should gather against me,
my heart shall not tremble.
Though they make war on me,
even then will I trust.
One thing I ask of the Lord;
this thing I seek;
To dwell in the house of the Lord
all the days of my life
That I may see the beauty of the Lord
and visit His temple.
For He will hide me in His dwelling
on the day of trouble;
He will conceal me in the shelter of His
dwelling.
He will set me high upon a rock.
Even now my head is held high
above my enemies on every side.
And I will offer in His dwelling
sacrifice with shouts of gladness;
I will sing and chant praise to the Lord.
Hear, O Lord, the sound of my voice;
have mercy on me and answer me.
My heart speaks of You, my eyes seek You;
I seek your presence, O Lord.
Hide not Your face from me;
do not drive off your servant in anger.
You are my helper, do not despise me;
forsake me not, O God my Savior.
Though my father and my mother forsake me,
yet will the Lord receive me.
Show me your way, O Lord, and lead me
in the right path because of my enemies.
Do not give me up to the wishes of my foes;
for false witnesses have risen up against me,
and such men as breathe violence.
I believe I shall see the goodness of the Lord
in the land of the living.

Wait for the Lord with courage;
be stouthearted, and wait for the Lord.
Praise the Lord from the heavens,
praise Him in the heights;
Praise Him, all His angels,
praise Him, all His warriors.
Praise Him, sun and moon;
praise Him, all shining stars.
Let them praise the name of the Lord
for He spoke and they were created;
He established them forever and ever;
He made a decree which shall not pass away.
Praise the Lord from the earth,
sea monsters and depths of the sea;
Fire and hail, snow and mist,
stormy winds fulfilling His word;
Mountains and all hills,
fruit trees and all cedars;
Wild beasts and all tame creatures,
things that creep and birds that fly.
Let the kings of the earth and all peoples,
the leaders and all the judges of the earth,
Young men too, and maidens,
old men and boys,
Praise the name of the Lord,
for His name alone is exalted;
May this be His praise from all His people,
from the children of Israel,
the people near to Him.

THE WISDOM OF SOLOMON

EOPLE OF Israel in those days sacrificed on hilltops, because there was no temple built to honor the name of the Lord.

King Solomon loved the Lord and followed the laws of David his father, but he too sacrificed and burned incense on hilltops. Often the king went to Gibeon to sacrifice there, for that was the most famous hilltop; a thousand burnt offerings Solomon offered upon that altar.

In Gibeon the Lord appeared to Solomon in a dream at night, and God said, "Ask of me whatever you want."

Solomon said, "You showed great mercy to your servant David, my father, because he walked before you in truth and in righteousness and was upright in his heart. You continued this great kindness to him in that you have given him a son to sit on his throne, as I do today.

"And now, O Lord my God, you have made your servant king instead of David my father, and I am like a little child: I do not know how to go out or come in. I, your servant, am in the midst of your great people whom you have chosen, so great a people that they cannot be numbered nor counted.

"Give, therefore, to your servant an understanding heart to judge your people, that I may judge between good and bad; for who is able to judge so great a people as yours?"

God was much pleased that Solomon asked this thing. And God said to him, "Because you have asked for this thing, and have not asked for long life for yourself, nor for riches for yourself, nor for the life of your enemies, but have asked for understanding to make wise judgments, you will see that I have done just as you asked. Lo, I have given you a wise and understanding heart, so that there has never been anyone like you before, nor shall anyone like you arise after you.

"And I have also given you that which you have not asked, both riches and honor, so that there will not be anyone who is your equal among the kings all your days.

"And if you will walk in my ways, to obey my laws and my commandments, as your father David did, then I will lengthen your days." Then Solomon awoke and knew that it was a dream. He went to Jerusalem and stood before the Ark of the Covenant of the Lord, and offered up burnt offerings and peace offerings, and made a feast for all his servants.

Then there came two women to the king, and stood before him.

The one woman said, "O my lord, this woman and I live in one house, and I bore a child in the house with her. And it happened that three days afterward, this woman bore a child, too. We were together, and there was no one else in the house with the two of us.

"This woman's child died in the night because she lay upon it, and she arose at midnight and took my son from beside me, while your handmaid slept, and she took him in her arms and laid her dead child in my arms.

"And when I rose in the morning to nurse my child, I saw that it was dead; but when I had looked at it in the daylight, I found that it was not my own son."

The other woman said, "No, the living is my son and the dead is your son."

And the first woman said, "No, the dead is your son and the living is my son."

Thus they argued before the king.

Then the king said, "The one says, 'This is my son that is alive, and your son is the dead child,' and the other says, 'No, your son is the dead one, and my son is the living.' " So the king said, "Bring me a sword," and they brought him a sword. "Divide the living child in two," he said, "and give half to the one and half to the other."

Then the mother to whom the living child belonged spoke to the king, for her heart ached for her son, and she said, "O my lord, give her the living child, and by no means kill it."

But the other said, "Let it be neither mine nor yours, but divide it."

Then the king answered and said, "Give the first woman the living child, and by no means kill it; she is the mother of it."

All Israel heard of the judgment which the king had handed down, and they respected the king. For they saw that the wisdom of God was in him, to give judgments.

And God gave Solomon great wisdom and understanding, and largeness of heart as the sand that is on the seashore. And Solomon's wisdom excelled the wisdom of all the children of the east country and all the wisdom of Egypt. For he was wiser than all men, and his fame spread through all nations round about.

And he spoke three thousand parables. He talked of trees, from the cedar tree that is in Lebanon even to the hyssop that springs out of the wall; he talked also of beasts, and of birds, and of creeping things, and of fish.

And people came from all lands to hear the wisdom of Solomon, from all the kings of the earth who had heard of his wisdom.

SOLOMON BUILDS THE TEMPLE

OW in the four hundred and eightieth year after the children of Israel had come out of the land of Egypt, in the fourth year of his reign, Solomon began to build a temple to the Lord.

The house of the Lord which King Solomon built was ninety feet long and thirty feet broad, and the height of it was forty-five feet. There was a broad porch before the temple, and it had windows and many chambers.

The house was built of stone made ready before it was brought there, so that there was no sound of a hammer or axe or any tool in the house while it was being built.

The walls and floors and ceilings of the house were of boards of cedar, and Solomon covered the floors with planks of fir.

And he adorned the whole house with pure gold, and the whole altar in the holy of holies was covered with pure gold. Within the holy of holies he had two cherubims of olive wood, each fifteen feet high, overlaid with gold, whose wings were spread wide to shelter the Ark of the Covenant.

All the walls and doors were carved with cherubims and palm trees, all covered with gold. And Solomon had all the vessels belonging to the house of the Lord also made of gold. The house was seven years in building, and then the work was finished which King Solomon had done for the house of the Lord.

Then it came to pass that a bright cloud filled the house of the Lord, and the glory of the Lord filled His house.

And Solomon said, "The Lord promised that He would dwell in a cloud!"

And Solomon stood before the altar of the Lord in sight of the assembly of Israel, and spread his hands before heaven, saying, "Lord God of Israel, there is no god like You in Heaven above or on earth beneath, who so keeps covenant and mercy with Your servants who have walked before You with all their heart. For You have chosen them to Yourself as an inheritance from among all other people of the earth, as You promised through Moses Your servant when You brought our fathers out of Egypt, O Lord God!"

ELIJAH AND THE POOR WIDOW

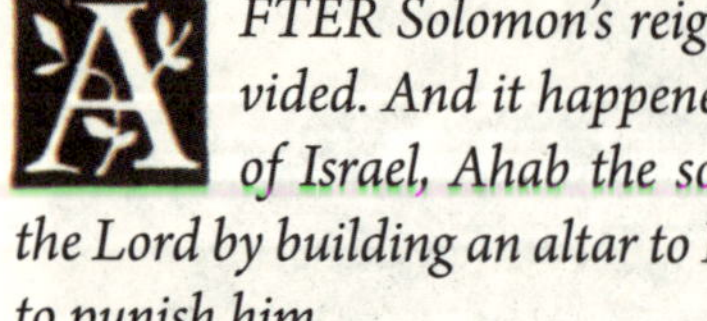

FTER Solomon's reign the kingdom was divided. And it happened that one of the kings of Israel, Ahab the son of Omri, displeased the Lord by building an altar to Baal. The Lord decided to punish him.

LIJAH THE Tishbite, an inhabitant of Gilead, said to Ahab, "As the Lord God of Israel lives, before whom I stand, there will not be dew nor rain for years, unless I say the word." Then the word of the Lord came to him, saying, "Get away from here and turn eastward and hide yourself by the brook Cherith, which is this side of Jordan. There you shall drink of the brook, and I have commanded ravens to feed you there."

So he went and did as the Lord had told him, and lived by the brook Cherith. And the ravens brought him bread and meat in the morning and bread and meat in the evening, and he drank of the brook.

But it came to pass, after a while, that the brook dried up, because there had been no rain in the land.

Then the word of the Lord came to him, saying, "Get up and go to Zarephath, which belongs to Sidon, and live there. You will find I have commanded a widow woman there to feed you."

So Elijah arose and went to Zarephath, and when he came to the gate of the city, he saw that the widow woman was there gathering sticks.

He called to her and said, "Fetch me, I beg of you, a little water in a vessel, so that I may have a

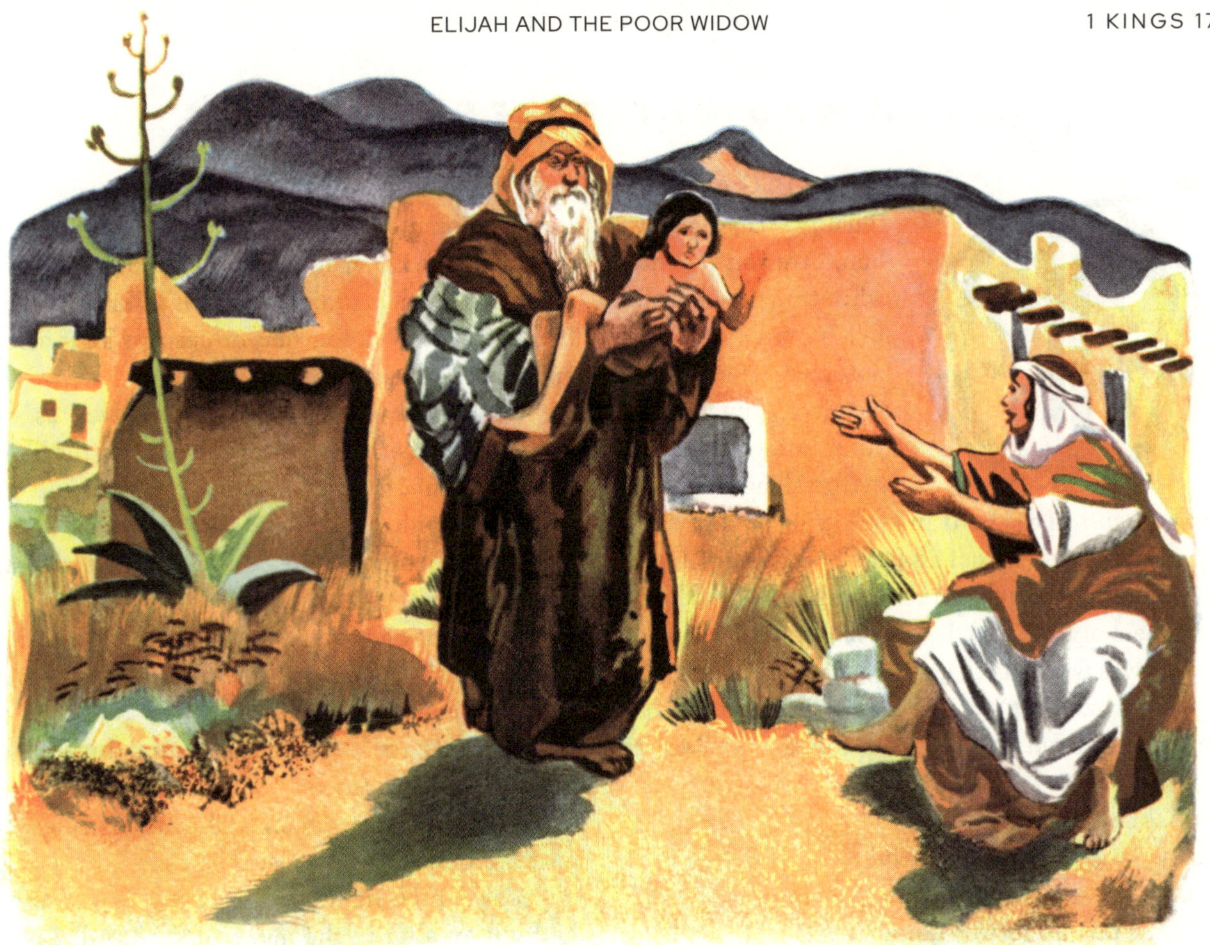

drink." And as she was going to fetch it, he called to her and said, "Please bring me a morsel of bread."

She said, "As the Lord your God lives, I have not a loaf, but only a handful of meal in a barrel, and a little oil in a jar. As you see, I am gathering a few sticks, that I may go in and prepare it for myself and my son, so that we may eat it and die."

Elijah said to her, "Do not fear; go and do as you have said; but first make me a little cake of the meal, and bring it to me, and afterward make some for yourself and for your son. For the Lord God of Israel has said, 'The barrel of meal shall not be empty, nor the jar of oil fail, until the day when the Lord sends rain upon the earth.'"

She went and did as Elijah told her, and she and Elijah and her household ate for many days.

But it happened, after these things, that the son of the woman, the mistress of the house, fell sick, and his sickness was so severe that there was no breath left in him.

She said to Elijah, "What have I done to you, O man of God? Have you come to me to remind me of my sins, and to kill my son?"

"Give me your son," he said to her, and he took him from her arms and carried him up to a loft where he stayed, and laid him upon his own bed.

Then he cried to the Lord and said, "O Lord my God, have You brought evil upon the widow with whom I am stopping, by killing her son?"

Then he stretched himself out upon the child three times and cried to the Lord, and said, "O Lord my God, I beg You, let this child's soul come back to him."

The Lord heard the voice of Ehas, and the soul of the child came into him again, and he breathed. Then Elijah took the child and brought him down from the chamber into the house, and gave him to his mother; and Elijah said, "See, your son lives!"

And the woman said to Elijah, "Now by this I know that you are a man of God, and that the word of the Lord which you preach is the truth."

ELIJAH AND THE PRIESTS OF BAAL

HEN KING Ahab saw Elijah, Ahab said to him, "Are you the man who troubles Israel?" Elijah answered, "It is not I who have troubled Israel, but you and your father's house, by forsaking the commandments of the Lord and following the Baals.

"Now you send out and gather together all Israel at Mount Carmel, and the four hundred and fifty prophets of Baal, and the four hundred prophets of the groves who eat at Queen Jezebel's table."

So Ahab sent word to all the children of Israel and gathered the prophets together at Mount Carmel.

Then Elijah came before all the people and said, "How long will you waver between two opinions? If the Lord is God, follow Him; if Baal, follow him."

The people answered not a word.

Then Elijah said to the people, "I, and I alone, remain a prophet of the Lord, but the prophets of Baal are four hundred and fifty men. Let them, then, get us two calves, and let them choose one calf for themselves and cut it in pieces and lay it on the wood, but put no fire under it. And I will dress the other calf and lay it on the wood, and put no fire under it.

"Then you call on the name of your gods, and I will call on the name of the Lord, and the God that answers with fire, let him be God." And all the people answered and said, "It is well spoken."

Elijah said to the prophets of Baal, "Choose one calf for yourselves and dress it first, for there are many of you. Call on the names of your gods, but do not put any fire under it."

They took the calf which was given them, and they dressed it and called on the name of Baal from morning until noon, saying, "O Baal, hear us." But there was no voice nor any answer, though they leaped upon the altar they had made.

At noon Elijah mocked them and said, "Cry aloud, for he is a god; either he is talking, or he is busy, or he is on a journey, or perhaps he is asleep and must be awakened."

They cried aloud and cut themselves, as was their custom, with knives and lances, until the blood gushed out upon their robes.

When midday was past, they worshiped before the altar until time for the evening sacrifice, and still there was neither a voice nor any answer nor any sign that their gods heard them as they prayed.

Then Elijah said to all the people, "Come near to me."

All the people gathered around him. Then he walked up to the altar of the Lord which had been broken down. Elijah took twelve stones, according to the number of the tribes of the sons of Jacob which made up Israel. With the stones he built an altar in the name of the Lord, and he made a trench around the altar, large enough to hold two measures of seed. He put the wood in order, and cut the calf in pieces and laid it on the wood.

Then he said, "Fill four barrels with water and pour it on the burnt sacrifice and on the wood." When they had done this he said, "Do it a second time," and they did it a second time. And he said, "Do it a third time," and they did it a third time.

The water ran around the altar, and he filled the trench with water, too.

Then, when it was time for the offering of the evening sacrifice, Elijah the prophet came near and said, "O Lord God of Abraham, Isaac, and Israel, let it be known today that You are the God in Israel, and that I am Your servant and have done all these things at Your command.

"Hear me, O Lord, hear me, that this people may know that You are the Lord God, and that You may have their hearts again."

Then the fire of the Lord came down and consumed the burnt sacrifice and the wood and the stones and the dust, and licked up the water that was in the trench.

When all the people saw it, they fell on their faces and said, "The Lord, He is God; the Lord, He is God."

THE PARTING OF ELIJAH AND ELISHA

FINALLY THE Lord decided to take Elijah up into Heaven in a whirlwind. At that time Elijah was with Elisha, his faithful follower. Elijah said to Elisha "Wait here, I beg you, for the Lord has told me to go to Bethel."

But Elisha said to him, "As the Lord lives and as your soul lives, I will not leave you." So they went down together to Bethel. Then the followers of the prophets who were at Bethel came out to meet Elisha and said to him, "Do you know that the Lord is going to take away your master from you today?"

"Yes, I know it," he said. "Hold your peace." And Elijah said to him, "Elisha, wait here, I beg of you. For the Lord has told me to go to Jericho."

And Elisha said, "As the Lord lives, and as your soul lives, I will not leave you."

So they went on to Jericho. Then the followers of the prophets who were at Jericho came to Elisha and said to him, "Do you know that the Lord is going to take away your master from you today?"

He said, "Yes, I know it. Hold your peace." And Elijah said to him, "Wait here, I beg you, for the Lord has told me to go to the Jordan." But Elisha said, "As the Lord lives, and as your soul lives, I will not leave you."

So the two went on. And fifty of the followers of the prophets went and stood at a distance to watch; and the two stood beside the Jordan.

Then Elijah took his mantle and folded it over, and struck the waters so that they were divided on either side, and the two men went across on dry ground.

It happened, when they had crossed over, that Elijah said to Elisha, "Ask what you will of me, before I am taken away from you." Elisha said, "Grant me a double portion (the eldest son's share) of your spirit, I beg you!"

"You have asked a hard thing," Elijah said. "Nevertheless, if you see me when I am taken from you, you shall have your wish; but if not, you shall not have it."

It happened, as they went on and talked together, that a chariot of fire appeared, and horses of fire, and swept them apart; and Elijah went up by a whirlwind into Heaven.

Elisha saw it, and he cried, "My father! The chariot of Israel, and its charioteer!" Then he could not see him any more, and he took hold of his own robe and ripped it in two.

He picked up Elijah's mantle which had fallen from him, and went back and stood by the bank of the Jordan. He took Elijah's mantle and struck the waters and said, "Where is the Lord God of Elijah?" And when he had struck the waters, they parted on either side of him, and Elisha crossed over.

When the followers of the prophets who had come to watch saw him, they said, "The spirit of Elijah rests on Elisha." And they came to meet him, and bowed themselves to the ground before him.

ELISHA CURES NAAMAN'S LEPROSY

NAAMAN, CAPTAIN of the army of the king of Syria, was a great man among his master's followers, and honorable. Through him the Lord had granted freedom to Syria. He was also a man of great courage; but he was a leper.

The Syrians had gone out by companies and had brought back as a captive out of the land of Israel a little girl; and she was a maidservant to Naaman's wife.

She said to her mistress, "I would to God my lord were with the prophet who is in Samaria, for he would cure him of his leprosy."

Someone went in and told the king, saying, "Thus and thus said the girl who is from the land of Israel."

The king of Syria said, "Go now, go, and I will send a letter to the king of Israel." Naaman departed with the letter, and took with him ten talents of silver, and six thousand pieces of gold, and ten complete changes of clothing.

He delivered to the king of Israel the letter, which said: "Now when this letter comes to you, you will see that I have sent to you with it Naaman, my servant, that you may cure him of his leprosy."

When the king of Israel had read the letter, he tore his clothes, and said, "Am I God, to kill and to make alive, that this man sends a man to me to be cured of his leprosy? Perhaps he is just trying to pick a quarrel with me."

Now when Elisha the man of God heard that the king of Israel was troubled, he sent word to the king, saying, "Why did you tear your clothes? Let the man come to me, and he shall know that there is a prophet in Israel."

So Naaman came with his horses and his chariot, and stood at the door of the house of Elisha.

Elisha sent a messenger to him, saying, "Go and wash in the Jordan seven times, and your flesh shall be healed again, and you will be well." Then Naaman was angry and went away, and said, "See now, I thought, 'He will surely come out to me and stand there and call on the name of the Lord his God and strike his hand on the place and cure the leprosy.' Are not Abana and Pharpar, the rivers of Damascus, better than all the waters of Israel? May I not wash in them and be cured?"

So he turned and went away in a rage.

His servants came up and spoke to him, and said, "My father, if the prophet had ordered you to do some great thing, would you not have done it? How much rather then obey when he says to you, 'Wash and be made well'?" Then he went down and dipped himself seven times in the Jordan, just as the man of God had said, and his flesh was once again like the flesh of a little child, and he was well.

He went back to the man of God, he and all his company, and came and stood before him, and he said, "Now I know that there is no God in all the earth but in Israel."

THE PROPHECY OF ISAIAH

AT THE time when King Uzziah died, I saw the Lord sitting on a throne lifted up on high, and His train filled the temple. Above it stood the seraphims. Each had six wings: With two He covered His face, and with two He covered His feet, and with two He did fly.

One cried to another and said, "Holy, holy, holy is the Lord God of hosts. The whole earth is full of His glory."

The posts of the door moved at the voice of him who cried, and the house was filled with smoke.

Then I said, "Woe is me! For I am ruined, because I am a man of unclean lips and I dwell in the midst of people of unclean lips, and now my eyes have seen the King, the Lord of hosts." Then one of the seraphims flew to me, bearing in his hand a live coal which he had taken from the altar with tongs. He laid it upon my mouth and said, "See, this has touched your lips, and your wickedness is taken away, and your sin purified."

Also I heard the voice of the Lord saying, "Whom shall I send' Who will go for us?" Then I said, "Here I am. Send me."

He said, "Go and tell this people: 'You hear, but you cannot understand. You see, but you cannot realize what you see.'

"Make the heart of this people sluggish, and make their ears heavy, and shut their eyes, lest they see with their eyes, and hear with their ears, and understand with their hearts, and change their ways and become healed."

Then I said, "Lord, how long?"

And He answered, "Until the cities are wasted and without inhabitants, and the houses are vacant, and the land is utterly desolate. Then the Lord will have removed the men far away, and the whole land will be forsaken."

(Isaiah was one of many prophets whose outlook for the future of Israel was very gloomy, but he saw a better day coming far ahead.)

The Lord Himself shall give you a king: You will see, a virgin will conceive and bear a son, and shall call His name Emmanuel. Butter and honey shall He eat, that He may know how to refuse the evil and choose the good.

The people who walked in darkness have seen a great light; upon those who dwell in the land of the shadow of death, the light has shone.

For unto us a child is to be born; unto us a son shall be given. And the government shall be upon His shoulders. His name shall be called Wonderful, Counselor, The Mighty God, The Everlasting Father, The Prince of Peace.

Of the spread of His kingdom and His peace there shall be no end, from now on, even forever. The zeal of the Lord of hosts will bring all this about.

JOSIAH AND THE BOOK OF THE LAW

JOSIAH WAS eight years old when he began to rule, and he ruled thirty-one years in Jerusalem. He did what was right in the sight of the Lord, and followed in the footsteps of David his forefather, and turned not aside to the right or to the left.

It happened in King Josiah's eighteenth year that the king sent Shaphan, the son of Azaliah, the son of Meshullam, the scribe, to the house of the Lord with these words:

"Go up to Hilkiah the high priest and have him add up the silver which is brought into the house of the Lord, which the keepers of the door have gathered from the people. Let them deliver it into the hands of the workers who oversee the house of the Lord, and let them give it to the workers in the house of the Lord, to repair the house. Get carpenters and builders and masons, and buy timber and hewn stone to repair the temple."

No records were kept of the money that was paid to the men, because they worked faithfully.

When Shaphan the scribe went to the temple, Hilkiah the high priest said to him, "I have found the book of the law in the house of the Lord." And Hilkiah gave the book to Shaphan, and he read it.

Shaphan the scribe came to the king and reported to the king: "Your servants have gathered up the money that was found in the temple, and have paid it to the workers who have the overseeing of the temple." Then Shaphan the scribe showed the king the book, saying, "Hilkiah the priest has delivered this book to me." And Shaphan read it before the king.

And when the king had heard the words of the book of the law (which we know as Deuteronomy), he tore his clothes, for he knew his fathers had not listened to the words of this book, to obey all the laws that were written down for them.

The king sent for all the elders of Judah and of Jerusalem; then he went up to the house of the Lord, taking all the men of Judah and all the inhabitants of Jerusalem with him, both the priests and the prophets and all the people, both small and great, and he read into their ears all the words of the book of the covenant which was found in the house of the Lord.

The king stood by a pillar and made a covenant before the Lord, to walk in His ways and to keep His commandments and follow His words and His laws, with all his heart and with all his soul, and to live up to the words of this covenant that were written in the book; and all the people stood to swear to the covenant.

Then the king commanded Hilkiah the high priest, and the priests of the second order, and the keepers of the door, to bring forth out of the temple of the Lord all the vessels that were made for Baal and his sacred wood, and for all the other gods; and he burned them outside Jerusalem in the fields of Kidron, and carried the ashes of them to Bethel.

He put down the idolatrous priests, whom the kings of Judah had ordained to burn incense in the high places in the cities of Judah and in the places round about Jerusalem, and also those who burned incense to Baal, to the sun, and to the moon, and to the planets, and to all the various gods. Josiah destroyed also the workers with ghosts and magic, and the wizards, and the images, and the idols, and all the evil things that were to be found in the land of Judah and in Jerusalem, so that he might live up to the words of the law which were written in the book that Hilkiah the priest found in the house of the Lord.

There had been no king like Josiah. For he turned to the Lord with all his heart, and with all his soul, and with all his might, according to all the law of Moses; neither did any come after him who were his equal.

THE MESSAGE OF THE PROPHETS

HERE were always men of God in Israel and Judah, no matter how wicked most of the kings, no matter how great the people's lack of faith. God sent special messengers, his chosen prophets, to each generation with His messages of warning and of comfort.

Through the prophets, God made it very clear that Israel and Judah would be punished for their idolatry and their unbelief. Yet a remnant of the people would be saved, and when the time for punishment was past a new king would come from the royal house of David — the king of whom ISAIAH spoke — who would rule all the earth and whose kingdom would have no end.

A PROPHECY OF AMOS

Behold, the eyes of the Lord are upon the sinful kingdom; and I will destroy it from the face of the earth.

But yet I will not completely destroy the house of Jacob — this is what the Lord says.

For behold, I will command, and I will sift the house of Israel among all nations as grain is sifted in a sieve.

But not one kernel shall fall to the ground.

All the sinners of my people shall fall by the sword, those who say "These evils shall not come near, and shall not come upon us!"

On that day I will raise up the tent of David which was fallen, and I will close up the tears in its walls and repair its damages,

And I will rebuild it as in the days of old.

A PROPHECY OF HOSEA

She (Israel) ran after false lovers and forgot me — this what the Lord says.

Therefore, behold, I will woo her and lead her into the desert and speak to her heart.

There she shall answer me as in her youth, as on the day when she came up out of Egypt.

I will take the names of Baals out of her mouth and she shall remember their names no more.

On that day I will make a covenant with her. I will destroy the bow, sword, and war from the land and make her sleep in safety.

Then I will wed you to myself forever, I will wed you to myself in righteousness and justice, in grace and mercy.

And I will wed you to myself in faithfulness that you may know I am the Lord.

A PROPHECY OF JEREMIAH

Behold, the days shall come — this is what the Lord says —

When I will make a new covenant with the house of Israel and with the house of Judah,

Not like the covenant I made with their fathers when I took them by the hand to bring them out of Egypt, the covenant they have broken despite my dominion over them;

But this shall be the covenant I will make with the house of Israel in those days — this is what the Lord says:

I will put my law within them and I will write it in their hearts, and I will be their God and they shall be my people. I will forgive their iniquity and I will remember their sin no more.

A PROPHECY OF EZEKIEL

I will make them one people in the land, upon the mountains of Israel, and one king shall be king over them all, and they shall no more be two nations nor be divided into two kingdoms.

My servant David shall be king over them, and they shall have one shepherd.

They shall walk in my judgments and keep my commandments, and shall fulfill them.

And I will make a covenant of peace with them. It shall be an everlasting covenant with them.

I will establish them and multiply them, and I will set my sanctuary among them forever.

A PROPHECY OF MICAH

It shall come to pass in the last days that the mountain of the Lord's house shall be established as high as the highest mountains, high above the hills, and people shall flow to it.

And many nations shall come in haste and say, "Come, let us go up to the mountain of the Lord and to the house of the God of Jacob that He may teach us His ways and we may walk in His paths."

And they shall beat their swords into plows and their spears into pruning hooks.

Nation shall not lift up sword against nation nor shall they learn war any more.

A PROPHECY OF JOEL

The Lord shall roar out of Zion, and He shall speak His voice from Jerusalem.

The heavens and the earth shall tremble, but the Lord shall be the hope of His people and the strength of the children of Israel.

"You shall know that I am the Lord your God, dwelling in Zion, my holy mountain.

Jerusalem shall be holy, and strangers shall pass through it no more.

It shall come to pass on that day that the mountains shall drip sweetness and the hills shall flow with milk and a fountain shall come from the house of the Lord to water the valley of thorns."

A PROPHECY OF ZECHARIAH

Rejoice greatly, O daughter of Zion; shout for joy, O daughter of Jerusalem!

Behold, your King comes to you. He is just, he is victorious.

He is humble, and he rides upon an ass and upon a colt, the foal of an ass.

He will destroy the chariots of Ephraim and do away with Jerusalem's war horses.

He will break the bow of war and shall bestow peace on the nations.

His rule shall extend from sea to sea and from the Euphrates to the ends of the earth.

Because of the blood of your covenant I will free your prisoners from the waterless pit.

A PROPHECY OF MALACHI

Behold, I will send my Angel and he shall prepare the way before my face.

And suddenly the Lord whom you seek, the Angel of the testament whom you desire, shall come to His temple!

Behold, He is coming—this is what the Lord of hosts says.

Who will endure the day of His coming? Who can stand in His presence?

For He is like the smelter's fire, and like the soapmaker's lye.

He shall sit down like a smelter and refiner of silver. And He shall purify the sons of Levi.

JONAH AND THE GREAT FISH

IN GALILEE there lived a prophet named Jonah, and the word of the Lord came to him, saying, "Arise, and go to Nineveh, the great city, and preach in it; for its wickedness has offended me." But Jonah fled from the face of the Lord and went down to Joppa to take a ship for Tarshish (in the opposite direction from Nineveh).

Then the Lord sent a great wind and the ship was in danger of being wrecked. The sailors said to one another, "Come, let us cast lots to find out why this evil has come upon us." So they cast lots, and the lot fell upon Jonah.

They said to him, "Tell us why this evil has come upon us. What is your business? What country are you from? Where are you going?" And he said to them, "I am a Hebrew, and I fear the Lord, the God of Heaven, who made both the sea and the dry land."

And they said to him, "What shall we do with you so the sea will be calm for us?"

And he said to them, "Throw me into the sea, for I know this storm has come upon you because of me."

The men tried to row to land, but they were not able for the sea was raging and tossing. They cried out to the Lord, and said, "We beg You, Lord, do not let us perish for this man's life and do not blame us for an innocent death, for You have done what pleased You!" They took Jonah and threw him into the sea, and the sea stopped raging. But the men were afraid.

Now the Lord made ready a great fish to swallow Jonah, and Jonah was in the belly of the fish three days and three nights. And Jonah prayed to the Lord out of the belly of the fish. At last the Lord spoke to the fish, and it vomited Jonah out on the dry land.

The word of the Lord came to Jonah a second time, saying, "Arise, and go to Nineveh, the great city, and preach there the preaching I tell you to."

And Jonah arose and went to Nineveh according to the word of the Lord. He walked about the city for one day's journey, crying out and saying, "In forty days, Nineveh will be destroyed!"

The men of Nineveh believed in God and proclaimed a fast, and put on sackcloth from the greatest of them down to the least.

The word came to the king of Nineveh, and he got up from his throne and threw off his robe, clothed himself in sackcloth and sat in ashes.

He caused it to be proclaimed in Nineveh from the mouth of the king and his princes, saying, "Let neither men nor beasts, oxen or sheep, taste anything. Let them not feed or drink water. Let men and beasts be covered with sackcloth and cry to the Lord with all their might. Let them turn everyone from his evil way and from the wickedness that they did.

"For who can tell whether God will turn again and forgive, and will turn away His fierce anger and we shall not perish?"

And God saw their works, and saw that they were turned from their evil ways. And God had mercy and did not send the punishment upon them He had said He would send.

THE PATIENCE OF JOB

JUST AND blameless man whose name was Job lived in the land of Uz. He had seven sons and three daughters, seven thousand sheep, three thousand camels, five hundred yoke of oxen, five hundred she-asses, and a great number of work animals, so that he was greater than any other man in the East.

One day Satan came before the Lord, and the Lord said to Satan, "Have you noticed my servant Job, that there is no one on earth like him, blameless and upright, fearing God and avoiding evil?"

But Satan answered, saying, "Have not You surrounded him and his family and all that he has with Your protection? Try putting forth Your hand and harming anything he has, and he will curse You to Your face."

The Lord said to Satan, "All he has is in your power, but do not harm his body."

And Satan went forth from the presence of God.

On a certain day, a messenger came to Job and said, "The oxen were plowing, and the asses were feeding beside them, and Sabeans carried them off in a raid. They killed the herdsmen with swords, and I alone escaped to tell you."

While he was yet speaking, another came and said, "Lightning came from heaven and struck the sheep and their shepherds and consumed them, and I alone escaped to tell you." While he was yet speaking, another came and said, "The Chaldeans came in three troops, seized the camels, carried them off, and killed those tending them with swords, and I alone escaped to tell you."

While he was yet speaking, another came and said, "Your sons and daughters were eating and drinking in their eldest brother's house when a great wind came across the desert and shook the house. It fell down on them and they are dead, and I alone escaped to tell you.

Then Job threw himself on the ground and said:

"I came naked from my mother's womb and naked I shall go back again. The Lord gave and the Lord has taken away. Blessed be the name of the Lord."

In all these things, Job did not say any sinful or foolish thing against God.

And Satan came before the Lord again and the Lord said to Satan, "Have you noticed my servant Job, that there is no one on earth like him, blameless and upright, fearing God and avoiding evil?"

But Satan answered, saying, "All that a man has he will trade for his life. But try putting forth your hand and harming his bone and flesh, and he will curse You to Your face."

The Lord said to Satan, "He is in your power, but spare his life." So Satan went on his way and struck Job with boils from the soles of his feet to the top of his head, and Job had to sit outside on a dunghill, scraping himself.

When three of Job's friends heard what had happened to him they set out to visit him: Eliphaz from Teman, Bildad from Shuh, and Zophar from Naamath. They came to Job and sat down on the ground with him seven days and seven nights, but did not speak to him for they saw the greatness of his grief. At last Job said:

"Perish the day on which I was born, the night they said, 'The child is a boy.' For what I fear overtakes me, and what I shrink from comes upon me. I have no peace or comfort. I have no rest, for trouble comes!"

But in none of his sufferings did Job curse God or complain against Him.

*HEN did Eliphaz the Temanite, and Bildad the Shuhite, and Zophar the Naamathite each made a speech for Job. They spoke of the justice of God. They spoke of His certain punishment for sinners. They said that the just man is always blessed in every way and need never fear suffering. Therefore, they said, Job had surely sinned against God to deserve the dreadful suffering which had come upon him.*

To each of these speeches Job could only answer that such was not the case. He had not sinned against God. He was suffering and did not know why.

Then Eliphaz the Temanite, and Bildad the Shuhite, and Zophar the Naamathite each made another speech for Job. They spoke again of the justice of God. They spoke again of His certain punishment for sinners. They said again that the just man is blessed in every way and need never fear suffering. Therefore, they said. Job had surely sinned against God to deserve the dreadful suffering which had come upon him.

To each of these speeches Job could only answer as before. He had not sinned. He was suffering and did not know why.

Then Eliphaz the Temanite, and Bildad the Shuhite, and Zophar the Naamathite each made one more speech for Job. They spoke once more of the justice of God. They spoke once more of His certain punishment for sinners. They said once more that the just man is blessed in every way and need never fear suffering.

At last Job could bear this no longer and he cried out to God, begging that He tell him the reason for his misery.

And the Lord spoke to Job out of a whirlwind, and said:

"Where were you when I founded the earth? Tell me, if you have understanding. Who decided its size; do you know? Who laid out the measuring line for it? Into what were its pedestals sunk, and who laid the cornerstone, while the morning stars sang in chorus and all the sons of God shouted for joy?

"Have you ever in your life ordered the morning to come or told the sun where to rise? Have you gone down to where the sea begins or walked about on the bottom of the deep? Have you measured out the width of the earth? Have you gone into the storehouse where the snow is kept or seen where all the hailstones are hidden?"

Then Job answered the Lord, and said:

"I know that You can do all things, that no purpose of Yours can be hindered. I have dealt with great things which I do not understand; things too wonderful for me, which I cannot know. I had heard of You by word of mouth, but now my eye has seen You. Therefore I disown what I have said, and repent in dust and ashes."

Then the Lord said to Eliphaz, "I am angry with you and with your two friends, for you have not spoken rightly concerning me as has my servant Job. Take seven bullocks and seven rams, and go to my servant Job, and offer a burnt offering for yourselves. And let my servant Job pray for you, for I will accept his prayer not to punish you too severely." Then Eliphaz and Bildad and Zophar did as the Lord commanded them. And the Lord accepted the prayer of Job.

And the Lord restored the prosperity of Job after he had prayed for his friends. The Lord even gave Job twice as much as he had before. Then all his brothers and sisters came to him, and all his old friends, and they ate bread with him in his house. They sympathized with him and comforted him for all the evil which the Lord had allowed to come upon him. And each of them gave him a piece of money and a golden ring.

Thus the Lord blessed the latter days of Job more than the first. For he had fourteen thousand sheep, six thousand camels, a thousand yoke of oxen, and a thousand she-asses. And he had seven sons and three daughters once more. In all the land there were no women as beautiful as the daughters of Job, and their father gave them an inheritance with their brothers.

After this Job lived a hundred and forty years. And he saw his children, and his grandchildren, and even his great-grandchildren. Then Job died, old and full of years.

THE STORY OF TOBIT

NOW TOBIT the elder was a just and holy man of the tribe of Naphtali, living in Nineveh, the great city of the Assyrians, for Shalmaneser the king of the Assyrians had taken his people captive. And because he was mindful of the Lord with all his heart, God gave him favor in the sight of Shalmaneser the king. But after a time Shalmaneser the king died and Sennacherib his son, who reigned in his place, had a hatred for the children of Israel. But Tobit, fearing God more than the king, went daily among all his people and gave as generously as he could to everyone. He fed the hungry, gave clothing to the naked, and carefully buried the dead and those who had been killed by the king.

Now it happened one day that being wearied with burying he came to his house and lay down by the wall to sleep. And as he was sleeping, hot dung from a swallow's nest fell into his eyes, and he was made blind. Tobit did not blame God for the blindness which had befallen him, but continued in the fear of God, giving Him thanks all the days of his life.

One day Tobit the elder called Tobias his son and said, "I tell you, my son, that I lent ten talents of silver to Gabael in Rages, a city of the Medes. Now therefore go to him and receive this sum of him, and restore to him his promissory note."

Then Tobias went forth and saw a handsome young man, dressed for a journey and ready to walk. Tobias asked him, "Do you know the way to the land of the Medes?" He answered, "I know it. I have often walked there."

Tobias brought the young man to his father, who asked him, "Can you take my son to Gabael at Rages?" The young man answered, "I will take him there and bring him back."

They set out on their journey and rested the first night by the river Tigris. But as Tobias went to wash his feet, a huge fish came up to bite him. The young man told him, "Take him by the gills and pull him to you." When the fish was on the shore the young man said, "Take out the gall of this fish and keep it, for it is a necessary medicine." And when he had done so they cooked and salted the fish for food.

When they reached the house of Raguel, the uncle of Tobias, Tobias stayed there a time and took Raguel's daughter, Sarah, for his wife.

Then Tobias called the young man to him and said, "I beseech you, go to Gabael at Rages and restore to him his note of hand, receive of him the money, and invite him to my wedding."

The young man found Gabael, gave him the note of hand, received of him all the money, and brought him back to attend the wedding.

When the wedding was ended Raguel gave Tobias half of all he owned, and Tobias started for home with his wife, Sara, and the young man.

On their joyful return, Tobias the younger, at the young man's direction, took some of the fish gall and anointed his father's eyes. He waited for half an hour and a white skin began to form, like the skin of an egg. Tobit took hold of it and pulled it from his eyes, and at once regained his sight. And for seven days they feasted and rejoiced with great joy.

Then the young man said to them, "Bless the God of Heaven, give glory to Him in the sight of all who live, for He has shown His mercy to you. I will open the truth to you and I will not hide the secret from you. I am Raphael, one of the seven who stand before the Lord. It is time that I return to Him who sent me, but bless God and proclaim His wonderful works!"

And when he had said these things he was taken out of sight and they saw him no more.

THE STORY OF JUDITH

OW IN the twelfth year of his reign Nebuchadnezzar, who ruled over all the East, called a great council of all his advisers and his governors and his officers of war and told them that he had decided to bring all the earth under his rule. This pleased them all, and Nebuchadnezzar called Holofernes, the general of his armies, and said to him, "Go out against all the kingdoms of the West. Do not spare any kingdom, and bring all the fortified cities under my yoke." Then Holofernes called the captains and the officers of the army and he gathered men for the expedition as the king had commanded him: a hundred and twenty thousand foot soldiers and twelve thousand archers with charioteers. And he went forth, he and all his army, with the chariots and the charioteers and the archers who covered the face of the earth like locusts.

Then the children of Israel who dwelt in the land of Judah heard these things and became afraid of him. And they fortified their towns and gathered grain to withstand a siege.

When it was told to Holofernes, the general of the army, that the children of Israel were preparing themselves to resist, he was greatly angered and began to rage furiously. On the next day he gave orders for his army to go up against the city of Bethulia. He ordered its aqueduct to be cut and its springs to be watched until there was hardly enough water left in the city to satisfy its people for a single day.

Then Uzziah, an elder of the city, stood up weeping and said, "Take courage, my brothers, and let us wait five days for mercy from the Lord. But if after five days are past there is still no help, then we must surrender to our enemies and put an end to our sufferings."

There was living in Bethulia a virtuous and beautiful widow named Judith. She was greatly respected by all because she feared the Lord very much, nor was there anyone who spoke ill of her. She sent for Uzziah and the elders and scolded them, "Who are you to tempt the Lord? You have set a time for the mercy of the Lord and have appointed a day for Him, just as it pleased you. But since the Lord is patient, let us be penitent and beg His pardon."

Uzziah and the elders said, "Everything you say is true. Now therefore pray for us, for you are a holy woman who fears God."

Judith went into her oratory and falling down before the Lord she cried out to Him for help. When her prayer was ended she called her maid, took off her widow's clothing, bathed herself, and dressed in her richest garments. Then she and her maid walked out the gate of the city toward the camp of the enemy.

And it came to pass as they went down the hill about break of day, that the watchmen of the enemy met them, and asked, "Where do you come from? Where are you going?" Judith answered, "I am a daughter of the Hebrews, but I fled from them because I knew that they will fall prey to you. For this reason I thought with myself, saying, 'I will go into the presence of the prince Holofernes and tell him their secrets.'"

When the men had heard this, they said to her, "You have saved your life by making this decision to come to our prince. Be sure that when you stand before him he will treat you well." They brought her to the tent of Holofernes and told him about her.

Judith saw Holofernes sitting under a canopy woven of purple and gold, looked on his face, and bowed to the ground before him.

Then Holofernes said, "Fear not. Never have I hurt anyone who was willing to serve Nebuchadnezzar. But why have you left your people and come to us?"

Judith said to him, "It is certain that our God is so offended with our sins that He has sent word by His prophets to our people that He will punish them because of their sins. Moreover, famine has come upon them, and for lack of water they are ready to die. And I, your handmaid, knew this and fled from them, and the Lord has sent me to tell you these very things."

Now in all of this Judith spoke the truth, and let Holofernes deceive himself through his own great pride.

All this pleased Holofernes and he ordered that she should go in where his treasures were kept, to stay there, for he planned to feed her from his own table. Judith asked that she might have liberty to go out at night and before daybreak for prayer, and he told his servants to let her go in and out freely.

She went out at night to the valley near Bethulia and prayed to the Lord, the God of Israel, that He would give her guidance to deliver her people. This went on for three days.

On the fourth day Holofernes gave a feast and invited Judith to come. Judith arose, dressed herself richly, and went before Holofernes. Holofernes said to her, "Drink now, and sit down, and be merry." And she ate and drank before him so that Holofernes was made happy because of her and drank more wine than he had ever drunk in his life.

When it was late the servants left, shutting the doors. Judith was left alone with Holofernes, but he was fast asleep on his bed and very drunk. Then Judith went to the pillar at the head of his bed and untied his sword which hung there. She drew it out of its sheath and took him by the hair, praying, "Strengthen me, O Lord God, at this hour!" She struck him twice on the neck, cutting off his head.

After a while she went out and gave the head to her maid for safekeeping and they went out of the camp as usual, no one stopping them.

When they reached Bethulia Judith said to the people, "Hear me, my brothers. Hang up this head on our walls. As soon as the sun rises, let every man take his weapons and rush out as though making an attack. Then the enemy watchmen, will go to wake their prince for battle, but they will find him without his head and they shall all be afraid. When you see them fleeing, go after them, for the Lord will destroy them under your feet."

This was done. The head of Holofernes was hung up and every man took arms and rushed out, making a great noise. The watchmen of the enemy ran to the tent of Holofernes and Holofernes was found dead. When all the army heard that Holofernes was beheaded, they tried to save themselves by flight, and the children of Israel, seeing them fleeing, came after them. And because the enemy was left leaderless they fled in disorder, so that the children of Israel were able to slay all they could catch.

Then Joakim the high priest came from Jerusalem to Bethulia with all his elders to see Judith, and they all blessed her, saying:

"You are the glory of Jerusalem.
You are the joy of Israel.
You are the honor of our people."

After this, all the people came to Jerusalem to worship the Lord, offering burnt sacrifices and vows. And for three months the joy of their victory was celebrated with Judith.

JERUSALEM IS DESTROYED

Yet even after Judith, the sins of the people doomed them to be destroyed by another king named Nebuchadnezzar.

URING THE ninth year of his reign, in the tenth month, on the tenth day of the month, Nebuchadnezzar, king of Babylon, came with all his Chaldean army to Jerusalem. They pitched their camp outside it and built forts facing it round about.

The city was besieged until the eleventh year of King Zedekiah's reign. And on the ninth day of the fourth month the famine spread over the city, and there was no bread for the people in the land.

The city was broken up, and the men of the army fled by night, by way of a gate between two walls, which was near the king's garden (for the Chaldeans were all around the city). And King Zedekiah went off toward the plain. The army of the Chaldeans pursued the king and overtook him on the plains of Jericho, and all his army was scattered.

So they took the king and brought him up to the king of Babylon at Riblah, and they passed judgment upon him. They bound him with chains and carried him to Babylon.

And in the fifth month, on the seventh day of the month, Nebuzaradan, captain of the guard, a servant of the king of Babylon, came to Jerusalem. He burned the house of the Lord, and the king's house, and all the houses of Jerusalem; every great man's house he burned with fire. And the army of the Chaldeans, which was with the captain of the guard, broke down the walls of Jerusalem all around the city.

The rest of the people who were left in the city, and the fugitives who fell into the hands of the king of Babylon, and the rest of the population, Nebuzaradan the captain of the guard carried away with him. But he left the poor of the land to care for the vineyards and the fields.

DANIEL AT NEBUCHADNEZZAR'S COURT

HEN THE reign of Jehoiakim, king of Judah, was in its third year, Nebuchadnezzar, king of Babylon, came to Jerusalem and besieged it. And the Lord gave Jehoiakim, king of Judah, into his hand, with part of the vessels of the house of God; and he carried them away into the land of Shinar, to the house of his god; and the vessels he brought into the treasure house of his god.

Then the king told Ashpenaz, the master of his household, to pick certain of the children of Israel, of the king's family, and of the princes, children who had no faults but were handsome and bright and quick to learn, who understood science and had abilities worthy to stand in the king's palace; to these they would teach the wisdom and the language of the Chaldeans.

Nebuchadnezzar allowed them a daily provision of his own food and wine, to nourish them so that at the end of three years they might stand before the king.

Now among these were some of the children of Judah: Daniel, Hananiah, Mishael, and Azariah. To all these the master of the household gave new names; he gave Daniel the name of Belteshazzar, to Hananiah the name of Shadrach, to Mishael, Meshach, and to Azariah, Abednego.

But Daniel decided in his heart that he would not pollute himself with the king's meat (which was not the food of the children of Israel) nor with the wine which he drank. Therefore he requested of the master of the household that he might not have to eat it.

Now God had filled the master of the household with love for Daniel. And the master of the household said to him, "I fear my lord the king, who has given orders for your food and drink. For why should he see your faces worse looking than the children who are in your group? If this happens, you will make me endanger my head with the king."

Then Daniel said to Malasar, whom the master of the household had put over Daniel, Hananiah, Mishael, and Azariah, "Test your servants, please, for ten days. Let them give us peas and beans to eat, and water to drink. Then look at our faces and at the faces of the children who eat some of the king's food, and then deal with your servants according to what you find."

He agreed to test them in this manner, and tried them for ten days. At the end of ten days their faces appeared fairer and plumper than any of the children who had eaten of the king's food. So Malasar took away their helpings of the meat, and the wine that they should drink, and gave them peas and beans.

As for the four children, God gave them knowledge and skill in all kinds of learning and wisdom; and Daniel had understanding of all visions and dreams.

Now at the end of the time when the king had said they should be brought in, the master of the household took them before Nebuchadnezzar.

The king talked with them, and among them all none was found like Daniel, Hananiah, Mishael, and Azariah; therefore they stayed before the king. And in all matters of wisdom and understanding in which the king tested them, he found them ten times better than all the magicians and astrologers that were in his realm.

And Daniel stayed on even until the first year of the reign of King Cyrus.

THE STATUE OF GOLD

EBUCHADNEZZAR THE king made a statue of gold ninety feet high and nine feet wide. He set it up on the plain of Dura, in the land of Babylon. Then Nebuchadnezzar the king sent out word to gather together the princes, the governors, and the captains, the judges, the treasurers, the counselors and the sheriffs, and all the rulers of the provinces, to come to see the statue.

Then the princes, the governors and captains, the judges, the treasurers, the counselors and the sheriffs, and all the rulers of the provinces gathered together to see the statue that Nebuchadnezzar the king had set up; and they stood before the statue.

Then a herald cried aloud, "To you it is commanded, O people, that when you hear the sound of the cornet, flute, harp, sackbut, psaltery, tambourine, and all kinds of music, you shall fall down and worship the golden image that Nebuchadnezzar the king has set up. And anyone who does not fall down and worship shall in that same hour be cast into the middle of a burning fiery furnace."

Therefore when the moment came, when all the people heard the sound of the cornet, flute, harp, sackbut, psaltery, and all kinds of music, they all fell down and worshiped the golden image that Nebuchadnezzar the king had set up.

Then certain Chaldeans came up and accused the Jews. They spoke to King Nebuchadnezzar and said:

"O King, live forever! You, O King, have sent out an order that every man who hears the sound of the cornet, flute, harp, sackbut, psaltery, and tambourine, and all kinds of music, shall fall down and worship the golden image, and that whoever does not fall down and worship shall be cast into the middle of a burning fiery furnace.

"Now there are certain Jews, whom you have put in charge of the affairs of the province of Babylon. They are Shadrach, Meshach, and Abednego; these men, O King, have not regarded your wishes. They do not serve your gods, nor do they worship the golden image which you have set up."

Then Nebuchadnezzar, in his rage and fury, commanded Shadrach, Meshach, and Abednego to be brought before him.

Nebuchadnezzar said to them, "Is it true, O Shadrach, Meshach, and Abednego, that you do not serve my gods, nor worship the golden image which I have set up?

"If you are ready, when you hear the sound of the cornet, flute, harp, sackbut, psaltery and tambourine and all kinds of music, to fall down and worship the image I have made, all is well; but if you will not worship, you will be cast, this same hour, into the middle of a burning fiery furnace; and who is the God who will deliver you out of my hands?"

Shadrach, Meshach, and Abednego answered and said to the king, "O Nebuchadnezzar, we do not need to think over our answer to you in this matter. If it be His will, our God, whom we serve, is able to save us from the burning fiery furnace, and He will save us from your hands, O King. But if not, you must know, O King, that we still will not serve your gods, nor worship the golden image which you have set up."

Then Nebuchadnezzar was full of fury, and his face hardened against Shadrach, Meshach, and Abednego. Therefore he spoke and commanded

that the furnace should be heated seven times more than usual. And he commanded the most mighty men in his army to bind Shadrach, Meshach, and Abednego, and to cast them into the burning fiery furnace.

Because the king had insisted that the furnace be exceedingly hot, the flame of the fire killed the men who led Shadrach, Meshach, and Abednego to it. But Shadrach, Meshach, and Abednego, in the midst of the burning fiery furnace, were unharmed.

Then Nebuchadnezzar the king was astonished, and rose up in haste and said to his counselors, "Did we not cast three men bound into the midst of the fire?"

They answered and said, "True, O King!"

He answered and said, "I see four men loose, walking in the midst of the fire, and they are unhurt; and the fourth man looks like an angel of God."

Then Nebuchadnezzar walked up to the mouth of the burning fiery furnace and said, "Shadrach, Meshach, and Abednego, you servants of the most high God, come forth and come here."

Then Shadrach, Meshach, and Abednego walked out of the fire. And all the princes, governors, and captains, and the king's counselors gathered together there and saw these men against whose bodies the fire had no power. Not a hair of their heads was singed, nor were their clothes burnt and there was no smell of fire upon them.

Then Nebuchadnezzar spoke and said, "Blessed be the God of Shadrach, Meshach, and Abednego, who has sent His angel and saved His servants who trusted in Him and who defied the king's word and risked their lives that they might not serve or worship any god except their own God.

"Therefore I make a decree: Any people, nation, or group who say anything against the God of Shadrach, Meshach, and Abednego, shall be cut in pieces, and their houses shall be made a dumping ground; for there is no other God who can save in this way."

Then the king promoted Shadrach, Meshach, and Abednego to high offices in the province of Babylon.

THE HANDWRITING ON THE WALL

UPON THE death of Nebuchadnezzar, his son Belshazzar became king. Belshazzar gave a great feast for a thousand of his lords and drank wine before the thousand. While he tasted the wine, Belshazzar commanded servants to bring the golden and silver vessels which his father Nebuchadnezzar had taken out of the temple which was in Jerusalem, so that the king and his princes, his wives, and the other women of his house might drink from them.

They brought the golden vessels that were taken out of the temple of the house of God, and his princes, his wives, and the other women drank from them. They drank wine and praised the gods of gold, and of silver, of brass, of iron, of wood, and of stone.

Within the same hour there appeared the fingers of a man's hand, writing upon the wall of the king's palace; and the king saw the part of the hand that wrote.

Then the king's face changed, and his thoughts troubled him so that the joints of his legs were loose and his knees knocked together.

The king cried aloud to bring in the astrologers, the Chaldeans, and the soothsayers, and the king said to these wise men of Babylon, "Whoever reads this writing and tells me the meaning of it shall be clothed in scarlet, and have a chain of gold about his neck, and shall be the third ruler in the country."

All the king's wise men came in, but they could not read the writing nor make known to the king the meaning of it.

Then King Belshazzar was greatly troubled, and his face changed, and his lords were dazed.

Now the queen, called by the king and his lords, came into the banqueting room, and the queen spoke and said, "O King, live forever! Do not let your thoughts trouble you, nor let your face change. There is a man in your kingdom who has in him the spirit of the holy gods. In the days of your father, light and understanding and wisdom like the wisdom of the gods was found in him. The king, Nebuchadnezzar, your father, made him master of the magicians, astrologers, Chaldeans, and soothsayers because of his excellent spirit and the knowledge and understanding, interpreting of dreams, explaining of hard sentences, and clearing up of doubts which Daniel, whom the king named Belshazzar, accomplished. Now let Daniel be called, and he will tell you the meaning of this."

Then Daniel was brought in before the king, and the king said to Daniel, "Are you that Daniel who is one of the children of the captivity of Judah, whom

the king my father brought out of the land of the Jews? I have heard of you, that the spirit of the gods is in you, and that light and understanding and excellent wisdom are found in you.

"Now the wise men and astrologers have been brought in before me to read this writing and tell me the meaning of it, but they could not interpret it for me. I have heard of you, and that you can give interpretations and clear up meanings. Now if you can read the writing and make the meaning of it clear to me, you shall be clothed in scarlet and have a chain of gold around your neck, and you shall be the third ruler in the kingdom."

Then Daniel answered and said to the king, "Keep your gifts for yourself and give your rewards to someone else, but I will read the writing to you, O King, and tell you the meaning of it.

"O King, the most high God gave Nebuchadnezzar, your father, a kingdom and majesty and glory and honor. And because of the majesty that He gave him all people, nations, and languages trembled and feared him — he killed whom he wanted to and kept alive whom he wanted to and raised men up or put them down as he liked. But when his heart was lifted up and his mind hardened in pride, his kingly throne was taken from him, and his glory was taken from him, until he knew that the most high God ruled in the kingdom of men, and that He chooses to rule over it whomever He wishes.

"And you his son, O Belshazzar, have not kept your heart simple, though you knew all this, but you have lifted yourself up against the Lord of Heaven. They have brought you the vessels of His house, and you and your lords, your wives and other women have drunk wine in them, and you have praised the gods of silver and gold, of brass, iron, wood, and stone, which do not see nor hear nor know; and the God in whose hands your breath of life is and whose ways should be yours, you have not praised.

"This hand, then, was sent from Him, and the writing was written by His hand. And this is the writing that was written:

MENE, TEKEL, PERES.

"This is the meaning of the thing: MENE, God has judged your kingdom and finished it; TEKEL, you have been weighed in the scales and found lacking; PERES, your kingdom will be divided and given to the Medes and Persians."

Then Belshazzar commanded that they clothe Daniel in scarlet and put a chain of gold about his neck; and he made a proclamation saying that he was to be the third ruler in the kingdom.

That night Belshazzar the king of the Chaldeans was killed. And Dari'us, the Mede, took the kingdom.

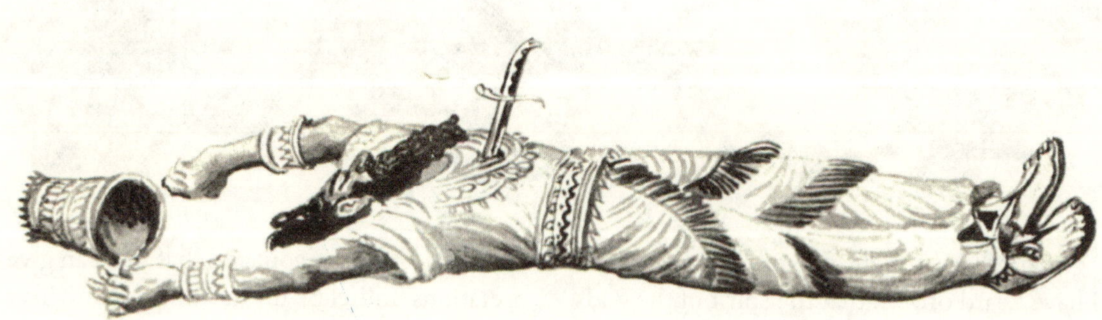

DANIEL IN THE LIONS' DEN

IT PLEASED Darius to set over the kingdom a hundred and twenty princes who were to rule the whole kingdom. And over these were three presidents, and of them Daniel was the first. The princes were to give account to them, so that the king would not have any troubles.

Daniel was put over the presidents and princes because of his excellent mind; and the king planned to put him over the whole kingdom. Then the presidents and princes tried to find some fault with Daniel concerning the kingdom, but they could find no fault, because he was faithful, and there was no error or fault to be found in him.

Then these men said, "We shall not find any grounds for complaint against Daniel except that he follows the laws of his God." Then these presidents and princes assembled together before the king and said to him, "King Darius, live forever! All the presidents of the kingdom, and the governors and the princes, the counselors and the captains, have consulted together about establishing a royal law, by a firm order, that whoever asks anything of any god or man for thirty days, except of you, O King, shall be cast into the den of lions.

"Now, O King, establish this order, and sign the writing, that it may not be changed, according to the law of the Medes and the Persians, which does not change."

Then King Darius signed the writing.

Now when Daniel knew that the law was signed, he went into his house and, his windows being open in his chamber facing Jerusalem, he knelt down three times a day and prayed and gave thanks to his God, just as he had before.

Then the men came together and found Daniel praying and entreating God. They hurried to the king and reminded him of his order.

"Did you not sign an order that any man asking a favor of any god or man within thirty days, except yourself, O King, shall be thrown into the den of lions?"

The king answered and said, "That is true, according to the law of the Medes and the Persians, which does not change."

Then they answered and said to the king, "That Daniel, who is one of the children of the captivity of Judah, does not respect you, O King, nor the order which you have signed, but makes his requests three times a day."

When he heard these words, the king was very much displeased with himself, and he set his heart on saving Daniel. He thought until the setting of the sun about how to save Daniel.

Then the men came before the king and said to him, "Remember, O King, that it is the law of the Medes and Persians that no order or law which the king lays down can be changed." Then the king commanded them to take Daniel and throw him into the den of lions. And the king said to Daniel, "Your God, whom you serve so faithfully, surely He will save you." Then a stone was brought and laid across the mouth of the den; and the king sealed it with his own signet, and with the signet of his lords, so that the plan might not be changed concerning Daniel.

Then the king went to his palace and passed the night in fasting. No musical instruments were brought in to him, and he did not sleep at all.

Very early in the morning the king arose and went in haste to the den of lions. When he came to the den, he cried out in a sorrowing voice to Daniel and said to him, "O Daniel, servant of the living God, has your God, whom you serve so faithfully, been able to save you from the lions?"

Then Daniel said to the king, "O King, live forever. My God has sent His angel and has shut the lion's mouths, so that they have not hurt me, because I was innocent in His sight; and I have done no harm to you either, O King."

Then the king was exceedingly glad for him and commanded that Daniel should be brought up out of the den. So Daniel was brought up out of the den, and no kind of wound was found on him, because he had believed firmly in his God.

Then the king gave commands, and they brought the men who had accused Daniel, and they cast them into the den of lions, and their children and their wives, too. And the lions broke all their bones into pieces.

Then King Darius wrote to all people and nations, and in all the languages of all the earth: "Peace be multiplied to you! I now command that in every part of my kingdom men tremble and fear before the God of Daniel, for He is the living God, unchanging forever, and His kingdom shall never be destroyed, and His power shall continue to the end. He rescues and saves, and He works signs and wonders in Heaven and on earth, He who has saved Daniel from the power of the lions."

So Daniel prospered in the reign of Darius, and in the reign of Cyrus the Persian.

THE TEMPLE IS REBUILT

SO THAT the word of the Lord might be fulfilled, the Lord stirred up the spirit of Cyrus, king of Persia, so that in the first year of his reign he sent out a notice throughout all his kingdom and put it into writing, saying:

"Thus says Cyrus, king of Persia: The Lord God of Heaven has given me all the kingdoms of the earth, and He has ordered me to build Him a house at Jerusalem, which is in Judea.

"Who is there among you who are of His people? May his God be with him and let him go up to Jerusalem, which is in Judea, and build the house of the Lord God of Israel in Jerusalem.

"And let all the rest wheresoever they dwell help him, every man from his place, with silver, and gold, goods and cattle, besides that which they offer freely to the temple of God in Jerusalem."

Then up rose the chief of the leaders of Judah and Benjamin, and the priests and the Levites, with all those whose spirits God had raised, to go up to build the house of the Lord in Jerusalem.

And all who were around them filled their hands with vessels of silver, with gold, with goods of all sorts, with cattle, and with precious things, besides all the free offerings.

And Cyrus the king brought out the vessels of the house of the Lord which Nebuchadnezzar had brought out of Jerusalem and had put in the house of his god.

When the seventh month was past, and the children of Israel were back in their cities, the people gathered together in Jerusalem.

And when the builders laid the foundation of the temple of the Lord, they set the priests in their robes with trumpets, and the Levites with cymbals, to praising the Lord, after the order of David, king of Israel.

And they sang together, praising and giving thanks to the Lord, because He is good, and His mercy toward Israel endures for ever. And all the people shouted with a great shout when they praised the Lord, because the foundation of the house of the Lord was laid.

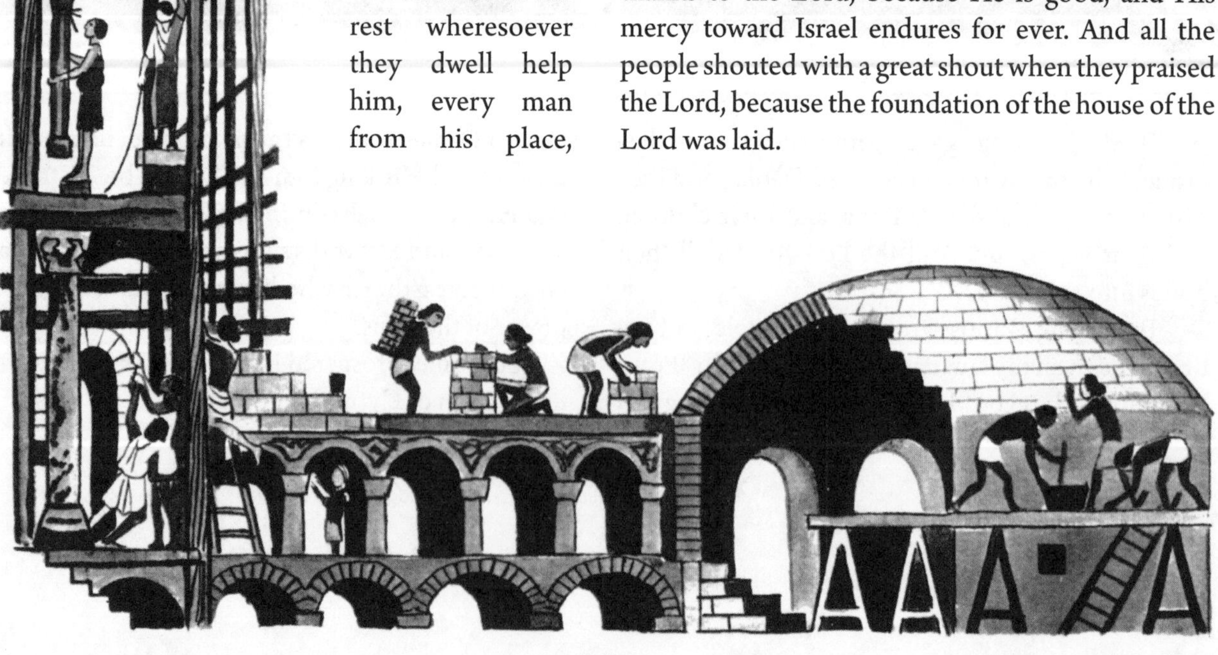

ESTHER SAVES HER PEOPLE

ONCE IN the days of King Ahasuerus, there lived in the king's palace a certain Jew named Mordecai, who had been carried away from Jerusalem with the captives whom Nebuchadnezzar the king of Babylon had carried away.

He brought up Hadassah, his brother's daughter, who was called Esther. The girl was fair and beautiful, and when her father and mother died, Mordecai took her for his own daughter.

The king came to love Esther above all women, and he set the royal crown upon her head and made her queen.

Now one day, Mordecai overheard the plotting of two of the king's chamberlains who planned to slay the king. Mordecai told Esther the queen, and Esther told the king. When the matter was looked into, it was found to be true, and the two men were both hanged on a tree.

But it happened that King Ahasuerus promoted a man named Haman, son of Hammedatha the Agagite, to a position above all the princes who worked with him. And Haman, who hated Mordecai and his people, said to King Asasuerus, "There is a certain people spread abroad in all the provinces of your kingdom. Their laws are different from those of other people, and they do not keep the king's laws. If it pleases the king, let a law be written that they may be destroyed."

The king said to Haman, "The people are yours, to do with them whatever seems good to you."

Then letters were sent by Haman into all the king's provinces, telling people to kill all Jews on one chosen day; and their belongings were to be taken as spoils.

When Mordecai learned all that had been done, he tore his clothes and put on sackcloth and ashes, and went out into the midst of the city, and cried loudly and bitterly.

Esther's maids and her chamberlain came and told her of this. Then the queen was exceedingly sad. She called for Hathach, one of the king's chamberlains, and sent him to Mordecai to ask what was wrong.

Mordecai told Hathach of Haman's plot and begged Esther to go in before the king to plead with him for her people.

When Hathach told Esther of Mordecai's words she sent an answer to Mordecai, saying, "All the servants of the king know that if anyone, whether man or woman, who has not been called shall come before the king, the king may put him to death. Only if the king shall hold out his golden scepter, he may live." But when Mordecai was told of Esther's words, he again urged her to save her people, even at the risk of her own life.

Then Esther sent this answer back to Mordecai: "Go, gather together all the Jews who live in this city and fast for me for three days, night and day. My maidens and I will fast likewise, and then I will go in before the king. And if I perish, I perish."

So Mordecai went his way and did all that Esther had commanded him.

On the third day, Esther put on her royal robes and went in before the king. And when the king saw Esther standing before him, she won his favor; and the king held out to Esther the golden scepter which was in his hand, and Esther drew near and touched the scepter.

Then the king said to her, "What would you like, Queen Esther? What is your request? It shall be given to you, even if it is half my kingdom.'"

And Esther answered, "If it seems good to the king, let the king and Haman come today to the banquet I have prepared for them."

So the king and Anian came to banquet with Esther the queen. And the king said again to Esther at the banquet, "What is your desire, Queen Esther?

It shall be granted to you. What is your request? It shall be done, even if it is half my kingdom."

Then Esther the queen answered and said "If I have found favor in your sight, O King, and if it please the king, let my life be given me at my desire, and my people be saved at my request. For we are sold, my people and I, to be destroyed, to be slain, to perish." Then King Ahasuerus answered and said to Esther the queen, "Who is he and where is he who dares in his heart to do this?"

And Esther said, "The foe and the enemy is the wicked Haman."

Then Haman was afraid before the king and the queen.

And Harbona, one of the chamberlains, said to the king, "Behold, there is a gallows, seventy-five feet high, which Haman has prepared for Mordecai, who spoke up well for the king once. It stands in the house of Haman."

Then the king said, "Hang him on it."

So they hanged Haman on the gallows which he had prepared for Mordecai. Then the king's anger was quieted.

On that day King Ahasuerus gave the house of Haman, the enemy of the Jews, to Esther the queen, and he sent orders to spare the Jews. And Mordecai came before the king, for Esther had told him what relation he was to her.

The king took off his ring, which he had taken back from Haman, and gave it to Mordecai. And Mordecai went forth from the presence of the king in royal robes of violet and sky color, and with a great crown of gold, and with a cloak of silk and purple; and all the city rejoiced and was glad.

And the Jews had light and gladness, and joy and honor.

THE HEROIC MACCABEES

OMING OUT of the land of the Greeks, Alexander, son of Philip of Macedon, overthrew Darius the king of the Persians and the Medes. He fought many battles and took everyone's strongholds and slew the kings of the earth. After these things Alexander knew that he would die. He called his servants to him and divided his kingdom among them. They made themselves kings, and there came from among them a wicked root, Antiochus.

King Antiochus the Illustrious wrote to all his kingdom that all his people should be one and that everyone should give up his own law. He sent letters by his messengers to Jerusalem and to all the cities of Judah that they should follow the customs of the pagan nations of the earth, that they should forbid burnt offerings and sacrifices and atonement offerings to be made in the temple of God, and that they should prohibit the celebration of the Sabbath and the festival days. He commanded the holy places to be profaned and pagan altars to be built, and temples, and idols, so that they should forget the law of God. And whosoever would not do according to the command of King Antiochus should be put to death.

And King Antiochus set up an abominable idol upon the altar of God, and they built altars throughout all the cities of Judah. They cut up and burned the books of the law of God, and everyone with whom the books of the law were found or who obeyed the law of God was put to death.

There arose in those days Mattathias, son of John, son of Simeon, a priest of the sons of Joarib, from Jerusalem, and he lived on the mountain of Modein with his five sons.

Many of the people of Israel who had consented to idolatry came to persuade them also, but Mattathias said with a loud voice, "Though all nations obey King Antiochus, I and my sons and my brethren will obey the law of our fathers. May God be merciful to us, for it would profit us nothing to forsake the law and the commandments of God."

So he and his sons fled into the mountains and left all that they had. And many who also desired justice and righteousness went down into the desert after them, and they lived there with their children and their wives.

They formed an army and slew the idolaters and wicked men, so that many fled to other nations for safety. And Mattathias and his friends went about throwing down the pagan altars, and all that they did came to prosper.

Now the days drew near that Mattathias should die, and he said to his sons:

"O my sons, be zealous for the law and give your lives for the covenant of your fathers. Call to mind the deeds of your fathers which they did in their generations and you shall receive glory and an everlasting name.

"Was not Abraham found faithful in temptation and it was reputed to him for justice?

"Joseph in the time of his distress kept the commandment and he was made lord of Egypt.

"Joshua who fulfilled God's word was made ruler in Israel.

"David by his mercy gained the throne of an everlasting kingdom.

"Elijah, full of zeal for the law, was taken up into Heaven.

"Hananiah and Azariah and Mishael by believing were delivered out of the fiery furnace.

"Daniel in his innocence was delivered out of the mouths of the lions."

And he blessed them and was joined to his fathers. And all Israel mourned for him.

Then his son Judas Maccabeus rose up in his stead. All his brothers helped him and all who had joined themselves with his father, and they fought the battle of Israel.

Now when King Antiochus heard these things he became angry, and he sent and gathered all the forces of his kingdom, an exceedingly strong army. He then delivered to Lysias, a nobleman of royal blood, half the army to destroy and to root out the strength of Israel and the remnant of Jerusalem, to take away the memory of them from that place.

Judas and his brothers saw that the army approached their borders and they knew of the orders the king had given to destroy their people. They gathered men and called an assembly that they might be ready for battle, and Judas said, "Prepare yourselves and be valiant men that you may fight those who are coming against us to destroy our people and the temple. Yet as God wills, so be it done!"

They joined battle and the enemy were routed and fled, and there fell of them to the number of three thousand men.

The next year, Lysias gathered together three score thousand chosen men and five thousand horsemen that he might subdue them. They joined in battle again, and there fell of the army of Lysias five thousand men.

After these victories Judas and his brothers said, "Behold, our enemies are overcome. Let us go up now to cleanse the holy places and to repair them." So all the army assembled together and they went up to Mount Zion. They saw the sanctuary desolate and the altar profaned, the gates burnt and shrubs growing in the courts as in a forest, and the rooms adjoining the temple thrown down.

Judas chose priests without fault, whose will was set on the law of God. They cleansed the holy places and took away everything that had been defiled with idol worship. They took uncut stones, according to the law, and built a new altar to replace the old one that had been defiled. They repaired the holy places and everything which was in the temple, and they sanctified the temple and its courtyards. They made new holy vessels and brought the lampstand, and the altar of incense, and the table for offering bread into the temple. They put incense on the altar and lighted the lamps that gave light in the temple. They set the loaves of bread on the table and hung up the veils, and finished all the things they had begun.

And they offered sacrifice, according to the law, on the new altar they had made. According to the exact time and according to the exact day on which the pagans had defiled it, on that day it was dedicated anew with hymns, and harps and lutes. And all the people worshiped, and they offered burnt offerings, and atonement offerings, and offerings of praise.

They adorned the front of the temple with crowns of gold and with shields, and they renewed the gates, and the rooms, and hung doors on them. And there was exceeding great joy among the people.

And Judas Maccabeus and his brothers and all the assembly of Israel decreed that the day of the dedication of the altar should be kept at this time from year to year for eight full days with joy and gladness.

LED by Judas Maccabeus and his brothers the children of Israel fought many more battles to defend their people and the temple. Finally, Judas Maccabeus had to send men to Rome to plead the Jewish cause. Rome was pleased with the ambassadors and an alliance was made between Rome and Jerusalem.

But other wars began and Judas Maccabeus was slain in battle. His brothers succeeded him in turn, while the fortunes of the Jewish nation rose and fell. Through it all the power of Rome grew ever stronger, till at last both Judea and Syria came under her rule and a new era of history began.

PERSONAL RECORD

NAME ______________________________

BORN ______________________________

IN ______________________________

BAPTISM ______________________________

PRIEST ______________________________

PARISH ______________________________

GODFATHER ______________________________

GODMOTHER ______________________________

FIRST COMMUNION ______________________________

PRIEST ______________________________

PARISH ______________________________

CONFIRMATION ______________________________

BISHOP ______________________________

PARISH ______________________________

SPONSOR ______________________________

CONFIRMATION NAME ______________________________

FAMILY RECORD

FATHER ______________________________

BORN ______________ IN ______________

MOTHER ______________________________

BORN ______________ IN ______________

BROTHERS AND SISTERS

______________ ______________

______________ ______________

______________ ______________

GRANDPARENTS

FATHER'S FAMILY MOTHER'S FAMILY

______________ GRANDFATHER ______________

______________ BORN ______________

______________ GRANDMOTHER ______________

______________ BORN ______________

THE NEW TESTAMENT

CONTENTS OF THE NEW TESTAMENT

CONTENTS OF THE NEW TESTAMENT

THE PROPHECY OF ISAIAH

THE PEOPLE who walked in darkness have seen a great light; those who dwell in the land of the shadow of death, upon them the light has shined. . . .

For unto us a child is born, unto us a son is given: and the government shall be upon His shoulders: and His name shall be called Wonderful, Counselor, The Mighty God, The Everlasting Father, The Prince of Peace.

Of the increase of His reign and His peace there shall be no end, upon the throne of David, and over all His kingdom, to order it, and to establish it with judgment and with justice from henceforth even for ever. . . .

THE CHILD JESUS

AN ANGEL VISITS MARY

IT HAPPENED in the days of Herod the king that the angel Gabriel was sent by God to a city of Galilee, named Nazareth, to a virgin betrothed to a man named Joseph, who was of the family of David. The name of the virgin was Mary.

The angel appeared to her and said, "Hail, you who are full of grace! The Lord is with you; you are blessed among women."

When she saw him, she was startled at what he had said, and she wondered to herself what this greeting could mean.

The angel said to her, "Do not be afraid, Mary; you have found favor with God. You are to have a son, and you shall call His name Jesus. He shall be great, and shall be called the Son of the Most High, and the Lord God shall give to Him the throne of His forefather David. He shall rule over the house of Jacob forever, and of His kingdom there shall be no end." Then Mary said to the angel, "How can this be, seeing that I do not know man?"

The angel answered and said to her, "The Holy Spirit shall come upon you, and the power of the Most High will overshadow you. So the Holy One who is to be born will be called the Son of God."

Mary said, "Behold the handmaid of the Lord. Let it be done to me as you have said." And the angel departed from her.

Mary rose up and started out in haste, and she went into the hill country to a town of Judah. She went to the house of Zachary and his wife, her cousin Elizabeth.

And Mary greeted Elizabeth with these words:

"My soul praises the Lord,

And my spirit rejoices in God my Savior,

For He has taken notice of His servant in her lowly station,

For, behold, from this time forth all generations shall call me blessed.

For He who is mighty has done great things for me.

And holy is His name!

His mercy shines on those who fear Him,

from generation to generation.

He has done a mighty deed with His arm,

He has scattered the proud in their plotting.

He has put down the mighty from their seats of power, and has lifted up the poor.

He has filled the hungry with good things, and the rich He has sent empty away.

He has helped His servant Israel, mindful of His mercy.

As He promised our fathers, to have mercy upon Abraham and His descendants forever."

Mary stayed with her cousin about three months, and then returned to her home.

THE BIRTH IN BETHLEHEM

IT HAPPENED in those days that a decree went out from Caesar Augustus (the emperor in far-off Rome) that all the world should be taxed. (And this taxing was first made when Quir-in'i-us was governor of Syria.)

Everyone went to be taxed, each to his own city. And Joseph too went up from Galilee, up from the city of Nazareth, into Judea, to the city of David, which is called Bethlehem, because he was of the house and family of David, to be taxed with Mary his wife, who was soon to have her child.

So it came about that, while they were there, the day arrived for her child to be born, and Mary brought forth her firstborn son, and wrapped him in swaddling clothes, and laid him in a manger, because there was no room for them in the inn.

There were in the same country shepherds staying in the field, keeping watch over their flocks by night.

An angel of the Lord appeared to them, and the glory of the Lord shone around them, and they were much afraid.

But the angel said, "Do not fear, for I bring you good news of a great joy which is coming to all your people. For to you today in the city of David, a Savior is born who is Christ the Lord. And this will be a sign to you: You shall find the babe wrapped in swaddling clothes, lying in a manger."

Suddenly there was with the angel a multitude from Heaven, praising God and saying: "Glory to God in the highest, and peace on earth among men of good will."

When the angels had left them and gone back into Heaven, the shepherds said to one another, "Let us go into Bethlehem, and see this thing which has happened, which the Lord has made known to us."

They went with all speed, and found Mary and Joseph, and the babe lying in a manger. And when they had seen it, they went about telling people what had been told them about this child. And all

who heard it marveled at the things which were told them by the shepherds.

But Mary treasured all these things, and thought about them in her heart.

And the shepherds returned, glorifying and praising God for all the things that they had heard and seen, as it had been told to them.

THE PRESENTATION IN THE TEMPLE

WHEN EIGHT days had passed, and it was time to circumcise the child, He was called Jesus. This was the name given Him by the angel who first announced His coming birth.

When the days of her purification were over, according to the law of Moses, they brought Him to Jerusalem, to present Him to the Lord (as it is written in the law of the Lord, "Every firstborn son shall be called holy to the Lord") and to offer a sacrifice according to the law of the Lord — a pair of turtledoves or two young pigeons.

Now there was a man in Jerusalem whose name was Simeon, and this man was upright and devout, waiting for the coming of the promised Messiah. The Holy Spirit was in him, and had revealed to him that he should not die before he had seen the Christ of the Lord.

The Spirit led him that day to the temple, and when the parents brought in the Child Jesus, to do for him what the law required, Simeon took Him up in his arms, and blessed God, and said: "Lord, now you dismiss your servant in peace, according to your word.

For my eyes have seen Your salvation Which You have prepared for all people —

A light to enlighten the Gentiles,

And the glory of Your people, Israel."

Joseph and the child's mother marveled at the things which were said of Him. But Simeon blessed them, and said to Mary, the child's mother, "This child is destined to bring about the fall and the rise of many in Israel. Many will speak against Him; and a sword will pierce your own soul, to reveal the thoughts of many." There was also one Anna, a prophetess, the daughter of Phanuel, of the tribe of Asher, who was a widow of about eighty-four years. She never left the temple, but served God with fastings and prayers night and day.

And she, coming in at that moment, gave thanks to the Lord, and spoke of Him to all those who were waiting for the freeing of Jerusalem.

When they had done everything according to the law of the Lord, they returned into Galilee, to their own city of Nazareth.

And the child grew and became strong. He was filled with wisdom, and the grace of God was upon Him.

THE VISIT OF THE WISE MEN

OW WHEN Jesus was born in Bethlehem of Judea, in the days of Herod the king, certain wise men from the East came to Jerusalem.

"Where is the newborn King of the Jews?" they asked. "For we have seen His star arise, and have come to worship Him."

When Herod the king heard this, he was troubled, and all Jerusalem with him. And when he had gathered all the chief priests and scribes of the people, he asked them where the Christ was to be born.

They said, "In Bethlehem of Judea, for this was written by the prophet:

'And you, Bethlehem, in Judah's land,
You are not the least among the leaders of Judah,
For from you will come a ruler Who will shepherd my people Israel.' "

Then Herod sent secretly for the wise men and asked them exactly what time the star had appeared. Then he sent them to Bethlehem, and said, "Go and search carefully for the young child. And when you have found Him, bring me word, that I may come and worship Him too." When they had heard the king's words, they departed. And the star which they had seen rise went before them, till it came to the place where the young child was; and there it stopped.

When they saw the star, they were exceedingly glad. They went into the house, and when they saw the young child with Mary His mother, they fell down and worshiped Him. They opened their treasures and presented gifts to Him, of gold and frankincense and myrrh.

Then, having been warned by God in a dream that they should not return to Herod, they went back to their own country by another way.

THE FLIGHT INTO EGYPT

WHEN THE wise men had departed, an angel of the Lord appeared to Joseph in a dream, saying, "Rise up, and take the young child and His mother, and flee to Egypt. And stay there until I bring you word. For Herod will seek the child to destroy Him."

So he arose and took the young child and His mother in the night, and went off to Egypt. And there they remained until the death of Herod, that the word of the prophet of the Lord might be fulfilled: "I have called my Son from Egypt." Herod, when he saw that the wise men had tricked him, was exceedingly angry. He sent men out to kill all the male children in Bethlehem, and in all the land around, under two years of age, for that was the time he had learned from the wise men.

Thus the saying came true which the prophet Jeremiah had spoken:

"A cry was heard in Ramah,
Weeping and loud lamentation,
Rachel weeping for her children,
and would not be comforted,
because they were no more."

But when Herod died, an angel of the Lord appeared in a dream to Joseph in Egypt, saying: "Rise up and take the young child and His mother, and go to the land of Israel. For those who sought the child's life are dead."

And he arose and took the young child and His mother, and went to the land of Israel. But when he heard that Archelaus reigned in Judea in the place of his father Herod, he was afraid to go there. So, being advised by God in a dream, he turned aside again into the region of Galilee.

He went and settled once more in the city called Nazareth, so that the words of the prophet might come true:

"He shall be called a Nazarene."

THE BOY JESUS IN THE TEMPLE

THE CHILD grew and became strong and thoughtful, and the blessing of God was upon Him.

Now His parents went to Jerusalem every year at the Feast of the Passover. And when He was twelve years old, they went up to Jerusalem as usual for the festival. When they had stayed the full number of days, they started back, but the child Jesus stayed behind in Jerusalem.

Joseph and Mary knew nothing of this. Supposing that He was in the caravan, they went a day's journey, and looked for Him among their relatives and acquaintances. But when they did not find Him, they turned back again to Jerusalem, seeking Him.

After three days, at last, they found Him in the temple, sitting among the teachers, both listening to them and asking them questions. And all who heard Him were astonished at His understanding and answers.

When His parents saw Him, they were amazed. And His mother said to Him, "Son, why have You behaved like this to us? Here Your father and I have been looking for You and worrying." And He said to them, "Why did you look for me? Did you not know that I must be about my Father's business?"

But they did not understand what He said. He went along with them to Nazareth, and was obedient to them. But His mother kept all these things in her heart.

And Jesus increased in wisdom as He grew, and in favor with God and man.

JESUS BEGINS HIS WORK

JESUS IS BAPTIZED

IN THOSE days John the Baptist appeared, preaching in the wilderness of Judea, and saying, "Repent, for the kingdom of Heaven is at hand." For it was He who was spoken of by the prophet ISAIAH, when he said, "Hear the voice of one crying in the wilderness, 'Prepare the way for the Lord, make His paths straight.'"

This same John wore clothing made of camel's hair, and a leather girdle about his waist. And his food was locusts and wild honey.

Then the people of Jerusalem, and all Judea, and all the region round about Jordan went out to him, and were baptized by him in the Jordan, confessing their sins.

But when he saw many of the Pharisees and the Sadducees (leaders in the temple) come to his baptism, he said to them, "You brood of snakes, who has warned you to flee from the wrath to come? Let us see you do worthy deeds, if you truly repent. And do not think it will be enough to say within yourselves, 'We have Abraham for a forefather.' For I say to you that God could produce children for Abraham from these stones.

"Now the axe is laid to the root of the trees, and every tree which does not bring forth good fruit will be cut down and cast into the fire.

"I baptize you with water in token of your repentance, but He who comes after me is so much mightier than I, that I am not even worthy to carry His sandals. He shall baptize you with the Holy Spirit, and with fire.

"His winnowing fan is in His hand, and He will thoroughly clean His floor after the harvest, and will gather His wheat in the barns, but the chaff He will burn up with unquenchable fire." (The harvest of which John spoke was a harvest of souls, and the wheat and chaff were the souls of the good and of the evil.)

Then Jesus came from Galilee to Jordan, and came to John, to be baptized by him. John tried to stop Him, saying, "I ought to be baptized by You, and do You come to me?"

Jesus answered him, saying, "Let it be so now. For it is right for us to fulfill all our duties to God."

Then John gave in to Him. And Jesus, when He was baptized, rose straight up out of the water. And the heavens opened to Him, and He saw the Spirit of God coming down like a dove, and lighting upon Him. And a voice from Heaven said, "This is my beloved Son, in whom I am well pleased."

And Jesus began His work at about thirty years of age.

THE TEMPTATION IN THE WILDERNESS

JESUS, FULL of the Holy Spirit, returned from the Jordan and was led by the Spirit into the wilderness. And for forty days He was tempted by the devil. In all those days He ate nothing, and when they were ended, he was famished.

The devil said to Him, "If You are the Son of God, command this stone to turn into bread." Jesus answered him, saying, "It is written that man shall not live by bread alone, but by every word of God."

Again the devil, taking Him up onto a high mountain, showed Him all the kingdoms of the world in a moment of time.

The devil said to Him, "All this power I will give to You, and the glory of them all; for it has been turned over to me, and I can give it to whomsoever I choose. If You will worship me, it shall all be Yours."

Jesus answered him and said, "Get thee behind me, Satan. For it is written, 'You shall worship the Lord your God, and Him only shall you serve.' "

Again he brought Him to Jerusalem, and set Him on a pinnacle of the temple, and said to Him, "If You are the Son of God, throw Yourself down from here. For it is written that He shall put His angels in charge of You, to keep You safe, and they will lift You up in their hands, lest You strike Your foot against a stone."

And Jesus answering, said to him, "It is said, 'You shall not tempt the Lord your God.' " When the devil had tried every temptation, he departed from Him for a time.

JESUS CHOOSES HIS DISCIPLES

NOW JESUS heard that John had been thrown into prison by Herod the governor, whom John had reproved for all the evil things he had done. Then Jesus left home and went out into Galilee. Leaving Nazareth, He went and lived in Capernaum, which is upon the coast of the Sea of Galilee, in the district of Zebulun and Naphtali. In this He was fulfilling the words of the prophet Isaiah:

"O land of Zebulun and land of Naphtali, by the road to the sea, beyond the Jordan, Galilee of the Gentiles, The people who sat in darkness have seen a great light. And upon those who sat in the land and shadow of death a light has dawned."

From that time on, Jesus too began to preach, saying, "Repent, for the kingdom of Heaven is coming."

It happened that one day as the people crowded around Him to hear the word of God, He was standing beside the Sea of Galilee. He saw two boats standing by the sea, but the fishermen had left them and were washing their nets.

He stepped into one of the boats, which was Simon's, and asked him to push out a little from the land. Then He sat down and taught the people from the boat.

When He had finished speaking, He said to Simon, "Row out to deep water, and let down your nets for a catch."

Simon answered Him, saying, "Master, we have worked all night, and we have taken nothing. Nevertheless, because You ask it, I will let down the nets."

When they had done so, the nets enclosed such a multitude of fish that they broke. Then Simon called to his partners, who were in the other boat, to come and help. They came, and filled both boats so full that they began to sink.

When Simon saw this, he fell down at Jesus' knees, saying, "Leave me, Master, for I am a sinful man." For he was astonished, as were all who were with him, at the catch of fish they had made. James

and John, the sons of Zebedee, who were partners with Simon, were astonished too.

Jesus said to Simon, "Do not be afraid. From now on you shall be a fisher of men."

And when they had brought their boats to shore, they left everything behind and followed Him.

And Jesus looked at Simon and said, "You are Simon, the son of John. You shall be called Cephas."

The next day Jesus found Philip and said to him, "Follow me."

Philip found Nathanael, and said to him, "We have found the one of whom Moses and the prophets wrote — Jesus of Nazareth, the son of Joseph."

Nathanael said, "Can any good thing come out of Nazareth?"

Philip replied, "Come and see."

When Jesus saw Nathanael coming, He said of him, "Here indeed is an Israelite in whom there is no deceit."

Nathanael said to Him, "How do you know me?"

Jesus told him, "Before Philip saw you, when you were under the fig tree, I saw you."

Nathanael answered and said to Him, "Teacher, you are the Son of God. You are the King of Israel."

Jesus said, "Do you believe in me because I said I saw you under the fig tree? You shall see greater

things than that. Truly, truly, I tell you, you shall see the heavens open and the angels of God going up and coming down upon the Son of Man."

One day at this time Jesus went up on a mountain top to pray, and continued all night in prayer to God. And when daylight came, He called to Him His disciples; of them He chose twelve, whom He also called apostles.

He appointed the twelve to be with Him, and also to go out to preach when He might send them, and to have the power to heal sicknesses and to cast out evil spirits.

There was Simon, whom He called Peter; there was James the son of Zebedee, and John the brother of James; and He called them Boanerges, the sons of thunder. There were Andrew and Philip and Bartholomew and Matthew and Thomas, and James the son of Alphaeus, and Thaddeus, and Simon the Cananaean. And there was Judas Iscariot, who betrayed Him.

THE MARRIAGE IN CANA

THE THIRD day there was a marriage in Cana of Galilee, and Jesus' mother was there. Jesus and His disciples were invited to the wedding, too. And when they ran short of wine Jesus' mother said to Him, "They have no more wine."

Jesus said to her, "What would you have me do? It is not time yet for me to act."

His mother said to the servants, "Do whatever He tells you."

There were six stone water pots standing there, for the purification rites of the Jews, each holding twenty or thirty gallons.

Jesus said to them, "Fill the water pots with water." And they filled them to the brim.

He said to them, "Draw some out now, and take it to the master of the feast." And they took it.

When the master of the feast tasted the water that was made wine, not knowing where it came from (but the servants who had drawn the water knew) the master of the feast called to the bridegroom and said to him, "Everyone else sets out his good wine at the beginning, and when men have drunk deeply, that which is poorer; but you have kept the good wine until now."

This, the first of the signs of His power, Jesus did in Cana of Galilee, and showed His glory. And His disciples believed in Him.

After this, He went down to Capernaum — He and His mother and His relatives and His disciples, and they stayed there a few days.

A PROPHET IN HIS OWN COUNTRY

JESUS WENT about in Galilee, full of the Holy Spirit, and His fame traveled through all the region. And He taught in their synagogues, being honored in them all.

He came to Nazareth, where He had been brought up, and, as His custom was, He went into the synagogue on the Sabbath Day, and stood up to read.

The book of the prophet ISAIAH was brought to Him, and when He had opened the book, He found the place where it says:

"The Spirit of the Lord is upon me, because He has blessed me to preach the gospel to the poor; He has sent me to heal the broken-hearted, to preach deliverance to the captives, and recovery of sight to the blind, to set free the oppressed, to proclaim the year of the Lord's grace."

He closed the book, and He gave it back to the attendant, and sat down. The eyes of all who were in the synagogue were fastened on Him. He began by saying to them, "Today this scripture is fulfilled in your hearing."

All spoke well of Him, and marveled at the winning words that came from His lips. But they said, "Is this not Joseph's son?"

He said to them, "No doubt you will repeat to me the proverb, 'Doctor, cure yourself. Whatever we have heard that you did in Capernaum, do here also in your own country.'" And He said, "Truly, I tell you, no prophet is accepted in His own country. But, I tell you, there were many widows in Israel in the days of Elijah, when the Heaven was shut up three years and six months, and there was great famine throughout all the land. But Elijah was not sent to one of them, but to a widow of Zarephath, a city of Sidon.

"And there were many lepers in Israel in the time of Elisha the prophet, and none of them was cured but Naaman the Syrian."

All the men in the synagogue, when they heard these things, were filled with anger. They rose up and drove Him out of the city, and led Him to the brow of the hill on which the city was built, so that they could throw Him down from it. But He made His way through the midst of the crowd and went off.

THE HEALING POWER OF JESUS

HE WENT down to Capernaum, a city of Galilee, and taught them on the Sabbath Days. They were astonished at His teaching, for His words had great power.

Now in the synagogue there was a man who had an unclean devil in his heart. He cried out with a loud voice, saying, "Let us alone. What have you to do with us, Jesus of Nazareth? Have you come to destroy us? I know who you are — the Holy One of God."

Jesus rebuked the devil, saying, "Be silent and come out of him."

The devil threw the man down before them all; then he came out of him, without doing him any harm. They were all amazed, and talked among themselves, saying, "What can this mean? He gives command to unclean spirits with power and authority, and they come out." And His fame spread to every place in the country round about.

He got up and left the synagogue and went to Simon's house. Simon's wife's mother was ill with a high fever, and they asked Him to help her.

He stood over her and rebuked the fever, and it left her.

Immediately she got up and waited on them.

Now as the sun was setting, everyone who had anyone sick with any disease at all brought them to Him. And He laid His hands on every one of them, and healed them.

Devils came out of many, too, crying out, and saying, "You are Christ the Son of God," and He rebuked them, forbidding them to speak, for they knew that He was Christ.

When it was day, He departed, and went off into a lonely spot. But the people sought Him out and came to Him, and tried to keep Him from leaving them.

And He said to them, "I must preach the kingdom of God to other towns, too, for that is what I have been sent to do."

And He preached in all the synagogues of Galilee.

THE HEALINGS AND TEACHINGS

THE CLEANSING OF THE LEPER

IT HAPPENED when He was in a certain city, a man came to Him who was full of leprosy. Seeing Jesus, he fell face down and begged Him, saying, "Lord, if only You will, You can make me clean and well."

So He put out His hand and touched him, saying, "I will; be clean." And immediately his leprosy was gone.

Jesus ordered him to tell no one, but to go and show himself to the priest and make an offering for his purification, according to the law of Moses, as evidence of his cure.

But the fame of Jesus spread abroad just so much more, and great multitudes gathered to hear Him, and to be cured by Him of their illnesses.

Jesus went off by Himself to a lonely place, and prayed.

THE FORGIVING OF SINS

IT HAPPENED that one day as He was teaching there were Pharisees and doctors of the law sitting by, who had come from every town of Galilee and Judea and Jerusalem. And the power of the Lord was in Him, to heal those who came.

Some men brought, on a bed, a man who was paralyzed, and they tried to find a way to bring him in, and to lay him before Jesus. And when they could not find a way to bring him in, because of the crowds, they went up on the housetop, and let him down through the tiling with his bed, into the middle of the crowd around Jesus.

And when He saw their faith, He said, "Man, your sins are forgiven."

Then the scribes and the Pharisees began to argue, "Who is this who speaks blasphemy? Who can forgive sins but God alone?"

But when Jesus saw what they were thinking, He said to them in reply, "What are you discussing in your hearts? Which is easier, to say, 'Your sins are

OF JESUS ANGER THE PHARISEES

forgiven,' or to say, 'Rise up and walk'? So that you may know that the Son of Man has power to forgive sins upon earth — (He turned to the paralyzed man) — I say to you, 'Rise up, pick up your bed, and go home.'" Immediately he rose up before them all, and took up the bed he had been lying on, and went off to his own house, praising God.

They were all amazed, and they praised God and were filled with fear, saying, "We have seen wonderful things today."

THE KEEPING OF THE SABBATH

ONE SABBATH soon afterward, it happened that His way led through the grain fields, and His disciples picked some heads of wheat, and ate them, rubbing them in their hands.

Certain of the Pharisees said to them, "Why do you do things which are against the rules of the Sabbath?"

Jesus, answering them, said, "Have you not read what David did, when he and his men were hungry? How he went into the house of God and took the temple bread, which it is not lawful for anyone but a priest to eat, and ate of it and gave some to those who were with him?" He said to them further, "The Son of Man is Lord also of the Sabbath."

It also happened on another Sabbath that He went into the synagogue and taught. And there was a man whose right hand was withered.

The scribes and Pharisees watched Him to see whether He would heal on the Sabbath Day, so they might find something to charge Him with.

But He knew their thoughts, and said to the man with the withered hand, "Rise and come forward."

The man arose and came forward.

Then Jesus said to them, "I want to ask you one thing: Is it lawful on the Sabbath Day to do good or to do evil? To save life or to destroy it?" And looking around at them all, He said to the man, "Stretch out your hand."

The man did so, and his hand was made as well as the other.

This filled the Pharisees with fury, and they discussed together what they could do to Jesus.

JESUS' GREATEST TEACHINGS

JESUS WENT all around Galilee, teaching in the synagogues, and preaching the gospel of the kingdom of God, and healing all kinds of sickness and all kinds of disease among the people.

His fame spread throughout all Syria, and they brought to Him all the sick people who suffered from different diseases and pain, and those who had evil spirits in their hearts, those who were sick in their minds, and those who were paralyzed; and He healed them.

Great crowds of people followed Him, from Galilee, from Decapolis, from Jerusalem, from Judea, and from beyond the Jordan.

When He saw these great crowds, He went up onto a hillside, and sat down, and His disciples came to Him. Then He opened His lips and began to teach them in these words:

THE BEATITUDES

"BLESSED are the poor in spirit, for theirs is the kingdom of Heaven.

"Blessed are the meek, for they shall possess the earth.

"Blessed are they who mourn, for they shall be comforted.

"Blessed are they who hunger and thirst for justice, for they shall be satisfied.

"Blessed are the merciful for they shall obtain mercy.

"Blessed are the clean of heart, for they shall see God.

"Blessed are the peacemakers, for they shall be called the children of God.

"Blessed are they who suffer persecution for justice's sake, for theirs is the kingdom of Heaven.

"Blessed are you, when men shall abuse you and persecute you and say all kinds of evil things about you falsely, for my sake. Rejoice and exult in it, for your reward in Heaven will be great; for that is the way they persecuted the prophets who came before you.

THE LIGHT OF THE WORLD

"YOU ARE the salt of the earth. But if the salt has lost its flavor, what can make it salty again? It is fit for nothing from then on but to be thrown out and trodden underfoot.

"You are the light of the world. A city that is set on a hill cannot be hid. Nor do men light a candle and put it under a bushel, but on a candlestick, where it gives light to all that are in the house.

"Let your light so shine before men, that they may see the good you do and glorify your Father in Heaven.

THE NEW COMMANDMENTS

"DO NOT think that I have come to destroy the old law or the prophets. I have come not to destroy but to fulfill. For I tell you, until Heaven and earth pass away, not one jot [the smallest letter] nor one tittle [the smallest part of a letter] shall be lost until all has been fulfilled.

"Therefore, anyone who breaks one of the least of these commandments, and teaches men to do so, shall be ranked the lowest of all in the kingdom of Heaven. But whoever obeys and teaches the law, he shall be called great in the kingdom of Heaven.

"For I tell you that unless your goodness excels that of the scribes and Pharisees, you will never enter into the kingdom of Heaven.

Do Not Store Up Anger

"You have heard that it was said by men in the days of old, 'You shall not kill; whoever kills will come up for sentence in the court.' But I tell you that whoever becomes angry with his brother without cause will be in danger of sentence by God. And whoever curses his brother shall be in danger of Hell fire.

"Therefore, if you bring your offering to the altar, and there remember that your brother has any grievance against you, leave your offering there before the altar, and go; first be reconciled to your brother, and then come and make your offering.

Do Not Swear Oaths

"Again, you have heard that it was said by men of old, 'You shall not swear falsely, but whatever you promise to the Lord, you must do.' But I tell you, Do not swear at all: neither by Heaven, for it is God's throne, nor by the earth, for it is His footstool, nor by Jerusalem, for it is the city of the great king. Neither shall you swear by your own head, because you have not the power to make one hair white or black. Let what you have to say be simply Yes or No, for whatever goes beyond these comes from the evil one.

Do Not Resist Injury

"You have heard that it has been said, 'An eye for an eye, and a tooth for a tooth.' But I tell you. Do not resist an injury; if anyone strikes you on the right cheek, turn the other to him also. If any man wants to sue you for your shirt, let him have your coat as well; and if anyone compels you to go one mile, go with him two. Give to him that asks, and if anyone wishes to borrow from you, do not turn away.

Love Your Enemies

"You have heard that it has been said, 'You shall love your neighbor and hate your enemy.' But I tell you, Love your enemies, bless those who speak ill of you, do good to those who hate you, and pray for those who harm you, so that you may be truly the children of your Father in Heaven. For He makes His sun rise on the bad and good alike, and sends His rain on the just and the unjust.

"For if you love only those who love you, what reward do you deserve? Do not even the tax-gatherers do as well? And if you greet your brothers only, what is remarkable about that? Do not even the Gentiles do that? You should be perfect, as your Father in Heaven is perfect.

Do Good Secretly

"Take care that you do not do your good deeds in public, in order to be seen by others; otherwise you will have no reward from your Father in Heaven. When you give charity, do not sound a trumpet before yourself as the hypocrites do in the synagogues and in the streets, to have the applause of men. I tell you truly, they have their reward in that. But when you give charity, do not let your left hand know what your right hand is doing, so that your charity may be in secret; and your Father who sees what you do in secret will reward you.

The Lord's Prayer

"And when you pray, you shall not be as the hypocrites are, for they love to pray standing in the synagogues and at the corners of the streets, so that men may see them. Truly I tell you, that is their reward.

"But you, when you pray, go into your room and when you have shut the door pray to your Father in secret. And your Father who sees what is in secret will reward you.

"But when you pray, do not use idle phrases, as the Gentiles do, for they imagine that they shall be heard for the amount they say. Do not be like them, therefore, for your Father knows everything you need, before you ask Him for it.

"In this manner, then, pray:

OUR FATHER Who art in Heaven,
Hallowed be Thy name.
Thy kingdom come.
Thy will be done
On earth as it is in Heaven.
Give us this day our daily bread.
And forgive us our trespasses.
As we forgive those who trespass against us.
And lead us not into temptation.
But deliver us from evil.

"For if you forgive others when they offend you, your heavenly Father will forgive you too; but if you do not forgive others when they offend you, neither will your Father forgive you for your offenses.

Do Not Store Up Earthly Treasures

"Do not store up treasures for yourselves upon earth, where moth and rust destroy them, and where thieves break in and steal. But store up treasures for yourselves in Heaven, where neither moth nor rust can destroy them, and where thieves do not break through and steal; for where your treasure is, your heart will be there, too.

"The lamp of the body is the eye; if, therefore, your eye is sound, your whole body will be full of light. But if your eye is unsound, your whole body will be full of darkness. If, therefore, the light (of the spirit) that is in you is darkened (by evil), how dense that darkness is!

"No man can work for two masters: for either he will hate one and love the other, or he will stand by one and despise the other. You cannot work both for God and for worldly wealth."

The Rich Man and His Soul

And He spoke to them in a parable, saying:

"The fields of a certain rich man yielded rich crops. And he thought to himself, 'What shall I do? I have no more room to store away all my riches.'

"Then he thought, 'This is what I will do: I will pull down my barns and build larger ones, and there I will store all my crops and my goods. And I will say to my soul, "Soul, you have enough wealth laid up for many years. Take your ease, eat, drink, and be merry." '

"But God said to him, 'O fool, tonight your soul shall be taken from you. Then to whom shall all these things belong, which you have laid by?'

"So it is with anyone who lays up earthly treasures for himself, instead of the riches of the spirit.

"Rather seek out the kingdom of God, and all the other things you need shall be given to you.

"And why do you worry about clothing? Consider the lilies of the field, and how they grow; they do not toil nor spin, and yet I tell you, even Solomon in all his glory was never clothed like one of them.

"Now if God so beautifully dresses the grass of the field, which blooms today and tomorrow is burned up, shall He not much more surely clothe you? O, how little faith you have!

The Lesson of the Lilies

"Therefore, do not worry, saying. What shall we eat? What shall we drink? or Where shall we find clothes? After all these things the Gentiles seek. Your heavenly Father knows that you need these things. But seek first the kingdom of God, and His goodness, and all these things will be freely given to you.

"Therefore, do not worry about tomorrow, for tomorrow will have worries of its own. The day's own troubles are enough for the day.

"Do not worry, I tell you, about your life—what you shall eat, or what you shall drink, nor about your body—what you shall wear. Is not life something more than food, and the body more than clothing?

"Look at the birds of the air, for they do not sow, nor harvest, nor gather food in barns. Yet your heavenly Father feeds them all. Are you not worth more than they?

"Which of you by worrying about it can add one footstep to the length of his life?

Do Not Judge Others

"Do not judge others, so that you may not be judged yourself. For as you judge others, so you shall be judged. And with the same measure you deal out to others, it shall be returned to you again.

"Why do you look at the splinter that is in your brother's eye, but ignore the plank that is in your own eye?

"How can you say to your brother, 'Let me pull the splinter out of your eye,' when there is a plank in your own eye? You hypocrite! First cast the plank out of your own eye, and then you will see more clearly to cast out the splinter from your brother's eye.

"Do not give what is sacred to dogs, nor cast your pearls before swine, lest they trample them under their feet, and turn about to attack you.

Ask, and You Shall Receive

"Ask, and it shall be given to you. Seek, and you shall find. Knock, and the door will be opened to you. For everyone who asks receives, and he who seeks finds, and to him who knocks the door shall be opened.

"What man of you is there who, if his son asks for bread, would give him a stone? Or if he asks for fish, would give him a snake? If you then, bad as you are, know how to give good gifts to your children, will not your Father in Heaven much more surely give good things to those who ask Him?

The Golden Rule

"Therefore, do to others everything that you would like them to do to you, for that is the meaning of the law and the prophets.

"Go in at the narrow gate; for wide is the gate and broad is the road that leads to destruction, and there are many who go in by it. But narrow is the gate and hard is the way that leads to life eternal, and few there are who find it."

Then He said, "What is the kingdom of God like? And what shall I say it resembles?

"It is like a grain of mustard seed, which a man took, and threw into his garden. And it grew and became a great tree, and the fowls of the air nested in its branches.

Be Ready for the Kingdom

"Fear not, little flock; for it is your Father's good pleasure to give you the kingdom.

"Sell what you have, and give it to the poor. Provide yourselves with purses which never wear out, a treasure in the Heavens which never fails, where no thief comes near nor moth devours. For where your treasure is, there will your heart be also.

"Always be dressed and ready, with your lights burning, like men who wait for their lord when he is about to return from a wedding, so that when he comes and knocks they may open the gates for him immediately.

"Blessed are those servants whom the lord finds watching when he comes. I tell you truly that he will fasten up his robe and make them sit down to the table, and he will come out and serve them.

"And if he comes in the middle of the night, or in the hours of dawn, and finds them so, blessed are those servants.

"You must be ready, too; for the Son of Man will come at an hour when you do not expect Him.

The House Upon the Rock

"Therefore, whoever hears these sayings of mine, and acts upon them, will be like a wise man who built his house upon a rock. And the rains fell, and the floods came, and the winds blew and beat upon that house; but it did not fall, for it had foundations in the rock.

"And everyone who hears these sayings of mine, and does not act upon them, will be like a foolish man, who built his house upon the sand; and the rains fell, and the floods came and the winds blew and beat upon that house; and it fell, and a great fall it was indeed."

When Jesus had finished His talk, the people were astonished at His teachings, for He taught them like one who had authority, and not like the scribes.

FORGIVING

ONE OF the Pharisees asked Jesus to come and eat with him. And He went into the Pharisee's house and sat down to dinner. Now there was a woman in that city who was a sinner, and when she learned that Jesus was having dinner at the Pharisee's house, she brought an alabaster box of ointment and stayed at His feet, behind Him, weeping. She began to wash His feet with tears, and wiped them with the hair of her head, and kissed His feet, and perfumed them with the ointment.

Now when the Pharisee who had invited Him saw this, he said to himself, "This man, if He were a prophet, would have known who and what kind of woman this is who touches Him; for she is sinful."

Jesus in answer said to him, "Simon, I have something to say to you."

And he said, "Master, speak."

"There was a certain money-lender to whom two men owed money. One owed him much, and the other little. When they had nothing to pay, he freely forgave them both.

"Tell me then, which of them will love him most?"

Simon answered and said, "I suppose he who had the most forgiven."

And He said to him, "You are right." Then, turning to the woman, He said to Simon, "Do you see this woman? I came into your house, and you gave me no water for my feet; but she has washed my feet with tears and wiped them with the hair of her head. You gave me no kiss, but this woman, since the moment I came in, has not stopped kissing my feet. You did not perfume my head with oil, but this woman has perfumed my feet with ointment.

"Therefore I tell you, her sins, which are many, are forgiven because she has loved me so much. But the man with little to be forgiven, he loves me little."

And He said to her, "Your sins are forgiven." Those who sat at dinner with Him began to say to themselves, "Who is this who forgives sins?

And He said to the woman, "Your faith has saved you; go in peace."

NICODEMUS ASKS HOW TO BE SAVED

NOW A certain Pharisee named Nicodemus, a ruler of the Jews, came to Jesus at night and said to Him, "Teacher, we know that You have come from God, for no one could do the miracles You do unless God were with him."

Jesus said, "I tell you truly, unless a man is born again he cannot see the kingdom of God." Nicodemus said, "How can a man be born when he is already grown up?"

Jesus said, "Unless a man is born of water and the Spirit he cannot enter God's kingdom." Nicodemus said, "How can this be?"

Jesus answered, "I speak of what I know and I testify to what I have seen. For no one is at home with the things of Heaven except the Son of Man who came down from Heaven. And just as Moses lifted up the serpent in the desert, so must the Son of Man be lifted up that those who believe in Him may have eternal life."

THE PARABLE OF THE SOWER

SOON AFTERWARD, it happened that He went out through every city and village around, preaching and telling the glad news of the kingdom of God. And the twelve disciples were with Him.

There were certain women, too, who had been healed of evil spirits and illnesses — Mary called Magdalene, out of whom seven devils had been driven, and Joanna the wife of Chuza, Herod's steward, and Susanna, and many others, who cared for Him out of their means.

When a great crowd was gathered together, with people who had come from all the towns around, He spoke to them in a parable:

"A sower went out to sow his seed. And as he sowed, some fell by the wayside, and it was trodden down, and the birds of the air devoured it.

"Some fell upon a rock, and as soon as it had sprung up, it withered away, because it lacked moisture.

"Some fell among thorns, and the thorns sprang up with it and choked it.

"And some fell on good ground, and sprang up and bore fruit a hundredfold."

And when He had finished, He said:

"He who has ears to hear, let him hear."

His disciples asked Him, saying, "What does this parable mean?"

And He said, "To you it is given to know the mysteries of the kingdom of God, but to the others I speak in parables, that seeing they may still not see (the truth), and hearing they may still not understand.

"Now this is the meaning of the parable:

"The seed is the word of God. Those by the wayside are those who hear; then the devil comes and takes away the word out of their hearts, lest they should believe and be saved.

"Those on the rock are they who, when they hear the word of God, receive it with joy; but having no roots, they believe for a while, but in time of temptation fall away.

"That which fell among thorns refers to those who, when they have heard, go out and are choked with the cares and riches and pleasures of this life, so that their faith never ripens.

"But the seed on the good ground means those who, having heard the word, keep it in an honest and good heart, and bring forth fruit with patience.

"Take care therefore how you listen; for to him who has (understanding), more shall be given; and whoever has it not, from him shall be taken away even that which he seems to have."

THE WINDS AND WAVES OBEY JESUS

NOW IT happened on a certain day that He went in a boat with His disciples, and He said to them, "Let us go over to the other side of the lake." So they set sail.

But as they sailed He fell asleep. And there came down a storm of wind, and the boat filled with water, so that they were in danger.

The disciples came to Him and awoke Him, saying, "Master, master, we are drowning."

Then He arose and rebuked the wind and the raging of the water, and they ceased and there was a calm.

And He said to them, "Where is your faith?"

They, being frightened, wondered at this, saying to one another, "What manner of man is this? For He commands even the winds and the water, and they obey Him."

JESUS CASTS OUT THE DEVILS

JESUS AND His disciples arrived at the country of the Gerasenes, which is across the lake from Galilee. When they stepped out onto the land, Jesus was met by a certain man from the city, who had been possessed by evil spirits for a long time, and wore no clothes; nor would he live in a house, but stayed among the tombs.

When he saw Jesus, he cried out and fell down before Him and said with a loud voice, "What have I to do with You, Jesus, Son of God Most High? I beg of You, do not torment me."

For Jesus had commanded the evil spirits to come out of the man. Often it seized him, and though he was bound with chains and fetters, he broke the bonds and was driven by the devil into the wilderness.

Jesus asked him, "What is your name?"

And he answered, "Legion" [six thousand], because there were many devils in him. And they begged Jesus not to send them back to hell. There was a herd of many pigs feeding on the mountainside, and they begged him to let them enter into the pigs. And He permitted it.

Then the devils went out of the man and entered into the pigs, and the herd rushed down the steep bank into the lake and were drowned.

When the herdsmen saw what had happened, they fled, and went and told their story in the city and in the countryside.

People went out to see what had been done; and they came to Jesus and found the man from whom the devils were gone, sitting at the feet of Jesus, clothed, and in his right mind; and they were afraid.

Those who had seen it, told them by what means he who had been possessed of the devils had been healed.

Then all the people of the countryside around begged Jesus to go away from them, for they were filled with a great fear. And He went back to His boat, and returned to the other side of the lake.

THE DAUGHTER OF JAIRUS

MAN CALLED Jairus came, a ruler of the synagogue; and he fell down at Jesus' feet, and begged Him to come to his house, for he had only one daughter, about twelve years of age, and she lay dying.

As Jesus was going, the people pressed about Him. And a woman who had been bleeding for twelve years and had spent all her savings upon physicians, but could not be healed, came behind Him and touched the border of His robe. And immediately her hemorrhage stopped. Jesus said, "Who touched me?"

When everyone denied it, Peter and those who were with him said, "Master, the multitude is crowding around and crushing against You. How can You say, 'Who touched me?' "

Jesus said, "Someone has touched me, for I can feel that power has gone out of me." When the woman saw that she had not escaped notice, she came trembling, and falling down before Him, she told Him before all the people why she had touched Him, and how she had been healed immediately.

And He said to her, "Daughter, be of good cheer. Your faith has healed you. Go in peace."

While He was speaking, someone came from the house of the ruler of the synagogue, saying to Him, "Your daughter is dead; do not trouble the Master."

But when Jesus heard this, He answered him, saying, "Do not fear; only believe, and she shall be well again."

When He came to the house, He did not permit anyone to go in, save Peter and James and John, and the father and mother of the girl.

They all wept and mourned for her, but He said, "Do not weep. She is not dead but asleep."

They laughed at Him, for they knew that she was dead. But He put them all out and took her by the hand, and spoke to her, saying, "Young girl, arise."

And her spirit returned, and she arose at once; and He directed them to give her something to eat.

Her parents were astonished, but He warned them to tell no one what had been done.

FEEDING THE MULTITUDE

JESUS TOOK the disciples and went off privately to a deserted place belonging to the town of Bethsaida. But the people, when they learned of it, followed Him. And He received them, and spoke to them of the kingdom of God, and healed those who needed healing.

And when the day began to wear away, the twelve came to Him and said, "Send the multitude away, so that they may go into the towns and country round about and find lodging and food, for we are in a lonely place here."

But He said to them, "Give them something to eat."

They said, "We have no more than five loaves and two fishes, unless we are to go and buy food for all these people." For there were about five thousand men.

He said to His disciples, "Make them sit down in groups of fifty." And they did so, and made them all sit down.

Then He took the five loaves and the two fishes, and looking up to Heaven, He blessed them and broke them and gave them to the disciples to serve to the people.

They ate, and were all filled, and there were twelve baskets of pieces that were left gathered up.

THE KEYS OF THE KINGDOM

ONE DAY, Jesus asked His disciples, "Who do people say I am?" And they said, "Some say that You are John the Baptist, some Elijah, and others Jeremiah or one of the old prophets come back to life."

Then He said to them, "But who do you say I am?"

And Simon Peter answered, saying, "You are the Christ, the Son of the living God."

Jesus said to him, "You are blessed indeed, Simon son of Jona, for flesh and blood have not revealed this to you, but my Father who is in Heaven. And I tell you this too: you are Peter the Rock, and upon this rock I will build my Church, and the gates of hell shall not prevail against it. And I will give to you the keys of the kingdom of Heaven; and whatever you bind on earth shall be bound in Heaven; and whatever you loose on earth shall be loosed in Heaven."

Then He sternly commanded them to tell no one about Him. For, He said, "The Son of Man must suffer many things, and be rejected by the elders and chief priests and scribes, and be killed, and rise again the third day."

And He said to them all, "If any man wants to follow me, let him deny himself and take up his cross, and follow me.

"For whoever wants to save his life shall lose it; but whoever gives up his life for my sake, that one will save it.

"For what is the advantage to a man, if he gains the whole world, and loses his own soul?

"For whoever is ashamed of me and my words, the Son of Man shall be ashamed of him when He comes in His own glory, and in the glory of His Father and of the holy angels. But I tell you truly, there are some standing here who shall not taste of death till they see the Son of Man enter His kingdom."

THE TRANSFIGURATION

ABOUT A week after this, He took Peter and John and James, and went up on a mountain to pray. And as He prayed, His face shone like the sun, and His garments became white as snow.

And behold, two men came to talk with Him — Moses and Elijah, who appeared gloriously and spoke of the death which awaited Him at Jerusalem.

Peter and those who were with Him were heavy with sleep; and when they awoke, they saw Jesus in His glory, and the two men who stood talking with Him.

As the two were leaving Him, Peter said to Jesus, "Master, it is good for us to be here. Let us make three shrines, one for you, and one for Moses, and one for Elijah."

Peter scarcely knew what he was saying. While he was speaking, a cloud came and overshadowed them, and they were frightened as the cloud came over them.

And a voice came out of the cloud, saying: "This is my beloved Son, with whom I am well pleased. Listen to Him."

When the disciples heard it, they fell on their faces, and were very much afraid.

Then Jesus came and touched them and said, "Rise up; do not be afraid."

And when they lifted up their eyes, they saw Jesus standing there alone. No one was with Him.

As they came down the mountain, Jesus commanded them, saying, "Do not tell anyone about this vision, until the Son of Man has risen from the dead."

THE GRAIN OF MUSTARD SEED

WHEN JESUS and His disciples came to the crowds of people awaiting them one day, a certain man came to Jesus, and kneeling down to Him, said, "Lord, have mercy on my son, for he is often out of his mind and sorely troubled; for oftentimes he falls into the fire, and often into the water. I brought him to Your disciples, but they could not cure him."

Jesus rebuked the evil spirit, and it went out of the boy, and the child was cured from that very hour.

Then the disciples came to Jesus privately, and said, "Why could we not cast it out?"

And Jesus said to them, "Because of your little faith. For I tell you truly, if you had faith as much as a grain of mustard seed, you could say to this mountain, 'Move over there,' and it would move; and nothing would be impossible for you."

JESUS BLESSES THE LITTLE CHILDREN

A DISPUTE arose among the disciples, as to which of them should be the greatest in the kingdom of Heaven. And Jesus, understanding the thought in their hearts, called a little child to Him, and set Him in the midst of them.

And He said, "Truly I tell you, unless you are changed in your hearts and become as little children, you shall not enter into the kingdom of Heaven. Therefore, whoever shall humble himself and become as this little child, that same one shall be the greatest in the kingdom of Heaven. And whoever shall welcome one such little child in my name, welcomes me.

"But whoever causes one of these little ones who believe in me to sin, it would be better for him if a millstone were hanged about his neck, and he were drowned in the depth of the sea.

"Take care that you do not look down upon one of these little ones; for I tell you, that in Heaven their angels always look upon the face of my Father who is in Heaven."

JESUS INSTRUCTS HIS DISCIPLES

IT HAPPENED that as they went along the road, a certain man said to Jesus, "Lord, I will follow You wherever you go."

Jesus said to him, "Foxes have holes, and birds of the air have nests; but the Son of Man does not have a place to lay His head."

And He said to another, "Follow me." But the man said, "Lord, let me go first and bury my father."

Jesus said to him, "Let the dead bury their dead, but you go and preach the kingdom of God."

Another also said, "Lord, I want to follow you, but let me go first to say farewell to my people at home."

And Jesus said to him, "No man, having put his hand to the plow, who looks back, is fit for the kingdom of God."

Some time after this, the Lord appointed seventy-two other disciples, and sent them out two by two to go before Him into every city and place where He Himself would go.

"The harvest (of souls) is truly great," He said to them, "but the laborers are few. Pray, therefore, to the Lord of the harvest that He may send out laborers into His harvest.

"Go your ways; you see, I send you out as lambs among wolves. Carry neither a purse nor wallet nor shoes, and greet no man along the way.

"Whenever you enter into a house, say first, 'Peace be in this house.' And if a man of peace is there, your peace shall rest upon it; if not, it shall return to you.

"Stay in the same house, eating and drinking whatever they give; for the laborer earns his board and keep. Do not go from house to house. And in whatever city you are, if they welcome you, eat whatever is put before you. And heal the sick that are there, saying to them, 'The kingdom of God has come close to you.'

"But if you enter into any city and they do not welcome you, go your way out into the streets of that city, and say, 'Even the very dust of your city, which clings to us, we wipe off against you; nevertheless be sure of this, that the kingdom of God is close to you.'

"And I tell you, it will be better in the day of judgment for Sodom than for that city. For he who hears you hears me; and he who looks down upon you, looks down upon me; and he who looks down upon me, has no use for Him who sent me."

Then the seventy-two went out. And they returned again, filled with joy, saying, "Lord, even the evil spirits obey us through Your name.

Jesus said, "Do not rejoice in this, that the spirits obey you, but rather rejoice because your names are written in Heaven."

THE GOOD SAMARITAN

A CERTAIN LAWYER stood up, and, to try Jesus out, said, "Master, what shall I do to inherit eternal life?"

Jesus said to him, "What is written in the law? How do you read it?"

And he, answering, said, "You shall love the Lord your God with all your heart, and with all your soul, and with all your strength, and with all your mind, and your neighbor as yourself."

And Jesus said to him, "You have answered correctly; do this, and you shall live forever."

But he, wishing to justify his question, said to Jesus, "And who is my neighbor?"

Jesus, answering, said: "A certain man went down from Jerusalem to Jericho, and fell among thieves, who stripped him of his clothing, and beat him, and went off, leaving him half dead.

"By chance a certain priest came down that way, and when he saw him, he passed by on the other side.

"A Levite also, when he reached the spot, came and looked at him, and passed by on the other side.

"But a certain Samaritan, as he journeyed, came where he was. And when he saw him, he took pity on him, and went to him, and bound up his wounds, pouring in oil and wine. And he set him on his own beast, and brought him to an inn, and took care of him.

"The next day, when he departed, he took out some coins, and gave them to the innkeeper, and said to him, 'Take care of him, and whatever you spend beyond this, when I come again I shall repay you.'

"Now which of these three, do you think, was neighbor to him who fell among the thieves?"

And he said, "He who took pity on him."

Then Jesus said to him, "Go, and do the same yourself."

MARY AND MARTHA

NOW IT happened, as they went about, that Jesus came into a certain village, and a woman named Martha welcomed him into her home.

She had a sister called Mary, who sat at Jesus' feet and listened to His words.

But Martha was very busy with many household duties, and once she came to Jesus and said, "Lord, do You not care that my sister has left me to do all the work alone? Tell her to help me."

Jesus answered and said to her, "Martha, Martha, you are concerned and troubled about many things. But only one thing is necessary and Mary has made the best choice, which shall not be taken away from her."

PARABLES OF FORGIVENESS

THE LOST IS FOUND

ALL THE tax-gatherers and sinners drew near to hear Jesus. When the Pharisees and scribes began to mutter, saying, "This man welcomes sinners, and eats with them," Jesus spoke to them in this parable:

"What man of you, if he has a hundred sheep and loses one, does not leave the ninety and nine in the wilderness, and go after the one which is lost, until he finds it? And when he has found it, he carries it on his shoulders, rejoicing. And when he reaches home, he calls together his friends and neighbors, saying to them, 'Rejoice with me, for I have found my sheep which was lost.'

"And I tell you, truly he rejoices more over that sheep than over the ninety and nine which did not go astray. In the same way, there is more joy in Heaven over one sinner who repents than over ninety and nine just people who need no repentance.

"Or what woman, having ten pieces of silver, if she loses one piece, does not light a candle and sweep the house, and search diligently until she finds it? And when she has found it, she calls her friends and neighbors together, saying, 'Rejoice with me, for I have found the coin which I had lost.'

"In the same way, I tell you, there is joy among the angels of God over one sinner who repents."

THE PRODIGAL SON

AND JESUS said, "A certain man had two sons; and the younger of them said to his father, 'Father, give me my share of the property.' So he divided his property between them.

"Not many days later, the younger son gathered together all his goods, and journeyed into a far country. And there he wasted his wealth in foolish living.

"When he had spent all he had, a great famine arose in that land, and he began to be in want. Then he went and hired himself out to a citizen of that country, who sent him into his fields to feed pigs. He was ready to fill himself with the husks the pigs ate, for no man gave him anything.

"When he came to himself, he said, 'How many hired servants in my father's house have bread enough and to spare, while I am perishing with hunger.

" 'I will rise up and go to my father, and will say to him, "Father, I have sinned against heaven and before you. I am not worthy any more to be called your son. Make me one of your hired servants." '

"He rose up and went to his father. But when he was still a long way off, his father saw him, and had pity, and ran and fell on his neck and kissed him.

"The son said to him, 'Father, I have sinned against Heaven, and in your eyes, and am not worthy any longer to be called your son.'

"But the father said to his servants, 'Bring out the best robe, and put it on him. And put a ring on his hand, and shoes on his feet. And bring out the fatted calf and kill it, and let us eat and be merry. For this son of mine was dead, and is alive again. He was lost, and is found.' And they began to be merry.

"Now his elder son was in the field. And as he came in and drew near the house, he heard music and dancing. He called one of the servants and asked what these things meant.

"He said to him, 'Your brother has come home. And your father has killed the fatted calf, because he has him back, safe and sound.'

"He was angry, and would not go in. So his father came out and pleaded with him.

"He answered his father, saying, 'Look, these many years I have served you, never at any time disobeying one of your commandments. And yet you never even gave me a young goat so that I could make merry with my friends.

" 'But as soon as this other son of yours came, who had eaten up your wealth with women of the streets, you killed the fatted calf for him.'

"And the father said to him, 'Son, you are always with me, and all that I have is yours. But it is right for us to make merry and be glad; for this your brother was dead, and is alive again; was lost, and is found.' "

THE KING AND HIS SERVANTS

THEN PETER came to Him, and said, "Lord, how often shall my brother sin against me and I forgive him? Seven times?'"

Jesus said to him, "I tell you, not seven times but seventy times seven.

"In that way the kingdom of Heaven is like a certain king who wanted to take an accounting of his servants. And when he had begun his figuring, one was found who owed him ten thousand talents [sixty million denarii]. Since he did not have it to repay, his lord commanded that he should be sold—he and his wife and his children and all that he had, and that payment should be made. But the servant fell down before him, pleading, and said, 'Lord, have patience with me and I will pay you all.'

"Then the lord of that servant was moved with pity, and freed him, and forgave him the debt. But the same servant went off and found one of his fellow servants who owed him only a hundred denarii. And he laid hands on him, and took him by the throat, saying, 'Pay me what you owe.'

"And his fellow servant fell down at his feet and begged him, saying, 'Have patience with me, and I will pay you all of it.'

"Still he would not, but went and cast him into prison until he should pay the debt.

"When his fellow servants saw what he had done, they were very sorry, and came and told their lord all that had been done.

"Then his lord, after he had called him in, said to him, 'O wicked servant, I forgave you all that debt, because you asked it of me. Should you not also have had pity on your fellow servant, as I had pity on you?'

"And his lord was angry, and delivered him to torturers, until he should pay all he owed.

"Just so shall my heavenly Father do to you, if you do not forgive all your brethren from your hearts."

PARABLES OF GOD'S JUSTICE

THE STORY OF THE VINEYARD

THE KINGDOM of Heaven is like an employer who went out early in the morning to hire laborers for his vineyard. When he had agreed with his laborers on a denarius a day (the usual daily wage), he sent them into his vineyard.

He went out about nine o'clock, and saw others standing idle in the market place, and said to them, "Go to my vineyard too, and whatever is right I will give you." And they went their way.

He went out again about noon and mid-afternoon, and did likewise. And near the end of the day he went out, and found others standing idle, and said to them, "Why do you stand here idle all day?"

They said to him, "Because no one has hired us.

He said to them, "You go to the vineyard, too, and whatever is right, you will receive." So when evening came, the lord of the vineyard said to his steward, "Call the laborers, and give them their wages, beginning from the last to the first."

And when those came who were hired near the end of the day, each one received a denarius. So when the first came, they expected that they would receive more; but they likewise received each one a denarius.

When they had been paid, they murmured against the man of the house, saying, "These last have worked only one hour, and you have made them equal to those of us who have borne the whole burden through the heat of the day."

But he answered one of them, and said, "Friend, I am doing you no wrong. Didn't you agree with me on a denarius? Take your share and go your way. I want to pay the last man just as I paid you. Is it not lawful for me to do as I wish with what is mine? Do you bear a grudge because I am generous?"

So the last shall be first, and the first last.

THE RICH MAN AND THE BEGGAR

THERE WAS a certain rich man, who was clothed in purple and fine linen, and dined richly every day. And there was a certain beggar named Lazarus who was laid at his gate, covered with sores, and wishing only to be fed with the crumbs which fell from the rich man's table. The dogs even came and licked his sores.

It came about that the beggar died, and was carried by the angels to Abraham's arms. The rich man also died, and was buried. And in hell he lifted up his eyes, being in torment, and saw Abraham far off, and Lazarus with him.

He cried out and said, "Father Abraham, have mercy on me, and send Lazarus, that he may dip the tip of his finger in water, and cool my tongue. For I am tormented in this flame."

But Abraham said, "Son, remember that you in your lifetime received your share of good things, and Lazarus his share of bad things; but now he is comforted and you are tormented. Besides, there is a great gulf set between you and us; so that those who would pass from here to you cannot; neither can those who would pass from your side to us."

Then the rich man said, "I beg you then, father, to send him to my father's house, where I have five brothers, so that he may warn them, lest they also come into this place of torment." Abraham said to him, "They have Moses and the prophets; let them listen to them."

And he said, "No, father Abraham, but if one went to them from the dead, they would repent."

And Abraham said to him, "If they do not listen to Moses and the prophets, they will not be persuaded, even if one rises from the dead."

THE TWO PRAYERS

HE SPOKE this parable to certain men who were proud of their own righteousness and looked down upon others: "Two men went up into the temple to pray: the one a Pharisee, the other a tax-gatherer.

"The Pharisee stood and prayed by himself in these words: 'God, I thank You that I am not like other men, greedy, unjust, adulterers, or like this tax-gatherer! I fast twice in the week. I give a tenth of all I own.'

"And the tax-gatherer, standing far off, would not so much as lift up his eyes to Heaven, but beat upon his breast, saying, 'God, be merciful to me, a sinner.'

"I tell you, this man went down to his house accepted by God rather than the other. For everyone who exalts himself shall be humbled, and he who humbles himself shall be exalted."

ZACCHAEUS, THE TAX-GATHERER

JESUS ENTERED and passed through Jericho. And it happened there was a man named Zacchaeus, who was the chief tax-gatherer, and very rich.

He tried to see Jesus, to learn who He was, but could not because of the crowd, for he was a small man. So he ran on ahead, and climbed up into a sycamore tree to see Him, for He was to pass that way.

When Jesus came to the place, He looked up and saw him, and said to him, "Zacchaeus, hurry down, for today I must stay at your house."

He came down quickly and welcomed Him joyfully.

But when the others saw it, they all murmured, saying, "He has gone to be the guest of a man who is a sinner."

Then Zacchaeus stood still and said to the Lord, "Look, Lord, half of my goods I will give to the poor. And if I have taken anything from any man falsely, I will repay it to him four times over."

Jesus said to him, "Today salvation has come to this house; for the Son of Man has come to seek out and to save those who were lost."

THE AMBITIOUS DISCIPLES

AS JESUS was on His way to Jerusalem, He took the twelve disciples aside along the way, and said to them: "You see, we are going up to Jerusalem; and the Son of Man shall be betrayed to the chief priests and the scribes, and they shall condemn Him to death, and shall deliver Him to the Gentiles to mock, and to scourge, and to crucify Him; and the third day He shall rise again."

Then the mother of Zebedee's children, the disciples James and John, came to Him with her sons, and, bowing down, she asked a certain favor of Him.

He said to her, "What do you wish?"

She said to Him, "Grant that these my two sons may sit, the one on Your right hand and the other on Your left, in Your kingdom."

But Jesus answered and said, "You do not know what you ask. Are you able to drink of the cup that I shall drink of, and to be baptized with the baptism I am being baptized with?" They said to Him, "We are able."

And He said to them, "You shall indeed drink of my cup, and be baptized with my baptism. But to sit on my right hand and on my left is not mine to give, but it shall be given to them for whom it has been prepared by my Father." When the ten heard this, they were filled with indignation against the two brothers.

But Jesus called them to Him and said, "You know that the princes of the Gentiles lord it over them, and that their rulers exercise great authority over them. But it shall not be so among you. Whoever wishes to be great among you, let him be your servant. And whoever wants to be chief among you, let him be your servant, even as the Son of Man came not to be served but to serve, and to give His life for the freeing of many."

And as they departed from Jericho, a great crowd followed Him.

STORM CLOUDS GATHER

THE BREAD OF LIFE

JESUS SPOKE to the people, saying:

"Do not work for the food which perishes, but for that food which endures unto everlasting life, which the Son of Man shall give to you."

Then they said to Him, "What sign do You show, that we may see it and believe in You? What can You do? Our fathers ate manna in the wilderness. As it is written, 'He gave them bread from Heaven to eat.'"

Then Jesus said to them, "Truly, truly I say to you, Moses did not give you this bread from Heaven, but my Father gives you the true bread from Heaven. For the bread of God is He who comes down from Heaven, and gives life to the world."

Then they said to Him, "Lord, give us this bread."

And Jesus said to them, "I am the bread of life; he who comes to me shall never hunger, and he that believes in me shall never thirst."

... The Jews then murmured at Him, because He said, "I am the bread which came down from Heaven." And they said, "Is not this Jesus, the son of Joseph, whose father and mother we know? How is it then that He says, 'I came down from heaven'?"

So Jesus answered and said to them, "Do not murmur among yourselves. I tell you truly, he who believes in me will have everlasting life. I am that bread of life.

"I am the living bread that came down from Heaven; if any man eat of this bread, he shall live forever. This bread that I will give is my flesh. I will give it for the life of the world."

The Jews then argued among themselves, saying, "How can this man give us His flesh to eat?" Jesus said to them, "I tell you truly, if you do not eat the flesh of the Son of Man and drink His blood, you shall not have life in you. He who eats my flesh and drinks my blood lives in me, and I live in him."

Many of His disciples, too, said, "This is a hard saying. Who can listen to it?"

But Jesus, knowing inwardly that his disciples were murmuring at this, said to them, "Does this shock you? Then what if you see the Son of Man go up to where He was before? It is the spirit that gives life; the flesh profits nothing. The words that I speak to you, they are spirit, and they are life. But there are some of you who do not believe."

And from that time, many of His followers turned away, and walked with Him no more.

Then Jesus said to the twelve, "Will you go away, too?"

But Simon Peter answered Him, "Lord, to whom shall we go? You have the words of eternal life."

After this Jesus went about in Galilee; for He would not go into Judea, because the Jews wanted to kill Him.

BACK TO JUDEA

NOW THE time had come for the Jewish Festival of Tabernacles. So His relatives said, "Leave this place and go to Judea, so that Your followers also may see the things that You do. For no man does things in secret if he wishes to be known openly." For even His relations did not fully believe in Him.

Then Jesus said to them, "My time has not come yet. But it is always time for you. The world cannot hate you, but it hates me, because I tell it that its ways are evil. You go up to this festival. I will not go up yet, for it is not quite time for me yet."

Having said these words, He stayed on in Galilee. But when His relatives had gone up, He also went, not openly, but in secret.

Now the Jews were looking for Him at the festival, and asking, "Where is He?"

There was much discussion among the people concerning Him, for some said, "He is a good man"; others said, "No, He deceives the people." But no one spoke openly of Him for fear of the Jews.

Now about the middle of the feast, Jesus went up into the temple and began to teach. The Jews were amazed, saying, "How is it this man is so learned, never having been to school?" Jesus answered them, and said, "My teaching is not my own, but is His that sent me."

Then some of the people of Jerusalem said, "Is not this the man they are trying to kill? See how boldly He speaks, and they say nothing to Him. Can it be that the rulers have discovered that He is truly the Christ? However, we know this man, and where He comes from; but when the Christ comes, no one knows where He will come from."

Then Jesus cried out as He taught in the temple, saying, "You know me, and also where I come from; but I have not come by myself, but He who sent me is true, whom you do not know."

Then they tried to arrest Him. But no one laid a hand on Him, because His time had not yet come.

And many of the people believed in Him, and said, "When Christ comes, will he do more miracles than those which this man has done?" The Pharisees heard that the people were whispering such things concerning Him, and the Pharisees and the chief priests sent officers to arrest Him.

But the officers came back to the chief priests and Pharisees; and they said to them, "Why have you not brought Him?"

The officers answered, "Never did a man speak like this man!"

Then the Pharisees answered, "Are you also deceived? Have any of the rulers or the Pharisees believed in Him? But these people who do not know the law are doomed."

DISPUTE IN THE TEMPLE

ON THE last day, that great day of the festival, Jesus stood up and cried out, saying, "If any man thirst, let him come to me and drink."

Many of the people there, hearing His sayings, said, "Truly this is a prophet."

Others said, "This is the Christ."

But some said, "Shall Christ come out of Galilee? Has not the Scripture said that Christ should come out of the family of David, and out of the town of Bethlehem, where David lived?"

So there was a division among the people concerning Him. And some of them would have arrested Him. But no one laid a hand on Him.

Jesus spoke again to them in the temple, saying, "I am the light of the world; he who follows me shall not walk in darkness, but shall have the light of life....

"Your father Abraham looked forward with joy to the day of my coming, and he saw it and was glad."

Then the Jews said to Him, "You are not even fifty years old, and you have seen Abraham?"

Jesus said to them, "Truly, truly I tell you, before Abraham was born, I AM."

Then they picked up stones to throw at Him; but Jesus hid Himself and, passing through the midst of them, went out of the temple and so passed by....

(Jesus went on with His teaching and preaching, despite the resentment and opposition of the Pharisees and others who were involved. He healed on the Sabbath a man born blind, and some of the Pharisees said, "This man does not come from God, for He does not keep the Sabbath." But others said, "How can a man who is a sinner do such marvelous things'" And there was a division among them.

"I am the good shepherd," He told them. "The good shepherd gives His life for His sheep. He who is only hired, whose sheep are not His own, when He sees a wolf coming, leaves the sheep and flees; and the wolf catches them, and scatters the sheep.

"I am the good shepherd. I know my sheep, and they know me, and I lay down my life for my sheep. No man takes it from me, but I lay it down by myself, and I have power to lay it down and to take it up again.")

"I AM THE CHRIST"

IT WAS at Jerusalem, during the Festival of Dedication, and it was winter.

Jesus was walking in the temple, in Solomon's porch, and the Jews surrounded Him and said to Him, "How long are you going to keep us in doubt? If you are the Christ, tell us plainly."

Jesus answered them, "I told you, and you did not believe me. The deeds that I do in my Father's name bear out my words.... My Father and I are one."

Then the Jews took up stones again to stone Him.

Jesus said to them, "I have shown you many good things from my Father. For which of these deeds are you stoning me?"

The Jews answered Him, saying, "It is not for your good deeds that we stone You, but for blasphemy; and because You, being a man, call yourself God."

Jesus answered them, "Do you say of Him whom the Father has blessed and sent into the world, 'You are blasphemous,' because I said, I am the Son of God? If I am not doing my Father's work, do not believe in me. But if I am, though you may not believe in me, believe in the deeds. Thus you may see, and believe, that the Father is in me, and I in Him."

For this they tried again to arrest Him; but He escaped from their hands, and went away again, beyond the Jordan to the place where John had first baptized. There He stayed and many came there to Him, and believed in Him.

JESUS BRINGS LAZARUS BACK TO LIFE

NOW A certain man was sick, Lazarus of Bethany, the village of Mary and her sister Martha. (It was the same Mary who anointed the Lord with ointment and wiped His feet with her hair, whose brother Lazarus was sick.)

Therefore his sisters sent word to Jesus, saying, "Lord, he whom You love is sick."

For Jesus loved Martha, and her sister and Lazarus.

When He heard that he was sick, then, He stayed two more days in the place where He was. After that He said to His disciples, "Let us go into Judea again."

His disciples said to Him, "Master, the Jews just recently tried to stone you. Are you going there again?"

Jesus said to them plainly, "Lazarus is dead. And I am glad for your sakes that I was not there, so that you may believe in me. But let us go to him."

Then Thomas, who was called the Twin, said to his fellow disciples, "Let us go, too, that we may die with Him."

When Jesus came, He found that Lazarus had been in the tomb four days already.

Now Martha, as soon as she heard that Jesus was coming, went out to meet Him; but Mary still remained in the house.

Then Martha said to Jesus, "Lord, if You had been here, my brother would not have died."

Jesus said to her, "Your brother will rise again."

Martha said to Him, "I know that he will rise again in the resurrection on the last day."

Jesus said to her, "I am the resurrection and the life. He who believes in me, even though he were dead, shall live again. And whoever lives and believes in me, shall never die. Do you believe this?"

She said to Him, "Yes, Lord, I believe that You are the Christ, the Son of God, who has come into the world." And when she had said this, she went away, and called Mary her sister secretly, saying, "The Master has come and is calling for you." As soon as Mary heard that, she arose quickly and went to Him.

Now Jesus had not yet come into the village, and when the Jews who were with her in the house saw Mary rise up hastily and go out, they followed her, saying, "She is going to the grave to weep there."

When Mary came to where Jesus was, and saw Him, she fell down at His feet, saying to Him, "Lord, if you had been here, my brother would not have died."

When Jesus saw her weeping, and the Jews who had come with her weeping too, He groaned within Himself, and was saddened. "Where have you laid him?" He said.

They said to Him, "Lord, come and see." Jesus, again groaning within Himself, came to the tomb. It was a cave, and a stone lay upon it.

Jesus said, "Take away the stone."

Martha, the sister of him who was dead, said to Him, "Lord, by this time he is decaying, for he has been dead four days."

Jesus said to her, "Did I not tell you that if you would believe in me, you would see the glory of God?"

Then they took away the stone from the grave. And Jesus lifted up His eyes and said, "Father, I thank you for having heard me. I know that you always hear me, but because of the people standing here I mention it, that they may believe that you have sent me." And when He had said this, He cried with a loud voice, "Lazarus, come out!"

And he who had been dead came out, bound hand and foot with graveclothes, and with his face bound up with a cloth. Jesus said to them, "Unbind him, and let him move."

Then many of the Jews who had come to Mary and had seen the things which Jesus did, believed in Him. But some of them went their ways to the Pharisees, and told them the things Jesus had done.

THE COUNCIL PLANS AGAINST JESUS

THE HIGH priests and the Pharisees gathered together in council, and said, "What shall we do? For this man does many marvelous things. If we continue to let Him alone, all our people will believe in Him, and the Romans will come and take away both our temple and our nation."

One of them, named Caiaphas, who was the high priest that year, said to them, "You do not know anything at all. You do not see that it is best for us that one man should die for the whole people, so that the nation may not perish."

He did not speak for himself alone, but being high priest that year, he prophesied that Jesus should die for the nation — and not for that nation only, but also that He might gather together in unity the children of God who were scattered abroad.

Then from that day on their plan was to put Him to death.

Jesus therefore did not go about openly any more among the Jews, but He went away from there to a place near the wilderness, to a city called Ephraim, and lived there with His disciples.

Now the Jewish Passover was close at hand, and many went up from the country to Jerusalem before the Passover, to purify themselves.

They looked around for Jesus, and wondered among themselves, as they stood in the temple, "What do you think? Will He not come to the festival?"

For both the chief priests and the Pharisees had given an order that if anyone knew where He was, he should tell it, that they might arrest Him.

SUPPER AT BETHANY

THE WEEK before the Passover, Jesus came to Bethany, where Lazarus was, whom He had raised from the dead.

There they made Him a supper, and Martha served it; and Lazarus was one of those at the table with Him.

Then Mary took a pound of ointment of nard, very costly, and anointed the feet of Jesus, and wiped His feet with her hair. And the house was filled with the odor of the ointment.

Then said one of the disciples — Judas Iscariot who was to betray Him — "Why was this ointment not sold for three hundred denarii, and given to the poor?" He said this, not because he cared for the poor, but because he was a thief, and had charge of the purse, and used to take what was in it.

Then Jesus said, "Let her alone. She has been keeping this for my burial day. For the poor you have always with you, but you will not always have me."

Many of the Jews knew that He was there, and they came, not only for Jesus' sake, but also that they might see Lazarus, whom He had raised from the dead.

But the chief priests planned together to put Lazarus to death, too, because on account of him many of the Jews left them and believed in Jesus.

CHRIST'S EARTHLY WORK NEARS

THE ENTRY INTO JERUSALEM

JESUS, WALKING ahead of His disciples, started the climb up to Jerusalem. And it happened that when He came close to Bethphage and Bethany, at the hill called the Mount of Olives, He sent two of His disciples on ahead, saying:

"Go into the village nearby. As you enter it you shall find a colt tied, on which no one has ever ridden. Untie him and bring him here.

"And if any man should ask you, 'Why do you untie him?' you shall say to him, 'Because the Lord needs him.'"

All this was done, to fulfill the saying of the prophet, which says:

"Tell the daughter of Zion,
'Look, your King comes to you.
Meek, and sitting upon an ass,
And a colt, the foal of an ass.'"

And the disciples who had been sent went their way, and found it just as He had told it to them.

COMPLETION

As they were untying the colt, the owners of it said to them, "Why are you untying the colt?" And they said, "The Lord needs him."

They brought him to Jesus, and they laid their robes upon the colt, and they set Jesus upon them. And as He went along, they spread their cloaks in the road.

And the crowds that had come to the festival, when they heard that Jesus was coming to Jerusalem, took branches of palm trees and went out to meet Him, and cried:

"Hosanna! Blessed is He who comes in the name of the Lord, the King of Israel!"

And when He came near, and reached the slope of the Mount of Olives, the whole crowd of the disciples began to rejoice and praise God with a loud voice for all the mighty deeds that they had seen, saying:

"Blessed is He who comes as king in the name of the Lord! Peace in Heaven, and glory in the highest!"

Some Pharisees who were in the crowd said, "Master, rebuke your disciples."

And He answered and said to them, "I tell you that if these people should hold their peace, the stones would immediately cry out."

And when He drew near, and saw the city before Him, He wept over it, saying:

"If only you knew, in this your day, the things which might work for your peace! But now they are hidden from your eyes.

"For the days shall come upon you, when your enemies will raise a wall about you, and surround you, and hem you in on every side.

"They shall raze you down to the ground, and your children with you; and they shall not leave one stone upon another, because you did not know when God visited you."

When He came into the city, with the crowds that went before and that followed Him shouting, "Hosanna to the Son of David, blessed is He who comes in the name of the Lord!" all the city was moved, and everyone asked, "Who is this?" The crowd replied, "This is Jesus, the prophet from Nazareth of Galilee."

And Jesus went into the temple of God, and drove out all those who sold and bought in the temple, and overturned the tables of the moneychangers and the seats of those who sold doves. For He said to them, "It is written, 'My house shall be called the house of prayer'; but you have made it a den of thieves."

And the blind and the lame came to Him in the temple, and He healed them.

But when the chief priests and scribes saw the wonderful things that He did, and heard the children crying in the temple, and saying, "Hosanna to the Son of David," they were very much displeased.

They said to Him, "Do you hear what these people say?"

And Jesus said to them, "Yes; have you never read, 'Out of the mouths of babes and infants you have drawn perfect praise'?"

Then He left them, and went out of the city to Bethany, and spent the night there.

THE FRUITLESS FIG TREE

NOW IN the morning, as He returned into the city, He was hungry. And when He saw a fig tree along the road, He went over to it, and found no figs on it, but leaves only. So He said to it, "Let no fruit grow on you from this moment forth forever." And at once the fig tree withered away.

When the disciples saw that, they were amazed, saying, "How soon the fig tree withered away!"

Jesus answered and said to them, "Truly I tell you, if you have unwavering faith, you can do not only what I have done to the fig tree, but also if you say to this mountain, 'Go away from here and throw yourself into the sea,' it shall be done. And everything, whatever it may be, which you ask in prayer, having faith, you shall receive."

ANOTHER PARABLE OF THE VINEYARD

WHEN JESUS came into the temple, the chief priests and the elders of the people came to Him as He was teaching, and said, "By what authority do you do these things?" Jesus would not answer their question because they were trying to trap Him, but He said:

"Listen to a parable:

"There was a certain man who planted a vineyard, and put a hedge around it, and dug a wine vat in it, and built a tower, and then rented it to workmen, and went into a distant land.

"When the time of ripe fruit drew near, he sent his servants to the workmen, to collect the fruits of the vineyard. But the workmen took his servants, and beat one, and killed another, and stoned another.

"Again he sent other servants; and they did the same to them.

"Last of all he sent his son to them, saying, 'They will respect my son.'

"But when the workmen saw the son, they said among themselves, 'This is the heir. Come, let us kill him and let us seize his inheritance.'

"And they caught him, and threw him out of the vineyard, and killed him.

"When the lord of the vineyard comes, what will he do to those workmen?" Jesus asked.

They said to him, "He will completely destroy those wicked men, and will rent out his vineyard to other workmen, who will pay him his share of the fruits when they ripen."

When the chief priests and Pharisees had heard His parable, they knew that He was speaking of them. But when they tried to lay their hands on Him, they were afraid of the crowds, because they took Him for a prophet.

TRIBUTE TO CAESAR

THE PHARISEES watched Jesus, and they sent out spies, who pretended to be honest men, so that they might make use of His words, to deliver Him to the power and authority of the governor.

And they questioned Him, saying, "Master, we know that you speak and teach the truth, favoring no one, but truly teaching the way of God. Now, is it lawful for us to pay taxes to Caesar, or not?"

He saw through their craftiness, and said to them, "Why do you try to trap me? Show me a coin. Whose name and likeness has it?"

They answered and said, "Caesar's."

And He said to them, "Pay to Caesar then the things which are Caesar's and to God the things which belong to God."

And they could not twist His words before the people. They were amazed at His answer, and held their peace.

THE WIDOW'S MITE

HE LOOKED up and saw the rich men casting their gifts into the treasury. And He saw also a certain poor widow casting into it two of the smallest coins, called mites.

And He said, "Truly I say to you that this poor widow has cast in more than all of them; for all these others have given out of their riches offerings to God, but she in her poverty has given all she had to live on."

THE PARABLE OF THE WEDDING GUESTS

AGAIN JESUS spoke to them by a parable, and said: "The kingdom of heaven is like a certain king, who prepared a marriage for his son, and sent his servants to call those who were invited to the wedding. And they would not come.

"Again, he sent out other servants, saying, 'Tell those who are invited that I have prepared my dinner; my oxen and my fat cattle are killed and everything is ready. Come to the marriage feast.'

"But they made light of it, and went their ways, one to his farm, another to his business. And the rest took his servants and treated them shamefully, and killed them.

"When the king heard of this, he was angry. He sent out his armies, and destroyed those murderers, and burnt up their city.

"Then he said to his servants, 'The wedding is ready, but those who were invited were not worthy. Go out into the highways now, and as many as you find, invite them to the marriage.'

"So those servants went out into the highways, and gathered together all the people they found, both bad and good, and the wedding was supplied with guests.

"When the king came in to see the guests, he saw a man there who was not wearing a wedding robe. And he said to him, 'Friend, how did you come in here, not having a wedding robe?'

"The man was speechless.

"Then the king said to his servants, 'Bind him hand and foot, and take him away, and cast him into outer darkness where there shall be weeping and gnashing of teeth.' For many are called, but few are chosen."

JESUS TELLS OF HIS COMING AGAIN

JESUS WENT to the temple, and as some of His disciples spoke to Him admiringly of the temple, how it was adorned with rich jewels and offerings, He said, "As for these things which you see today, the days will come when there shall not be one stone left upon another, that has not been thrown down."

And as He sat upon the Mount of Olives, His disciples came to Him privately, saying, "Tell us when these things shall be, and what shall be the sign when these things shall begin to happen?"

And Jesus answered and said to them, "Take care that no one deceive you. For many shall come in my name, saying, 'I am Christ,' and shall deceive many. And you shall hear of wars and rumors of wars; see that you do not become troubled, for all these things must happen, but they are not the end.

"For nation shall rise against nation, and kingdom against kingdom; and there shall be famines, and pestilences, and earthquakes in different places. All these are the beginning of sorrows.

"For then there shall be great troubles, such as there have never been since the beginning of the world, no nor ever shall be. And unless those days should be shortened, no living things could be saved; but for the sake of my chosen ones, those days shall be shortened.

"Then if any man shall say to you, 'See, here is Christ, or 'There,' do not believe him.

"For as the lightning comes out of the east and flashes to the west, so shall the coming of the Son of Man be.

"Immediately after the misery of those days the sun shall be darkened, and the moon shall not give her light, and the stars shall fall from Heaven, and the powers of the heavens shall be shaken.

"Then the sign of the Son of Man shall appear in the heaven, and then shall all the peoples of the earth mourn. And they shall see the Son of Man coming in the clouds of heaven with great power and majesty. And He shall send His angels with a great sound of a trumpet, and they shall gather together His chosen ones from the four winds, from one end of Heaven to the other.

"Now learn a lesson from the fig tree: when its branch is still tender and putting forth leaves, you know that summer is near. So in the same way, when you see all these things, know that the end is near, even at the doors.

"Truly I say to you, this generation shall not pass away, until all these things have been fulfilled. Heaven and earth shall pass away, but my words shall not pass away.

"But no man knows the day and hour, no, not even the angels in Heaven, but my Father only. Watch therefore, for you do not know at what hour your Lord will come.

"But know this, that if the man of the house had known at what time the thief would come, he would have watched, and would not have allowed his house to be broken into.

"Therefore you should be ready, too; for at the time you expect it least, the Son of Man will come.

"Blessed is the servant whom his lord shall find doing his duty when he comes. Truly I tell you, he shall put him in charge of all his goods."

THE PARABLE OF THE WISE AND FOOLISH VIRGINS

THEN THE kingdom of Heaven shall be like the ten virgins who took their lamps and went out to meet the bridegroom. And five of them were wise, and five were foolish.

Those who were foolish took their lamps, and took no oil with them. But the wise ones took oil in their flasks with their lamps.

As the bridegroom was delayed, they all grew drowsy and fell asleep. But at midnight the cry went up, "Look! The bridegroom is coming. Go out and meet him!"

Then all the virgins rose up and trimmed their lamps.

And the foolish said to the wise, "Give us some of your oil, for our lamps have gone out." But the wise answered, saying, "We cannot, lest there should not be enough both for us and for you. Go instead to the dealers in oil, and buy some for yourselves."

And while they went to buy, the bridegroom came, and those who were ready went in with him to the marriage, and the door was shut.

Afterward the other virgins came, saying, "Lord, Lord, open the door for us."

But he answered and said, "Truly, I do not know you."

Therefore watch, for you know neither the day nor the hour in which the Son of Man shall come.

THE PARABLE OF THE MONEY

FOR THE kingdom of Heaven is like a man about to go on a long journey, who called his servants and entrusted his wealth to them.

To one he gave five talents, to another two, and to another one — to each according to his abilities. And then he started off on his journey.

He who had received the five talents went and traded with them, and made five talents more. Similarly, the one who had received two made two more. But he who had received one went and dug in the earth and hid his lord's money.

After a long time the lord of those servants came home and settled up with them. He who had received the five talents brought out five more, saying, "Lord, you gave me five talents; see, I have earned five more with them."

His lord said to him, "Well done, good and faithful servant. You have been faithful over small things; I will make you responsible for large ones. Come, share with your lord in his good fortune."

Also he who had received two talents came and said, "Lord, you gave me two talents; see, I have earned two more with them."

His lord said to him, "Well done, good and faithful servant. You have been faithful over small things; I will make you responsible for large ones. Come, share with your lord in his good fortune."

Then he who had received the one talent came and said, "Lord, I knew that you are a hard man, harvesting where you have not sown, and gathering where you have not threshed; and I was afraid, and went and hid your money in the earth. See, here you have what is yours."

His lord answered and said to him, "You wicked and lazy servant! You knew that I reap where I have not sowed, and gathered where I have not threshed. Therefore, you should have loaned out my money, and then at my homecoming I should have had my money back with interest.

"Therefore take away the money from him, and give it to him who has ten talents. For to every one who has (kept faith) more shall be given, and he shall have abundance. But from him who has not, even that which he has shall be taken away.

"Now cast the good-for-nothing servant into outer darkness. There shall be weeping and gnashing of teeth."

THE DAY OF JUDGMENT

WHEN THE Son of Man shall come in His glory, and all the angels with Him, then He shall sit upon His glorious throne, and before Him shall be gathered all the nations of the world. And He shall separate them one from the other, as a shepherd divides his sheep from the goats. He shall set the sheep on His right hand, but the goats on the left.

Then the King shall say to those on His right hand, "Come, you whom my Father has blessed, inherit the kingdom prepared for you from the beginning of the world.

"For I was hungry, and you gave me food; I was thirsty, and you gave me drink; I was a stranger, and you took me in; without clothing and you clothed me; I was sick, and you visited me; I was in prison, and you came to me." Then the just will answer Him, saying: "Lord, when did we see You hungry, and feed You? Or thirsty, and give You drink? When did we see You a stranger, and take You in? Or without

clothing, and clothe You? Or when did we see You sick, or in prison, and come to You?"

And the King shall answer and say to them, "Truly I tell you, inasmuch as you have done it to the least of these my brothers, you have done it to me."

Then He shall also say to those on His left hand, "Be off, you accursed ones, into everlasting fire, prepared for the devil and his angels. For I was hungry and you did not give me food; I was thirsty, and you gave me nothing to drink; I was a stranger, and you did not take me in; lacked clothing, and you did not clothe me; I was sick and in prison, and you did not visit me."

Then they too will answer Him, saying, "Lord, when did we see You hungry, or thirsty, or a stranger, or without clothing, or sick, or in prison, and did not wait upon You?"

Then He shall answer them saying, "Truly I say to you, inasmuch as you did not do it for one of the least of these my brothers, you did not do it for me."

And these shall go away into everlasting punishment; but the just shall enter into eternal life.

THE LAST SUPPER

NOW THE Feast of the Unleavened Bread drew near, that feast which is called the Passover.

The chief priests and the scribes and the elders of the people gathered together at the palace of the high priest, Caiaphas. And they planned how they might take Jesus by stealth and kill Him. But they agreed that it could not be on the feast day, lest there be an uprising among the people.

Then Satan entered into one of the twelve disciples, called Judas Iscariot; and he went to the chief priests and captains and said to them, "What will you give me if I deliver Him to you?" They were pleased, and they promised him thirty pieces of silver. And from that time on he watched for an opportunity to betray Jesus when there was no crowd around.

Then came the Day of Unleavened Bread, when the Passover lamb had to be killed. And Jesus sent Peter and John, saying, "Go and prepare the Passover feast, so that we may eat."

They said to Him, "Where do you want us to prepare it?"

He said, "When you have come into the city, you will meet a man carrying a pitcher of water. Follow him into the house he enters. And say to the man of the house, 'The Master says to you, "Where is the guest chamber, where I shall eat the Passover feast with my disciples?"'

"And he will show you a large upper room, well furnished. Make your preparations there." They went, and found it all as He had told them, and they prepared for the Passover feast.

When the evening came, Jesus sat down with the twelve. And He said to them, "How greatly I have wished to eat this Passover with you before I suffer. For I tell you, I shall not eat another until it is fulfilled in the kingdom of God." Then taking a cup, He gave thanks and said.

"Share this among you. For I tell you, I shall not drink of the fruit of the vine until the kingdom of God has come."

He took bread and gave thanks and broke it into pieces and gave it to them, saying, "This is my body which is given for you; do this in remembrance of me."

In the same manner, He took the wine cup after supper and gave thanks, saying, "This is the New Covenant in my blood, which is shed for you and for many, for the forgiveness of their sins."

When supper was ended, Jesus rose from the table, laid aside His robe, and fastened a towel about Him. Then He poured water into a basin, and began to wash the disciples' feet, and to wipe them with a towel.

When He came to Simon Peter, Peter said to Him, "Lord, are you washing my feet?"

Jesus answered and said to him, "What I am doing you do not understand now, but you will understand later on."

Peter said, "You shall never wash my feet."

Jesus answered him, saying, "If I do not wash you, you have no share with me."

Then Peter said to Him, "Lord, not my feet only, but also my hands and my head."

But Jesus replied, "He who is truly cleansed needs only to wash his feet to be entirely clean; you are clean — but not all of you." For He knew who was to betray Him. That was why He said, "You are not all clean."

So after He had washed their feet, and had put on His robe and was seated again, He said to them, "Do you understand what I have done to you? You call me Master and Lord, and rightly so, for I am. If I then, your Lord and Master, have washed your feet, you also ought to wash one another's feet. For I have set an example, that you should do as I have done to you. For I tell you truly, the servant is not greater than his lord, nor is the messenger greater than he who sent him. If you know these things, it will be well for you to do them.

"I am not speaking of you all. I know whom I have chosen; but the Scripture must be fulfilled that says, 'He who eats bread with me has lifted up his heel against me!' "

When Jesus had said this, He became very sad, and He said solemnly, "I tell you truly that one of you shall betray me."

Then the disciples looked at one another, wondering of whom He spoke.

Now close beside Jesus at the table was one of the disciples, he whom Jesus loved. Simon Peter therefore beckoned to him, that he should ask who it was of whom Jesus spoke.

He then, leaning toward Jesus, said to Him, "Lord, who is it?"

Jesus answered, "It is he to whom I shall give a piece of bread, when I have dipped it in the bowl." And when He had dipped the bread, He gave it to Judas Iscariot, the son of Simon.

And after he took the bread, Satan entered into him.

Then Jesus said to him, "What you must do, do quickly."

Now no one at the table understood what He meant in saying this to him. For some of them thought it was because Judas had the purse that Jesus said to him, "Buy the things we shall need for the festival," or that he should give something to the poor.

As soon as he had received the bread, he went out at once. And it was then night.

JESUS' FAREWELL TO HIS DISCIPLES

AS SOON as Judas had left, Jesus said, "My little children, for only a little while longer I shall be with you. You will look for me, but, as I said to the Jews, where I am going, you cannot come, so I tell you now.

"I give you a new commandment, that you love one another; as I have loved you, so you should also love one another. By this all people will know that you are my disciples, if you love one another.

"Greater love no man can have than this, that a man lay down his life for his friends. You are my friends, if you do as I command you. No longer do I call you servants, for a servant does not know what his lord does; but I have called you friends, for all the things that I have heard from my Father, I have made known to you.

"Do not let your hearts be troubled. You believe in God; believe in me too. In my Father's house there is room for many. If it were not so, I would have told you. I go to prepare a place for you. And if I go and prepare a place for you, I will come again, and take you back with me, that where I am, you may be also.

"Peace I leave with you; my peace I give to you. Not as the world gives it do I give it to you.

Simon Peter said to Him, "Lord, where are you going?"

Jesus answered him, "Where I am going, you cannot follow me now, but you shall follow me later."

Peter said to Him, "Lord, why cannot I follow You now? I would lay down my life for Your sake."

Jesus answered him, "Will you lay down your life for my sake? I tell you truly, the cock will not crow before you have denied me three times."

And He said to them, "When I sent you out without purses or wallets or shoes, did you want for anything?"

They said, "Nothing."

Then He said to them, "But now, he who has a purse, let him take it, and also his wallet. And he who has no sword, let him sell his robe and buy one (like an outlaw). For I tell you, the Scripture must be fulfilled in me (and in those who follow me): 'And he was counted as an outlaw.' For what is written of me is coming to completion."

And they said (not understanding Him), "Lord, see, here are two swords."

And He said to them, "Enough."

CHRIST'S BITTER CUP AND GLORIOUS VICTORY

GETHSEMANE

AFTER SINGING a psalm, they went out to the Mount of Olives. Then Jesus said to them, "You will all desert me tonight; for it is written, 'I will smite the shepherd, and the sheep of the flock will be scattered.' But after I have risen again, I will go back to Galilee before you."

Peter answered and said to Him, "Though everyone else may desert you, I will never desert you.

Jesus said to him again, "I tell you truly, that tonight before the cock crows, you will deny that you know me three times."

But Peter said to Him, "Even though I should die with you, I would never deny you."

And all the disciples said the same.

Then Jesus walked with them to a place over the brook Kidron, where there was a garden called Gethsemane. And He said to the disciples, "Sit here, while I go over there and pray." He took with Him Peter and the two sons of Zebedee; and He began to be very sorrowful and heavy of heart. Then He said to them, "My heart is full of sorrow, almost to death. You stay here and keep watch with me."

He went on a little farther and fell on His face and prayed, saying, "O my Father, if it is possible, let this cup pass away from me. Yet, let it be not as I will, but as You will."

And He came back to the disciples and found them asleep, and said to Peter, "What, could you not watch with me one hour? Watch now, and pray that you do not fall into temptation; the spirit is indeed willing, but the flesh is weak." He went away again a second time, and prayed, saying, "O my Father, if this cup cannot pass away from me unless I drink it, Your will be done."

And He came back and found them asleep again, for their eyes were heavy. Then He left them, and went away again, and prayed a third time, saying the same words.

An angel from Heaven appeared to Him, strengthening Him. Then, being in agony, He prayed more earnestly, and His sweat fell to the ground as great drops of blood.

After that He came to His disciples, and said to them, "Sleep on now and take your rest. The hour has come when the Son of Man shall be betrayed into the hands of sinners.

"Rise up! Let us be going. See, here comes the one who shall betray me."

And while He was still speaking, lo, Judas, one of the twelve, came, and with him a great crowd with lanterns and torches and swords and clubs, from the chief priests and the elders of the people.

Now he who was to betray Him gave them a signal, saying, "Whomever I kiss, He is the one. Seize hold of Him."

And with that he came to Jesus, and said, "Hail, Master," and kissed Him.

Jesus said to him, "Friend, why have you come?'' Then they came and laid hands on Jesus and arrested Him.

Simon Peter, having a sword, drew it and struck a servant of the high priest, and cut off his right ear.

But Jesus said to him, "Put up your sword again in its place, for all who draw the sword shall die by the sword. Do you think that I could not now pray to my Father, and have Him send me at once twelve legions of angels? But how then would the Scriptures be fulfilled which say that this must happen this way?" And He touched the man's ear and healed him.

At the same time He said to the crowd, "Have you come out as if against a thief, with swords and clubs, to arrest me; I sat daily with you, teaching in the temple, and you never laid a hand on me." But all this was done that the words of the prophets might be fulfilled.

Then all the disciples deserted Him and fled.

PETER DENIES CHRIST

THOSE WHO had arrested Jesus led Him to Caiaphas the high priest, with whom the scribes and elders were meeting.

But Peter followed Him at a distance to the palace of the high priest, and went in and sat with the servants, to see how it should end.

Now the chief priests and elders, and all the council, tried to get false testimony against Jesus, so they could sentence Him to death. But they found nothing. Although many people came to testify falsely, still they found nothing.

At last two false witnesses came. And one said, "This man said, 'I could destroy the temple of God and build it again in three days.' "

The high priest arose and said to Him, "Have you no answer to make? What about this story against you?"

But Jesus was silent.

Then the high priest said to Him, "I order you in

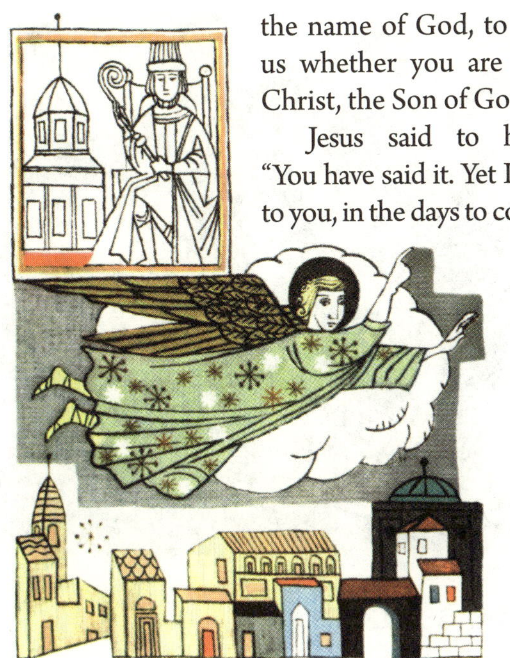

the name of God, to tell us whether you are the Christ, the Son of God."

Jesus said to him, "You have said it. Yet I say to you, in the days to come you shall see the Son of Man sitting on the right hand of the All-powerful, and coming on the clouds of Heaven."

Then the high priest tore his clothes, saying, "He has spoken blasphemy! What further need have we of witnesses? Look, you have heard His own words of blasphemy now! What do you think?"

They answered and said, "He deserves death."

Then they spat in His face, and struck Him, and others hit Him with the palms of their hands, saying, "Now give us a prophecy, you Christ! Who is it that struck You?"

Now Peter, when the servants had kindled a fire in the middle of the courtyard and sat down together, sat down among them.

But a certain maid noticed him as he sat by the fire, and after looking searchingly at him, said, "This man was with Jesus of Galilee."

And he denied Him, saying, "Woman, I do not know Him."

And when he had gone out into the porch, another maid saw him, and said to those who were there, "This man was also with Jesus of Nazareth."

And again he denied Him with an oath, saying, "I do not know the man."

And after a while some of the others who were standing around came up to him, and said to Peter, "Surely you are one of them too; for your accent betrays you." Then he began to curse and to swear, saying, "I do not know the man." And immediately the cock crowed.

Then Peter remembered the words of Jesus, when He said to him, "Before the cock crows, you will deny me three times." And he went out, and wept bitterly.

JESUS BEFORE PONTIUS PILATE

WHEN THE morning came, all the chief priests and elders of the people made plans against Jesus, to have Him put to death. And when they had bound Him, they led Him away to the hall of judgment, and delivered Him to Pontius Pilate. They themselves could not go into the judgment hall, lest they should be ceremonially defiled, for they wanted to be able to eat their Passover supper. So Pilate came out to them, and said, "What charge do you bring against this man?"

They answered and said to him, "If He were not an evildoer, we would not have delivered Him to you."

Then Pilate said to them, "Take Him and judge Him according to your law."

But the Jews said to him, "It is not lawful for us to put any man to death."

Then Pilate went back into the judgment hall and called Jesus to him, and said to Him, "Are You the King of the Jews?"

Jesus answered him, "Are you asking this of yourself, or have others told you this about me?" Pilate said, "Am I a Jew? Your own people and the chief priests have delivered you to me. What have You done?"

Jesus answered, "My kingdom is not of this world. If my kingdom were of this world, my servants would have fought against my being delivered to the Jews. No, my kingdom is elsewhere."

Then Pilate said to Him, "You are a king then?"

Jesus answered, "You have said it: I am a king. For that purpose I was born, and for this I came into the world, that I should bear witness to the truth. Everyone who is on the side of the truth listens to my voice."

Pilate said to Him, "What is truth?" And when he had said this, he went out again to the Jews, and said to them, "I find no fault at all in Him. But you have a custom, that I should release to you one prisoner at the Passover. Do you want me then to release to you the King of the Jews?"

Then they all cried out again, saying, "Not this man but Barabbas." Now Barabbas was a robber and murderer.

As Pilate was sitting on the judgment seat, his wife sent a message to him, saying, "Have nothing to do with harming that just man; for I have just suffered greatly in a dream about Him." But the chief priests and elders persuaded the crowd that they should ask for Barabbas and put Jesus to death.

Then Pilate took Jesus and had Him flogged. And the soldiers braided a crown of thorns and put it on His head, and they put a reed in His right hand, and they dressed Him in a purple robe.

They bowed the knee before Him and mocked Him, saying, "Hail, King of the Jews!" And they spat on Him, and taking the reed from His hand they struck Him on the head.

Pilate went out again then, and said to the Jews, "Look, I bring Him out to you, so that you may know that I find no guilt in Him."

Then Jesus came out, wearing the crown of thorns and the purple robe. And Pilate said to them, "Behold the man!"

When the chief priests and officers saw Him, they cried out, saying, "Crucify Him, crucify Him!"

And when Pilate saw that he could not convince them, but rather that a riot was beginning, he took water and washed his hands before the crowd, saying, "I am innocent of the blood of this just man. You take Him and crucify Him, for I can find no guilt in Him."

Then all the people answered and said, "Let His blood be on us, and on our children."

And he released Barabbas to them, and delivered Jesus to be crucified.

THE END OF JUDAS

HEN JUDAS, who had betrayed Him, when he saw that Jesus was condemned, repented, and brought the thirty pieces of silver back to the chief priests and elders, saying, "I have sinned in that I have betrayed the life of an innocent man."

And they said, "What is that to us? That is your affair."

Then he threw down the pieces of silver in the temple, and went out and hanged himself.

And the chief priests took the silver pieces and said, "It is not lawful for us to put them into the treasury, because it is the price of a life."

And they discussed it among themselves, and bought with the silver the potter's field, to bury strangers in. That is why the same field has been called the Field of Blood until this day.

THE CRUCIFIXION

HEY TOOK Jesus and led Him away; and He, bearing His cross, went out to a place called The Place of the Skull, which in Hebrew is called Golgotha.

And as they led Him along, they laid hands on one Simon, from Cyrene, coming in from the country, and put the cross on his shoulders, so that he could carry it, following after Jesus.

And there followed Him a great group of people, and of women who lamented Him with loud wails.

But Jesus turned to them and said, "Daughters of Jerusalem, do not weep for me. Weep rather for yourselves and for your children. For the days are coming in which they will say, 'Blessed are the childless, and the women who have never borne or nursed children.'

"Then they shall begin to say to the mountains, 'Fall on us!' And to the hills, 'Cover us!' For if this is what they do when the wood is green, what will they do when it is dry?"

There were also two others, common criminals, led out with Him to be put to death. And when they

had come to the place, which is also called Calvary, they crucified Him there, and the two criminals, one on the right hand and the other on the left.

Then Jesus said, "Father, forgive them, for they know not what they do."

Then the soldiers, when they had crucified Jesus, took His garments, and divided them into four piles, one to each soldier. They took His robe, too. Now the robe was seamless, woven from the top down. Therefore they said among themselves, "Let us not tear it, but let us draw lots for it, to see whose it shall be."

This was so that the Scripture might be fulfilled which says, "They divided my clothing among them, and for my robe they drew lots." All these things, therefore, the soldiers did.

Now close by the cross of Jesus stood His mother, and His mother's sister, Mary the wife

of Clopas, and Mary Magdalene. When Jesus saw His mother and John, the disciple whom He loved best, standing by, He said to His mother, "Woman, this is your son."

Then He said to the disciple, "This is your mother." And from that hour that disciple took her into his own home.

Now the people stood watching Him, and the rulers joined them in jeering at Him, saying, "He saved others; let Him save Himself if He is Christ, the chosen one of God."

The soldiers also mocked Him, coming to Him and offering Him a sponge filled with vinegar, and saying, "If You are the King of the Jews, save Yourself."

And there was a sign above His head, written in letters of Greek and Latin and Hebrew:

JESUS OF NAZARETH,
KING OF THE JEWS.

One of the criminals who were hanged with Him scoffed at Him, saying, "If You are Christ, save Yourself and us."

But the other answering rebuked him, saying, "Do you not fear God, seeing that you are condemned to the same fate? And we are here justly, for we are getting the just payment for our deeds, but this man has done nothing wrong." And he said to Jesus, "Lord, remember me when You come into Your kingdom."

And Jesus said to him, "I tell you truly, today you shall be with me in paradise."

It was about noon; and darkness fell over all the earth until three in the afternoon. The sun was

darkened, and the veil of the temple was tom down the middle. The earth shook, rocks split, and tombs were opened.

And when Jesus had cried out with a loud voice, He said, "Father, into Your hands I commend my spirit." And having said this, His soul left His body.

Now when the captain of the guard saw the earthquake and all that had happened, he praised God, saying, "Truly this was the Son of God." And all the people who had come to watch the spectacle, seeing what had happened, beat their breasts and went home.

And many who knew Him, and the women who had followed Him from Galilee, stood far off, watching all these things.

THE TOMB IN THE GARDEN

AFTER THIS Joseph of Arimathea, who was a disciple of Jesus, but secretly, for fear of the Jews, asked Pilate if he might take away the body of Jesus, and Pilate gave him permission.

He came, then, and took the body of Jesus. And Nicodemus came too, he who had first visited Jesus by night, and brought a mixture of myrrh and aloes, about a hundred pounds.

They took the body of Jesus and wound it in linen cloths with the spices, in the Jewish manner of burial.

Now in the place where He was crucified there was a garden; and in the garden was a new tomb in which no man had ever been laid. They laid Jesus there, because it was the Jews' day of preparation, and the tomb was near at hand.

And the women, too, who had come from Galilee, followed along, and saw the tomb and how His body was laid in it. Then Joseph rolled a great stone to the door of the tomb, and departed.

Now the next day, that followed the day of preparation, the chief priests and Pharisees came in a body to Pilate, saying, "Sir, we remember that that deceiver said, while He was still alive, 'After three days I will rise again.'

"Therefore command that the tomb be made secure until the third day, lest His disciples should come by night and steal Him away, and say to the people, 'He has risen from the dead.' Then the final deception would be worse than the first."

Pilate said to them, "You have your guard. Go, and make it as secure as you can."

So they went and made the tomb secure, sealing the stone and setting a guard over it.

CHRIST HAS RISEN

AT THE end of the Sabbath, as it began to dawn on the first day of the week, Mary Magdalene and the other Mary came to see the tomb.

And they found there had been a great earthquake; for the angel of the Lord had come down from Heaven and rolled back the stone from the door, and was sitting on it. His face was like lightning, and his garments were white as snow.

For fear of him, the guards trembled, and fainted away like dead men.

But the angel spoke and said to the women, "Do not be afraid; for I know that you are looking for Jesus, who was crucified. He is not here, for He has risen as He said He would. Come, see the place where the Lord was laid.

"Now go quickly and tell His disciples that He has risen from the dead, and that He is going on ahead into Galilee, where you shall see Him. There, I have told you."

And they departed quickly from the tomb, with fear and great joy, and ran to bring His disciples word. And as they hurried to tell His disciples, Jesus met them, saying, "Greetings." And they came and held Him by the feet and worshiped Him.

Then Jesus said to them, "Do not be afraid. Go tell my brethren that they should go into Galilee, and there they shall see me."

CHRIST ON THE ROAD TO EMMAUS

NOW IT HAPPENED that two of the disciples went that same day to a village called Emmaus, which was about seven miles from Jerusalem, and they were talking together of all these things which had happened. And it happened that as they were discussing together and arguing, Jesus Himself came near and walked along with them, but their eyes were kept from recognizing Him.

He said to them, "What sort of things are these that you are discussing among yourselves as you walk, and why are you so sad?"

And one of them, whose name was Cleopas, answered and said to Him, "Are you just a stranger in Jerusalem, that you do not know about the things which have happened here these last days?"

And He said to them, "What things?"

And they said to Him, "Concerning Jesus of Nazareth, who was a prophet mighty in word and deed before God and all the people, and how the chief priests and our rulers delivered Him up to be condemned to death and have crucified Him.

"We had faith that He would save Israel, and besides, today is the third day since these things were done, and some of our women who went early to the tomb have astonished us, because they did not find His body, but they came back saying that they had seen a vision of angels who said that He was alive.

"And some of those who were with us went to the tomb and found things just as the women had said, but did not see Him."

Then He said to them, "O fools and slow of heart to believe all that the prophets have spoken! Was Christ not supposed to suffer these things, before entering into His glory?" And beginning at Moses and all the prophets, He explained to them in all the Scriptures the things concerning Himself.

They came near to the village where they were going, and He acted as though He would have gone further. But they urged Him, saying, "Stay with us, for it is nearly evening, and the day is far gone." So He went in to stay with them.

And it happened, as He sat at supper with them, that He took bread, and blessed it and broke it, and gave it to them. Then their eyes were opened, and they recognized Him; but He vanished from their sight.

And they said to one another, "Didn't our hearts burn within us, while He talked to us along the road, and while He explained the Scriptures to us?"

And they got up that same hour, and returned to Jerusalem, and found the eleven gathered together, and some others with them, and they told all that had taken place along the road, and how He made Himself known to them in the breaking of bread. And as they were telling it, Jesus Himself stood among them, and said to them, "Peace be to you all."

CHRIST VISITS THE DISCIPLES

THAT SAME day at evening, the first day of the week, when the doors were shut where the disciples gathered, for fear of the Jews, Jesus came and stood among them, and said to them, "Peace be to you all." And when He had spoken, He showed them His hands and His side. The disciples were glad when they saw the Lord.

Then Jesus said to them again, "Peace be to you all. As my Father sent me, just so I send you." And when He had said this, He breathed on them, and said to them, "Receive the Holy Spirit! Anyone whose sins you forgive, they shall be forgiven to him, and anyone whose sins you retain, they shall be retained.

"Go all of you now, and make disciples in all nations, baptizing them in the name of the Father, and of the Son, and of the Holy Spirit, teaching them to observe all the commandments I have given you; and you shall see, I am with you always, even to the end of the world."

But Thomas, one of the twelve, known as the Twin, was not with them when Jesus came. So when the other disciples said to him, "We have seen the Lord," he said to them, "Unless I see the prints of the nails in His hands, and put my finger into the print of the nails, and thrust my hand into His side, I will not believe it."

After a week, again the disciples were in the same room, and Thomas with them. Then Jesus came, though the doors were shut, and stood among them,

and said, "Peace be to you all." He said to Thomas, "Reach out your finger and touch my hands, and put your hand here and thrust it into my side, and do not be a doubter, but believe in me."

Thomas answered and said to Him, "My Lord and my God."

Jesus said to him, "Thomas, because you have seen me, you have believed; blessed are they who have not seen me, and yet believe in me."

JESUS APPEARS TO THE FISHERMEN

AFTER ALL these things, Jesus appeared again to the disciples at the Sea of Tiberias, and this was the way in which He appeared.

Simon Peter and Thomas called the Twin, and Nathanael of Cana in Galilee, and the sons of Zebedee, and two others of His disciples were there together.

Simon Peter said to them, "I am going fishing.

They said to him, "We will go with you."

They went out and took a boat immediately, but all night they caught nothing.

But when the morning came, Jesus stood on the shore, though they did not know that it was Jesus.

Then Jesus said to them, "Young men, have you any fish?"

They answered Him, "No."

And He said to them, "Cast the net on the right side of the boat, and you will find some." So they cast, and were not able to draw the net in, for all the fish in it.

Then John said to Peter, "It is the Lord." Now when Simon Peter heard that it was the Lord, he wound his fisherman's coat about him, and jumped into the water to swim ashore. The other disciples came in the little boat — for they were not far from land, perhaps a hundred yards — dragging the net full of fish.

As soon as they had come to land, they saw a fire of coals there, and fish laid on it, and bread.

Jesus said to them, "Bring some of the fish which you have caught."

Simon Peter went and drew the net to land, full of large fish, a hundred and fifty-three, and though there were so many, still the net was not broken.

Jesus said to them, "Come and eat."

And none of the disciples dared ask Him, "Who are you?" knowing that it was the Lord.

Then Jesus came and served them with bread and fish. And this was the third time that Jesus showed Himself to His disciples after He had risen from the dead.

JESUS ASCENDS INTO HEAVEN

JESUS APPEARED to His disciples for forty days, speaking of the things pertaining to the kingdom of God. And while He met with them, He commanded them not to leave Jerusalem, but to wait there for a promise from the Father.

"For John baptized with water, but you shall be baptized with the Holy Spirit not many days from now. You shall receive power when the Holy Spirit comes to you, and you shall be witnesses to me in

Jerusalem, and in all Judea, and in Samaria, and to the farthest ends of the earth."

Then Jesus led the disciples out as far as Bethany, and He lifted up His hands and blessed them. And it happened as He was blessing them, He was parted from them, and carried up into Heaven, and a cloud hid Him from their sight.

And while they stood looking steadily toward Heaven as He went up, two men stood beside them in robes of white, and they said, "You men of Galilee, why do you stand gazing up into Heaven? This same Jesus whom you saw taken up into Heaven shall come again in just the same way as you have seen Him go."

And they bowed down before the wonder of the sight, and returned to Jerusalem filled with joy, and were constantly in the temple, praising and blessing God. Amen.

THE APOSTLES CARRY ON THE LORD'S WORK

THE GIFT OF LANGUAGES

WHEN THE DAYS of Pentecost were ending, the disciples all gathered together with one accord. And suddenly there came a sound from Heaven like a violent wind, and it filled all the house where they were sitting.

And they saw tongues like flame appear and rest on each of them. And they were all filled with the Holy Spirit, and began to speak in other languages, whatever the Spirit bade them say.

There were living in Jerusalem devout Jews from every country under Heaven. And when this news was noised abroad, a great crowd of them gathered, and were amazed, because every man heard them speak in his own language.

They were all astonished and wondered, saying to one another, "Look, are not all these people who are speaking Galileans? How is it that each of

us hears the language of the land in which he was born? Parthians and Medes and Elamites, and the men of Mesopotamia, and of Judea, and Cappadocia and Pontus and Asia, of Phrygia and Pamphylia, of Egypt and the parts of Libya around Cyrene, and visitors from Rome, Jews and proselytes, Cretans and Arabs, we all hear them tell in our own languages the wonderful works of God."

They were all amazed, and bewildered, saying to one another, "What does this mean?" Others, mocking, said, "These men are full of new wine."

But Peter, standing up with the eleven (for they had chosen Matthias to replace Judas), lifted up his voice and said to them, "You men of Judea, and all you who live in Jerusalem, listen to my words and know this. These are not drunken men, as you may suppose, for it is only nine in the morning. But this is the fulfillment of the words of the prophet Joel:

"'And it shall come about in the last days,' God says, 'that I will pour out my Spirit upon all men. And your sons and your daughters will be prophets, and your young men shall see visions, and your old men shall dream true dreams. And I will show wonders in Heaven above, and signs in the earth beneath — blood and fire and clouds of smoke. The sun shall be turned to darkness and the moon into blood, before that great day of the Lord comes. And it shall come about that whoever calls on the name of the Lord shall be saved.'" And he told them of Jesus the Christ, the Son of God.

Then those who gladly received his word were baptized, and that same day about three thousand joined them, and gave themselves willingly to the apostles' teaching and fellowship, breaking bread together and praying.

Awe overcame everyone, and many wonders were done by the apostles.

All the believers stayed together, and shared everything. They sold their possessions, and divided the money among all the people, as each had need of it.

Day after day they went together to the temple, and ate their meals in one house or another, with gladness and unity of heart, praising God and respected by all the people. And the Lord added to their number each day those who would be saved.

THE LAME MAN AT THE BEAUTIFUL GATE

NOW PETER and John went together into the temple at the hour of prayer, which is the middle of the afternoon. And a certain man, lame from birth, was carried daily to the gate of the temple which is called Beautiful, and laid there to beg from those who entered the temple.

Seeing Peter and John about to go into the temple, he asked them for something. And Peter, fastening his eyes upon him, as did John, said, "Look at us."

He looked at them, hoping to receive something from them. Then Peter said, "Silver and gold I do not have, but what I have I shall give to you. In the name of Jesus Christ of Nazareth, rise up and walk!"

And he took him by the right hand and lifted him up. Immediately his feet and ankle bones became strong, and he, leaping up, stood and walked, and went with them into the temple, walking and leaping and praising God.

All the people saw him walking and praising God, and they knew that it was he who had sat begging at the Beautiful Gate of the temple; they were filled with wonder and amazement at what had happened to him.

As the lame man now healed held onto Peter and John, all the people hurried to gather around them in the porch which is called Solomon's, full of wonder.

When Peter saw this, he said to the people, "You men of Israel, why are you so surprised? Why do you stare at us so, as though by our own power or holiness we have made this man walk?

"The God of Abraham, and of Isaac, and of Jacob, the God of our fathers, is thus glorifying His Son Jesus, whom you delivered up and denied in the presence of Pilate, when he was determined to let Him go. But you denied the Holy One and the Just, and demanded that a murderer be set free to you; you killed the Author of life, whom God has raised from the dead. Of that we are witnesses. And His name through faith has made strong this man whom you all know."

As they spoke to the people, the priests and the captain of the temple and the Sadducees came upon them, and were annoyed because they were teaching the people and preaching the resurrection of Jesus from the dead. They arrested them, and locked them up until the next day.

However, many of those who had heard them believed their story, and the number of their group grew to about five thousand.

THE APOSTLES ESCAPE FROM PRISON

IT HAPPENED the next day that the rulers and elders and scribes, Annas the high priest and Caiaphas, and John and Alexander and those who were of the family of the high priest were gathered together at Jerusalem.

They conferred among themselves, saying, "What shall we do with these men? For that was indeed a wonderful thing which they did, and it is known to all the people of Jerusalem, and we cannot deny it. But so that it shall not spread any further, let us sternly threaten them, so that they will not speak to anyone any more in His name." And they called them, and commanded them not to speak at all nor teach in the name of Jesus.

But Peter and John answered and said to them, "Whether it would be right in the sight of God to pay more attention to you than to God, you can judge. For we can only speak of the things we have seen and heard."

So when they had threatened them further, they let them go. Then great wonders were worked among the people by the hands of the apostles, so much so that the people brought out the sick into the streets, and laid them on beds and couches, so that at least the shadow of Peter passing by might fall upon them.

Crowds of people came too from the towns around Jerusalem, bringing sick folk and those who were troubled with evil spirits, and they were cured, every one.

Then the high priest stood up, and all the Sadducees who were with him, and they were filled with indignation. They laid their hands upon the apostles and put them into the public prison.

But the angel of the Lord opened the prison doors by night, and brought them out, and said, "Go, stand up in the temple and speak to the people all the words of life."

When they heard that, they went into the temple early in the morning, and taught.

But the high priest came, with all those around him, and called the Sanhedrin together, and all the elders of the children of Israel, and sent to the prison to have them brought.

When the officers went and found that they were not in the prison, they came back and reported it. Then someone came and told them, "Look, the men whom you put in prison are standing in the temple and teaching the people." When the high priest and the captain of the temple and the chief priests heard these things, they wondered gloomily what would come of it.

STEPHEN, THE FIRST MARTYR

NOW STEPHEN, a man full of faith and power, did great wonders and miracles among the people.

Some members of the synagogue tried to debate with him, but they were no match for the wisdom and the Spirit who spoke through him. Then they aroused men to say, "We have heard him speak blasphemous words against God and against Moses."

They stirred up the people and the elders and the scribes, and they came upon him and seized him and brought him before the Sanhedrin.

They set up false witnesses, who said, "This man constantly blasphemes against this holy place and the law, for we have heard him say that this Jesus of Nazareth will destroy this place and change the customs which Moses gave us." And all those who sat in the Sanhedrin looked sternly at him, and saw that his face was like the face of an angel.

Then the high priest said, "Is this so?"

He said, "Men, brothers, fathers, listen to me. The Most High does not dwell in temples made with hands; as the prophet says, '"Heaven is my throne, and the earth is my footstool. What house

can you build for me?" says the Lord, "or in what place can I rest? For has not my hand made all these things?"'

"You are proud and heathen in heart and ear! You always resist the Holy Spirit; just as your fathers did, you do too. Which of the prophets did your fathers not persecute? And they killed those who foretold the coming of the Just One, whom you have just now betrayed and murdered — you who received the law from the angels, but have not kept it!"

When they heard these things, they were cut to the heart, and ground their teeth at him. But he being full of the Holy Spirit, looked steadily up into Heaven, and saw the glory of God, and Jesus standing on the right hand of God.

He said, "Look! I see the heavens opened, and the Son of Man standing on the right hand of God!"

Then they cried out in loud voices, and stopped up their ears, and rushed at him in one body. They threw him out of the city, and stoned him. The witnesses laid down their cloaks at the feet of a young man named Saul.

They stoned Stephen, who was calling upon God and saying, "Lord Jesus, receive my soul." He fell to his knees and cried out with a loud voice, "Lord, do not count this sin against them." And when he had said this, he fell asleep in death.

SAUL ON THE ROAD TO DAMASCUS

NOW SAUL was making havoc of the Church, breaking into every home, and dragging out men and women to put them into prison.

Still breathing out threats of slaughter against the disciples of the Lord, Saul then went to the high priest, and asked from him letters to the synagogues in Damascus, so that if he found any who followed Christ's way, whether they were men or women, he could bring them bound to Jerusalem.

But as he journeyed, approaching Damascus, suddenly there shone around him a light from Heaven; and he fell to the earth, and heard a voice saying to him, "Saul, Saul, why do you persecute me?"

And he said, "Who are You, Lord?"

And the Lord said, "I am Jesus, whom you persecute."

And he, trembling and astonished, said, "Lord, what do You want me to do?"

And the Lord said to him, "Get up and go into the city, and you will be told what you must do."

The men who were traveling with him stood speechless, hearing a voice, but seeing no one.

Saul got up from the ground, but when he opened his eyes, he could see no one, and they led him by the hand into Damascus. For three days he was without his sight, and neither ate nor drank.

Now there was a certain disciple in Damascus, named Ananias. And the Lord appeared to him in a vision, calling him by name. And he said, "Lord, here I am."

The Lord said to him, "Get up and go into the street called Straight, and ask in the house of Judas for a man called Saul of Tarsus, for he is praying, and has seen in a vision a man named Ananias coming in and putting his hand upon him, that he might see again."

Then Ananias said, "Lord, I have heard from many people about this man, and how much evil he has done to Your people in Jerusalem. And he has come here with authority from the chief priests to arrest everyone who calls upon Your name."

But the Lord said to him, "Go; for he is the means I have chosen to carry my name to the Gentiles, and to kings, and to the children of Israel. For I will show him how much he must suffer for my sake."

Ananias went his way, and came to the house, and, laying his hands on him, said, "Brother Saul, the Lord Jesus, who appeared to you along the road as you came, has sent me that you may have your sight back and be filled with the Holy Spirit."

Immediately it was as if scales fell from his eyes, and he received his sight back at once and got up and was baptized.

When he had eaten, he felt stronger; and Saul stayed on for some days with the disciples who lived in Damascus.

And at once he began preaching in the synagogues that Jesus is the Son of God. And all who heard him were amazed, saying, "Is not this the man who made havoc on those who called on Christ's name in Jerusalem, and came here for the purpose of bringing them in chains to the chief priests?"

But Saul grew constantly in strength, and so confused the Jews who lived in Damascus, by proving that this was indeed the Christ, that after some days had passed they plotted to kill him.

But Saul knew that they were lying in wait for him, and that they watched the gates day and night, to kill him. So the disciples took him by night, and let him down over the wall in a basket.

And when Saul came to Jerusalem, he joined the disciples there.

CORNELIUS, THE GOOD CENTURION

THERE WAS a certain man in Caesarea called Cornelius, a centurion of the Italian division. He was devout and Godfearing, as was all his household, and gave much alms to the people, and prayed constantly to God.

He saw in a vision, late one afternoon, an angel of God come to him and say, "Cornelius!"

When he looked at him, he was frightened, and he said, "What is it, Lord?"

And the angel said to him, "Your prayers and your good deeds have come up before God and have been remembered. Now send men to Joppa, and ask for one Simon, whose other name is Peter. He is staying with one Simon a tanner, whose house is by the seaside."

When the angel who spoke to Cornelius had gone away, he called two of his household servants and a God-fearing soldier of his personal guard, and when he had told them all these things, he sent them to Joppa.

On the next day, as they went along on their journey, and came near to the city, Peter went up upon the housetop for his noonday prayers. And while he was there the men whom Cornelius had sent, having made inquiry for Simon's house, came and stood before the gate and called out, asking whether Simon called Peter was staying there.

The Holy Spirit said to Peter, "Look, three men are searching for you. Get up and go down and go with them. Do not worry about anything, for I have sent them."

Then Peter went down to the men whom Cornelius had sent to him, and said, "See, I am the one you seek. Why have you come?"

And they said, "Cornelius the centurion, a just man and one who loves God, a man of good reputation among the Jewish people, was told by a holy angel of God to send for you to come to his house, so that he could hear you speak."

Then he called them in and gave them lodging. And the next day Peter went away with them, and certain of the brethren from Joppa went with him.

The following day they came into Caesarea, and Cornelius was waiting for them, having called together his kinsmen and close friends.

As Peter came in, Cornelius met him, and fell down at his feet, and bowed down before him, but Peter pulled him up, saying, "Stand up. I too am only a man." And as they talked together, he went in, and found that there was a large group gathered.

And he said to them, "You know that it is an unlawful thing for a man who is a Jew to keep company with anyone of another people, or to visit them; but God has taught me not to call any man common or unclean.

"Therefore I came to you without question, as soon as I was sent for. Now may I ask what your purpose was in sending for me?"

Cornelius told him of his vision.

Then Peter began to speak and said, "Truly I can see that God is no respecter of persons, but in every

nation the man who loves God and lives a good life is acceptable to Him."

While Peter was still speaking to them, the Holy Spirit fell on all those who heard his words. And all the disciples of the Jewish people who had come with Peter were astonished, because the gift of the Holy Spirit was poured down upon the Gentile as well. For they heard them speak in strange languages and glorify God.

Then Peter said, "Can any man deny them water to be baptized, these who have received the Holy Spirit as well as we?" And he commanded them to be baptized in the name of the Lord.

Then they begged him to stay with them there for several days.

PETER IN PRISON

NOW ABOUT that time Herod the king reached out to harass certain of the followers of Christ. He had James the brother of John killed with the sword; and because he saw that it pleased the Jews, he went on to arrest Peter, too, during the days of the Festival of Unleavened Bread.

When he had seized him, he put him in prison and assigned four squads of soldiers to guard him, intending after the Passover to bring him out for public punishment.

So Peter was kept in prison, but the prayers of the Church went up unceasingly to God for him.

When Herod was about to have him brought out, that same night Peter was sleeping between two soldiers, bound with two chains; and the keepers at the gates guarded the prison.

Lo, an angel of the Lord came to him, and a light shone in the prison, and he struck Peter on the side and raised him up, saying, "Get up quickly." And his chains fell off his hands. The angel said, "Dress yourself and put on your sandals." And he did so. Then he said to him, "Put your cloak around you and follow me."

And he went out, following him, but still did not believe that all this was really being done by the angel, but thought he was dreaming.

When they had passed the first and the second guard, they came to the iron gate that led into the city. It opened to them of its own accord, and they went out and passed along one street — and then the angel departed from him.

When Peter came to himself, he said, "Now I know most certainly that the Lord has sent His angel and has delivered me from the hand of Herod, and from all that the Jewish people were hoping for."

When he had realized this, he went to the house of Mary the mother of John, whose other name was Mark, where many of the faithful were gathered together praying.

As Peter knocked at the outer doorway, a maiden named Rhoda came to answer it. And when she recognized Peter's voice, she was so happy that she did not even open the gate but ran in and told the others that Peter was standing at the gate.

They said to her, "You are mad." But she kept insisting that it was so. Then they said, "It is his guardian angel."

But Peter continued knocking, and when they finally opened the door and saw him, they were astonished. But he, motioning them with his hand to be silent, told them how the Lord had brought him out of the prison. And he said, "Tell this thing to the brethren." And he went on, and went to another place.

Now as soon as it was day, there was no little worry among the soldiers, as to what had become of Peter. And when Herod asked for him and found that he was not there, he questioned the guards and commanded that they should be put to death.

THE SPREAD OF THE CHURCHES

NOW IN the church at Antioch there were certain prophets and teachers, as Barnabas, and Simeon who was called Niger, and Lucius of Cyrene, and Manaen, who had been brought up with Herod the governor, and Saul, who was also called Paul. And as they were performing public worship and fasting, the Holy Spirit said, "Set Barnabas and Saul apart for me for the work for which I have chosen them."

And when they had fasted and prayed together, and laid their hands on them, they sent them away. So they, being sent out by the Holy Spirit, left Seleucia, and sailed from there to Cyprus.

This was the beginning of a long journey for Paul, for in Paphos, Pamphylia, and Pisidia he spoke in the synagogues and in the streets, bringing the message of Jesus to Jews and Gentiles alike; for as Paul said to the crowds who flocked to hear him, "The Lord gave us this command: 'I have made you to be a light to the Gentiles, to be a means of salvation to the very ends of the earth.'"

Often the unbelieving Jews stirred up their own people and the Gentiles as well against Paul and Barnabas. Sometimes they were driven out of town, and once Paul was stoned and left for dead. But still they went on, now through Syria and Cilicia, teaching, baptizing, and setting up new churches for the followers of Christ.

APOSTLES MISTAKEN FOR GODS

THERE WAS a certain man of Lystra who, being a cripple from birth, had never walked. He heard Paul speak, and Paul, looking at him, and seeing that he had enough faith to be healed, said in a loud voice, "Stand up on your feet." And he leaped up and walked.

When the people saw what Paul had done, they lifted up their voices in their own language, crying: "The gods have come down to us in human form!" They called Barnabas Zeus and Paul Hermes, because he was the chief speaker.

Then the priest of Zeus, whose temple was outside the city, brought oxen wreathed with garlands to the gates, and prepared to offer a sacrifice with the people.

When the apostles, Paul and Barnabas, heard of this, they tore their clothes and ran among the people, crying out, "Sirs, why do you do these things? We are only human beings, with feelings like your own, and are preaching to you that you should turn from these vain worships to the living God, who made heaven and earth, and the sea, and all things in the world.

"In times past He let all peoples walk in their own ways, but He did not leave you without reminders of Himself, in that He did good things for you, and gave you rain from heaven and fruitful seasons, filling your hearts with food and gladness."

Even with these words, they barely stopped the people from offering sacrifices to them.

THE STORY OF EUTYCHUS

UPON THE first day of the week, when the disciples in Troas met together for the Eucharist, Paul, who was ready to depart the next day, preached to them, and continued talking until midnight.

There were many lamps burning in the upper room where they were gathered together. And in one window sat a certain young man named Eutychus, who was getting very sleepy. As Paul preached on and on, he went fast asleep, and fell from the third floor, and was picked up dead.

Paul went down and threw himself upon him, and putting his arms around him said, "Do not worry; he is still alive."

When he came up again, he broke bread and ate and talked a long while, until break of day, and then he departed. And they brought the young man home alive, and were not a little comforted.

PAUL IN PRISON

WHEN PAUL said farewell to the presbyters of the church at Miletus, he told them that he would not see them again, because, "I am going, compelled by the Holy Spirit, to Jerusalem, not knowing what may happen to me there."

In Jerusalem, Jews from Asia Minor, when they saw him in the temple, stirred up all the people, and seized him with great shouts. Then the whole city was stirred up, and people hurried together, and they took Paul and dragged him out of the temple, slamming the doors behind him.

As they were about to kill him, word came to the captain of the soldiers that all Jerusalem was in an uproar. He at once took soldiers and centurions and ran down to the place; and when the crowd saw the chief captain and his soldiers, they stopped beating Paul.

Then the chief captain came up and arrested him, and ordered him to be bound with two chains, and demanded to know who he was and what he had done.

Some cried one thing, some another, among the crowd, and since he could not learn anything for all the shouting, the captain ordered Paul to be carried into the castle.

When he came to the stairs, he had to be actually carried by the soldiers, because of the violence of the crowd; for most of the people followed after him, crying, "Away with him!"

Paul Is Spirited Away

Some of the Jews even took an oath not to eat or drink until they had killed Paul. But when Paul's

nephew brought word of this to Paul, and through him to the captain of the garrison (who knew Paul was a Roman citizen), the captain ordered two hundred armed soldiers and seventy horsemen and two hundred spearmen to escort Paul by night, on horseback, to the custody of Felix, the governor at Caesarea.

Felix the Governor

Now Felix the governor had some knowledge of the way of Christ's followers. After a few days he came with his wife Drusilla, who was a Jewess, and sent for Paul and listened to him talk about the faith of Christ. But when Paul spoke of the need for morality, and the coming judgment, he became frightened and would not listen. Still he had Paul kept safe, and let him have some liberty and as many visitors as came to see him. So Paul stayed in prison two years, until Porcius Festus took Felix's place.

Paul Appeals to Rome

When Festus came into the province, he called Paul before him and asked if he was willing to go to Jerusalem and stand trial there before him as governor. But Paul, knowing how the Jews of Jerusalem hated him, and knowing too his special rights as a citizen of Rome, said, "I will stand trial in Caesar's court at Rome; I have done the Jews no wrong, as you know."

King Agrippa Hears Paul

Some days later, King Agrippa and his sister Bernice came to Caesarea to pay their respects to Festus. And when they had been there for a while, Festus told the King about Paul's case — how the men of Jerusalem demanded his death, but the governor could find no harm in him, and how now Paul had appealed to Caesar, so that he would have to be sent to Rome for trial.

"I would like to hear this man myself," said Agrippa to Festus.

"Tomorrow," said Festus, "you shall hear him. Perhaps from your examination of him I may get something to put into writing about him; for it seems to me absurd to send a prisoner to Rome without stating what crimes he is charged with."

The next day, when Agrippa and Bernice had been ushered into the audience hall with great pomp, with the chief officers and principal men of the city about them, at Festus' command, Paul was brought in.

Then Agrippa said to Paul, "You may speak for yourself."

So Paul stretched out his hand and spoke of his beliefs; he spoke so movingly that Agrippa said, "You would soon persuade me to be a Christian."

And Paul said, "Sooner or later, I would to God that not only you but all who are listening to me today might be just as I am, except for these chains."

When he had finished speaking, the king stood up, and the governor, and Bernice, and those who had been with them; and when they had left the room, they talked among themselves, saying, "This man has done nothing worthy of death or prison."

Then Agrippa said to Festus, "This man might have been set free, if he had not appealed to Caesar."

Shipwreck on the Way to Rome

When it was decided that Paul should go to Italy, they turned him over, with some other prisoners, to a centurion named Julius, an officer in Augustus' forces. Boarding a ship of Adramyttium, they put to sea, intending to sail along the coast of Asia.

The next day they put in at Sidon, and Julius courteously gave Paul liberty to go ashore to be welcomed by his friends.

When they left there, they sailed along the coast of Cyprus, for the wind was against them. After some time, they came to Myra, a city of Lycia, where the centurion found a ship out of Alexandria sailing to Italy, and he transferred his prisoners to it.

For some time they sailed slowly, without favorable winds. When they came to a place called Fair Havens, near the city of Lasea, much time had passed, so that it was a dangerous season for sailing — for the Day of Atonement (mid-September) was already past.

Paul warned them, "Sirs, I foresee that this voyage will bring damage and loss, not only of the cargo and ship, but also of our lives."

Nevertheless the centurion believed the captain and the owner of the ship more than Paul's words. And because the harbor was not well suited for wintering in, they still thought it better to leave, if it would be at all possible to get to Phoenix in Crete, and winter there.

When the south wind blew softly, thinking that they could reach their goal, they weighed anchor and sailed along close to Crete. But it was not long before a real tempest of wind came up, and caught the ship. Since it could not face into the wind, they let it be driven along.

Running under the lee of a small island called Cauda, they had a hard time with the ship's rowboat; but when it had been taken aboard, they could run ropes under the ship to re-enforce it. Then, afraid of being caught in the quicksand, they lowered the sails and let the ship drift.

Being violently tossed about by the storm, the next day they threw some of the cargo overboard to lighten the ship; and the following day with their own hands they threw away the ship's extra equipment.

When neither sun nor stars appeared for many days, and the great tempest still raged, everyone gave up hope of being saved.

But after going without food for a long time, Paul stood up and spoke to them, telling them to be of good cheer, for an angel of the Lord had appeared to him, promising that not a life should be lost among them, but only the ship, and that they would be cast ashore upon some island.

When the fourteenth day came, and the sailors felt, about midnight, that they were coming close to land, they checked the depth of the water and put out four anchors, and let down the rowboat, planning to flee the ship.

But Paul said to the centurion and his men, "Unless these sailors stay aboard, we cannot be saved." So the soldiers cut the rowboat loose.

Then as day came on, Paul prevailed upon them all to take some food, for they had gone fourteen

days without eating. He took bread, and gave thanks to God before them all, and when he had divided it, he began to eat. Then they all cheered up and began to eat, too. And when they had eaten their fill, they lightened the ship by throwing the rest of the wheat into the sea.

When daylight came, they did not recognize the nearby shore, but they found a bay with a beach, where they planned, if possible, to run the ship ashore. When they had cut away the anchors and left them in the sea, they untied the steering rudders, and raised the mainsail to the wind, and made for shore.

Striking a reef, they ran the ship aground, and the bow stuck fast, while the stem was hammered to pieces by the waves.

The soldiers plotted to kill the prisoners, lest any of them should swim away and escape. But the centurion, wanting to save Paul, kept them from that plan, and commanded those who could swim to throw themselves first into the sea, and get to land. Then the rest came, some on boards, some on broken pieces of the wreck, and all got safely to the land.

Paul's Winter on Malta

After their escape, they discovered that the island was called Malta; and the people there were very kind. They kindled a fire and welcomed them all to it, because of the rain and the cold.

When Paul had gathered a bundle of sticks and laid them on the fire, a viper crawled out because of the heat, and fastened itself on his hand.

When the natives saw that poisonous snake hanging from his hand, they whispered among themselves, "No doubt this man is a murderer whom justice will not permit to live, even though he has escaped the sea."

But he shook the snake off into the fire, and was not harmed. They kept watching for him to swell up, or to fall down dead suddenly; but after they had watched a great while, and saw no harm come to him, they changed their minds, and said that he was a god.

The estates of the headman of the island, Publius by name, were nearby. There he welcomed Paul and entertained him pleasantly for three days. . . .

During this time, Paul cured the father of Publius, and after that all the sick on the island also came and were cured. They heaped honors upon Paul, and when he sailed away, after three months, they loaded him down with all he might need.

After three months he departed on a ship of Alexandria which had wintered on the island, and came at last, by easy stages, to Rome.

Paul in Rome

When they reached Rome, the centurion turned over his prisoners to the captain of the guard; but Paul was allowed to live by himself, with a soldier to guard him.

Now when the brethren at Rome had heard of his coming, they came to meet him as far as the Appian forum and the Three Taverns; and when Paul saw them, he thanked God and took courage again.

Since the Jews of Rome were still open-minded about him, Paul lived for two whole years in his own rented house, and welcomed all who came to him, preaching the kingdom of God and teaching about the Lord Jesus Christ with full confidence, and no one hindered him.

PAUL'S LETTERS

ON HIS MANY travels and during his stay in Rome, first in a house of his own and later in prison, Paul kept in touch by letter with the churches he had founded.

Timothy, his beloved assistant, often wrote these letters as Paul dictated them, and went himself as a messenger to deliver them to the people. Many other faithful members of the young churches also took their turns in carrying these letters full of advice, encouragement, instruction, and affection.

Letters from Paul and some of the other apostles make up most of the rest of the New Testament. Here are some of the most beautiful parts of Paul's letters.

Faith, Hope, and Charity

Though I speak in the languages of men and of angels, if I have not charity, I am like a noisy gong or a tinkling cymbal. And though I have the gift of prophecy, and understand all mysteries and all knowledge, and though I have all faith, so that I could move mountains, if I do not have charity, I am nothing.

And though I give all my goods to feed the poor, and though I give my body to be burned, if I do not have charity, it is worth nothing.

Charity is patient, and is kind; charity is not jealous or boastful, is not puffed up; does not make any parade, seeks nothing for itself, is not easily provoked, thinks no evil. Charity is never pleased by wickedness, but rejoices with the truth; bears all things, believes all things, hopes all things, endures all things.

Charity never fails; but where there are prophecies, they shall end; where there is the gift of languages, it shall fall silent; where there is knowledge, it shall vanish.

For we know in part, and we prophesy in part; but when that which is perfect comes, that which was imperfect shall pass away.

When I was a child, I spoke as a child, I understood as a child, I thought as a child; but when I became a man, I put away childish things.

For now we see as in a dim mirror, darkly; but then, face to face. Now I understand in part, but then I shall understand as clearly as God understands me.

Now these three remain: faith, hope, and charity; but the greatest of these is charity.

The Armor of God

Be strengthened in the Lord, and in the strength of His power. Put on the armor of God, so that you may be able to stand up against the plots of the devil. For we wrestle not against flesh and blood, but against the princedoms and powers and rulers of the darkness of this world, against supernatural forces of spiritual wickedness.

Therefore take up the armor of God, so that you may be able to resist in the day of evil, and to stand perfect in all things.

Take your stand, then, with the belt of truth about your waist, and wearing the breastplate of justice, and on your feet the swift shoes of the gospel of peace. Above all, take the shield of faith, with which you will be able to put out all the flaming darts of the wicked. And take the helmet of salvation, and the sword of the Spirit, which is the word of God.

Paul Views His Own Work

Are there servants of Christ? (I speak in jest) I am more! Harder at work, beaten countless times, in prison more often, and often in danger of death.

Five times I have been given thirty-nine lashes by the Jews. Three times I was beaten with rods, once I was stoned. Three times have I suffered shipwreck; once I was adrift on the sea for a day and a night.

Often on my journeys I have been in danger from flooded rivers, in danger from robbers, in danger from my own people, in danger from the Gentiles, in danger in the city, in danger in the wilderness, in danger among false brethren.

I have known labor and hardship, nights without sleep, hunger and thirst, many fasts, and cold and lack of shelter. Besides all these things thrust upon me from outside, there is that which is with me every day, my anxiety for all the churches.

But now I am already being poured out in sacrifice, and the time of my deliverance is near.

I have fought the good fight; I have finished the race; I have kept the faith. Now there awaits me a crown of justice, which the Lord, the just judge, will give me on that day — and not to me only, but to all those who have lovingly waited for his coming.

When all men forsook me, the Lord stood by me and strengthened me; and the Lord shall deliver me from all evil, and will bring me safely to His heavenly kingdom; to Him be glory forever and ever. Amen.

THE VISION OF GLORY

THE NEW Church had some sad and difficult days. Peter and Paul were both put to death in Rome for their faith, and many others suffered also for Christ. To encourage the faithful, by reminding them of the rewards in store for them in the life to come, Saint John wrote a vivid account of his vision of the kingdom of Heaven, saying in part:

And I saw a new Heaven and a new earth: for the first Heaven and the first earth had passed away, and there was no more sea.

And I heard a great voice from the throne saying, "Behold, the dwelling of God with men, and He will dwell with them, and they shall be His people, and God Himself shall be with them as their God. And God shall wipe away every tear from their eyes; and there shall be no more death, nor mourning nor crying; neither shall there be any more pain; for the former things have passed away."

And he carried me away in the spirit to a great and high mountain, and showed me the holy city, Jerusalem, descending out of Heaven from God, having the glory of God. And her light was like a most precious stone, even like a jasper stone, clear as crystal. The city had a wall great and high, with twelve gates, and at the gates twelve angels.

Now the wall was of jasper; and the city was pure gold, as clear as glass. And the foundations of the wall of the city were adorned with all kinds of precious stones. And the twelve gates were twelve pearls, each gate was of one pearl; and the street of the city was pure gold, like transparent glass.

I saw no temple in it, for the Lord God almighty and the Lamb of God are the temple of it. And the city had no need of the sun, nor of the moon, to shine in it; for the glory of God lighted it, and the Lamb of God is its light.

And he showed me a river of the water of life, clear as crystal, flowing out of the throne of God. In the middle of the golden street, on both sides of the river grew the tree of life, which bore twelve kinds of

fruit, and yielded a fruit every month; and the leaves of the tree were for the healing of the nations.

The throne of God shall be there, and His servants shall serve Him, and they shall see His face, and His name shall be on their foreheads. And they shall need neither candle nor the light of the sun, for the Lord God gives them light; and they shall reign forever and ever.

And he said to me, "These words are trustworthy and true; and the Lord, the God of the spirits of the prophets, sent His angel to show to His servants what must come shortly to pass. Blessed is he who keeps the words of the prophecy of this book.

"And my reward is with me, to render to each one according to his works. I am the beginning and the end. I, Jesus, have sent my angel to testify to you concerning the churches. I am the root and offspring of David, the bright morning star."

The grace of Our Lord Jesus Christ be with all.

THE STORY OF THE BIBLE

HEN WE read the Bible, we should remember that it is not one book, but many. It was not all written at the same time, or in the same place, or even in the same language. The writing of its various books went on for a thousand years. Some were written by prophets, others by poets, wise men, and apostles and evangelists. Some books were written in Palestine; others were written in Egypt or Babylonia, at Antioch or Rome. Most of the Old Testament books were written in Hebrew, though some are in Greek. The books of the New Testament are all in Greek because this was the language most widely used in our Lord's time.

In spite of their differences, the books of the Bible belong together. They have one message. They are held together by one wonderful fact — they were all written by God. The Bible is really the Word of God. Men held the pens that wrote the words, but God gave them His knowledge and His understanding; He shared His truth with them. There is nothing in the Bible that God did not want to be written. There is nothing in it that He did not inspire. The Bible is His word. His book. His truth.

The Bible tells the story of God's dealings with men from the beginning to the end of the world. It starts in Genesis with the creation of the universe. It ends, in St. John's Revelation, with the coming of God's kingdom. The whole span of history, the beginning and the end of time, is contained in this Book of Books. It begins with the creation of Heaven and earth and closes with the creation of "a new Heaven and a new earth."

Between these two events a plan unfolds. The plan is God's redemption of mankind. After man was created and placed in the Garden of Eden, he betrayed God's trust and committed the first sin. By this sin, Adam lost the gift of eternal life for himself and all his children. But God promised to give mankind a new Adam — a Savior who would come to deliver us from sin. This Savior, the Messiah, is spoken of throughout the Old Testament. Slowly, our picture of Him becomes clearer, more definite, more wonderful.

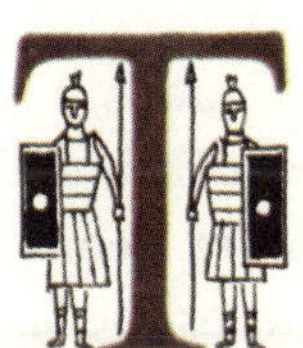

HE OLD Testament is a book of prophecy, a book of hope. It tells us what is to come and prepares the way for the Savior. It is also a book of promise, of an agreement — or testament — between God and man. Abraham and his sons promised to worship and obey God. God promised to make them a great nation, to give them the Land of Canaan, and to send a Savior to deliver them from sin. The promise which God made to Abraham was to be fulfilled in Him who is both the son of Abraham and the Son of God — Jesus Christ.

The Old Testament tells us that a Savior will come. It records God's promise that He would bring the children of Abraham into a land "flowing with milk and honey" and keep them safe, if they would serve Him and keep His commandments. The commandments were not kept, God was disobeyed, and the Jews were carried away as slaves to Babylon. But God's great promise of a Savior still remained.

In the reign of Caesar Augustus, when "all the world was at peace," the Savior came. Christ was born at Bethlehem, God's promise was fulfilled, and a new way of life began. The books of the New Testament record the testament of forgiveness brought by Christ, the testament of grace begun on Calvary — a testament not only promised, but fulfilled. The Redeemer who had been spoken of in prophecy has really come. The salvation which God promised to Adam has come in the new Adam — Christ Our Lord.

JUST AS the two Testaments differ, though both contain God's word to men, so the various books differ from each other. Each book of the Bible was written for a special purpose. Some of them are historical. Others are prophetic. Some teach wisdom or give advice. Others were written chiefly to praise God. One of them, the Psalms, is really a collection of hymns.

The historical books — including Genesis, Exodus, Numbers, Joshua, Judges, Kings, Ezra and Maccabees — tell the story of God's chosen people, the children of Israel. Genesis, which means "beginning," tells the story of creation and the beginning of the people of Israel. In Exodus, which means "going out," we read of the miraculous escape of the Israelites from Egypt. The book of Numbers tells of their entry into the Promised Land of Canaan. Joshua relates their fight to win the land. Judges tells of the heroes who defended Israel after Joshua's death. The books of Kings tell of the division of the people into two warring camps, the idolatries of their kings, and the final carrying away into Babylon. The books of Ezra tell of the joyful return to Palestine, and the books of the Maccabees bring us almost to the time of Christ.

Besides history, the Bible contains books which are almost novels. There are two love stories, that of Ruth and that of Tobias, and stories of two great heroines who saved their people, Judith and Esther.

The book of Job, like the book of Psalms, is a book of wisdom. It tells how even suffering can bring us closer to God. The Psalms, which were begun by David, are a collection of sacred hymns used in the Temple worship. The various books of the prophets contain the warnings of God's messengers telling His people of the punishment which would come for their sins. But when punishment had come, the prophets foretold God's forgiveness and the return home. Among the greatest of them was ISAIAH, who told of the sufferings of the Messiah, and Daniel, who bore witness to God in Babylon before a pagan king.

NOT IN words alone, however, is the message of the Bible contained. The events it describes really happened. The wisdom it teaches is a light for all men. Its prophecies have been fulfilled. But the Bible also contains hidden pictures of things to come. The escape of Israel from slavery in Egypt is one of these — a picture of our release from original sin through Baptism. Like the children of Israel, we pass through a sea — not the Red Sea, but the water of the baptismal font. Like Israel, we are redeemed by the blood of a lamb — not the Passover Lamb, but the Lamb of God. Like Israel, we share a sacred meal — not the Passover supper, but the Eucharist. Like Israel, we offer sacrifice to God — not the sacrifice of sheep and oxen, but the perfect sacrifice of Calvary.

Christ Himself showed us one of these pictures when He compared Himself to the prophet Jonah, telling His apostles that just as Jonah was three days in the belly of the "great fish," so He would be three days in the "belly of the earth." And, like Jonah, He would come out again.

IN THE beginning of the New Testament we find the four Gospels which tell the story of Christ's earthly life. Though they are four books, they have one message, one story. The Gospel of Matthew stresses the human side of our Lord's life. For this reason, Matthew and his Gospel are usually represented under the symbol of a manlike being — an angel. The Gospel of Mark tells of Christ's kingly power and of His many miracles, and so Mark and his Gospel are often shown under the symbol of kingship — a lion. The Gospel of Luke tells of Christ's death for mankind. His perfect sacrifice for us on Calvary. Luke and his Gospel are therefore often represented by the symbol of sacrifice — an ox. John's Gospel tells us of Christ's Divinity. He and his Gospel are represented as an eagle, whose farseeing eyes can pierce the heights of Heaven.

After the Gospels comes the Acts of the Apostles, written by St. Luke, which tells of the earliest days of the Church. In the Acts we learn of the heroic death of Stephen, the first martyr, and of the travels and labors of St. Peter and St. Paul. Following the Acts are various Epistles, or letters, written by the apostles to the first Christians. Most of these were the work of St. Paul.

With the Revelation of St. John, the only book of prophecy in the New Testament, our Bible comes to an end. The Apocalypse, which means "removing the veil," tells of the Church's struggle against evil and godless men, the final victory of Christ, and the coming of the new and heavenly Jerusalem — the eternal city of God. Heaven and earth will be made new, and the saints will live and rejoice with Him forever. The plan which began in Genesis is at last complete. Mankind will come to eternal happiness, the perfect knowledge and love of God for which God created him. The Revelation "removes the veil" from the work of God and shows His perfect plan for us.

This is our Bible, "the library of God," as St. Jerome called it.

HE MISSIONARY WORK of the apostles among people who spoke Greek — and almost everyone spoke some Greek in those days — was made much easier by having a Greek translation of the Old Testament to quote from. This version is called the Septuagint, or "Seventy," because it was said to have been made by seventy wise men who all agreed with each other. But the translation was really made by Greek-speaking Jews of Alexandria, Egypt, about three hundred years before the birth of Christ.

The Septuagint contains certain books which seem to have been written originally in Greek, not in Hebrew, and were not much read in Palestine. When the Jews of Palestine collected their sacred books, which were all in Hebrew, these books in Greek were left out of the list. That is why most Protestants, who follow the list of Old Testament books made in Palestine, do not have these "extra" books in their Bibles.

TAKING THE Bible as their guide, archaeologists have been able to find long-lost cities and uncover many ancient ruins. Walls have been found at Jericho, broken by some great force, just as the book of Joshua relates. Historians have found that the book of Acts — which tells the story of St. Paul's missionary journeys — gives an accurate picture of the world during the first century A.D. The Bible and history have often gone hand in hand, each shedding light on the other, each confirming what the other says.

The Church has always loved the Bible. Priests and deacons suffered martyrdom rather than surrender the sacred books to pagans. The Gospel book is still honored with incense at a solemn Mass, as though it were Christ Himself. Often the Gospels were placed on a throne to take Christ's place at Church councils.

The Church uses the Bible as a foundation for her teaching and the source of her art. The great cathedrals of Europe are full of carvings, mosaics, and paintings based on the Bible. The first book printed, in 1452 by Gutenberg, was St. Jerome's Latin version of the Bible. The Church's clergy, theologians, and scholars must know and study the Bible, for as St. Jerome said, "Ignorance of the Bible is ignorance of Christ."

Next to the Blessed Sacrament of the Altar, the Bible is the Church's greatest treasure. And, like the Eucharist, it too contains Christ — not in His Body and Blood, but in His word and His truth.

THE HOLY SACRIFICE OF THE MASS

The Priest Comes to the Altar

WHEN WE attend Mass on Sundays and Holydays, we are obeying the command that Jesus gave us at the Last Supper when He said, "Do this in memory of Me."

At that first Mass, on the first Holy Thursday, He gave His own Body and Blood to His Apostles under the appearance of bread and wine. The Church teaches us that when Christ said "This is My body" and "This is My blood" the bread and wine were truly changed into His Body and Blood — to be our spiritual food and a way to eternal life.

The next day, the first Good Friday, Christ completed His giving of Himself to us by dying on the cross for our sins. His gift of Himself as our food and His gift of Himself as a sacrifice for our sins are really one gift, one sacrifice.

Because the Mass and Calvary are one sacrifice, one gift, they can never be separated. Every time we go to Mass, we share in the sacrifice of Calvary and offer the same victim, Jesus Christ, to God the Father. Every time we receive Holy Communion, we receive the same Body and Blood that Christ gave to the Apostles at the Last Supper.

Through the centuries, the Church has obeyed Christ's command, "Do this in memory of Me," and has brought the Mass to every nation and people. What began in a little room in Jerusalem has spread throughout the world. And the Mass will continue until Christ comes again in glory at the end of time.

Only through the Mass can we offer to God the perfect victim — Jesus Christ, His Son, Our Lord.

Prayers of Preparation

WE BEGIN the Mass by making the Sign of the Cross and by confessing our sins to God and asking for His forgiveness. The priest and altar boys stand at the foot of the altar.

In the Confession prayer, the *Confiteor,* we ask for the prayers of the Virgin Mary and all the saints to free us from sin and bring us into everlasting life with them.

After the prayers of preparation, the priest goes to the altar and kisses it. This kiss represents the great love between Christ and His Church. It is also a greeting to the martyrs whose relics are kept in the altar stone.

The Introit

THE PRIEST now goes to the right, or Epistle, side of the altar to read the *Introit.* These are verses taken from the book of Psalms.

In Latin, *Introit* means "he enters." It was originally sung when the bishop or priest entered the church to begin Mass. The words of the *Introit* are chosen to fit the theme of the Mass about to be celebrated and to prepare our minds for prayer. Thus it is important to follow the text in our Missals.

When he has finished the *Introit,* the priest returns to the center of the altar to begin the *Kyrie.*

The Kyrie

THE PRIEST now says, alternately with the server, *"Kyrie, eleison*—Lord, have mercy" and *"Christe, eleison*—Christ, have mercy."

The *Kyrie* is a prayer to the Blessed Trinity. The first petition, *"Kyrie, eleison,"* is said three times and is addressed to God the Father.

The second petition, *"Christe, eleison,"* is said three times and is addressed to God the Son. The third petition, again *"Kyrie, eleison,"* is also said three times and is addressed to God the Holy Spirit.

This prayer reminds us that at Mass we worship the three Persons of the Blessed Trinity.

The Gloria

AFTER THE *Kyrie,* the priest says the *"Gloria in Excelsis*—Glory to God in the highest," which begins with the words the angels sang at Christ's birth. Like the *Kyrie,* the *Gloria* honors the Blessed Trinity. It is omitted in Lent, Advent, and Masses for the dead.

After the *Gloria,* the priest turns to us and spreads his hands in greeting, saying, *"Dominus, vobiscum*—The Lord be with you." We answer, *"Et cum spiritu tuo*—And with your spirit." This greeting occurs many times in the Mass. It reminds us of the unity between priest and people and tells us that something important is about to begin.

The Collect

THE PRIEST goes to the right side of the altar to read the *Collect,* or *Prayer,* which changes every Sunday and feast day.

The word *Collect* is from the Latin *"collecta,"* which means "gathering." It represents the intentions of the congregation gathered together for Mass.

Every *Collect* begins with a greeting to God and usually mentions some great thing He has done for us. It then asks for a special gift or help from Him and offers the entire prayer "through Jesus Christ, Your Son, Our Lord, who lives and reigns with You in the unity of the Holy Spirit."

The Epistle

AFTER THE *Collect,* the priest reads a lesson usually taken from one of the Epistles. During the reading, the priest keeps his hands on the book as a sign that we should not only hear the Word of God but do it.

After the *Epistle,* the priest reads two Psalm verses called the *Gradual* from *"gradus*—step" because of the place from which the Gradual was sung in the early Church.

After the *Gradual* comes an *Alleluia* verse to prepare us for the "good news" of the Gospel. In penitential seasons, a longer set of verses called the *Tract,* from the Latin word for "long," is read instead.

The Gospel

THE PRIEST goes to the center of the altar, bows low, and asks God to cleanse his "heart and lips." He then greets us with *"Dominus vobiscum"* and announces the *Gospel,* telling us the name of the evangelist from whose writings the reading is taken. With his thumb, he makes a small Sign of the Cross on the page to mark the beginning of the reading, then makes three more crosses on his forehead, lips, and breast while we do the same. These crosses are a sign that we must prepare our minds, lips, and hearts to receive the words of Christ.

After we answer, *"Gloria tibi, Domine*— Glory to You, O Lord," he reads the *Gospel.*

The Creed

AFTER THE *Gospel* reading, the priest goes to the center of the altar to say the Nicene Creed, the Church's hymn of faith.

Like the Kyrie and Gloria, the Creed praises the Trinity. Its first part tells us of "the Father almighty, Creator of heaven and earth." The second speaks of "Jesus Christ, the only-begotten Son of God." At the words "and He was incarnate by the Holy Spirit of the Virgin Mary And Was Made Man," we genuflect with the priest to honor Christ's Incarnation.

The third part tells us of the Holy Spirit, "the Lord and Giver of Life, who spoke through the prophets."

The Offertory Verse

THE PRIEST turns and greets us with *"Dominus vobiscum"* to call our attention to the offering of bread and wine which is about to take place.

Until now, the Mass has been very much like the ancient synagogue service with its readings, psalms, and prayers. Now the sacrificial part of the Mass is about to begin.

The priest reads the *Offertory Verse* chosen especially for each Mass. This verse was once sung while the people brought their gifts of bread and wine to the altar.

The *Offertory Verse* encourages us to give ourselves to Christ in order that He may bring us to His Father in heaven.

Offering the Bread

THE PRIEST raises the paten and host, saying, "Receive, Holy Father, almighty and everlasting God, this spotless host which I, Your unworthy servant, offer to You . . . for all who are present here and for all faithful Christians, both living and dead."

The bread and wine used at Mass were once brought to the altar in a great procession in which the people carried their gifts of bread and wine. The procession meant that we should not only offer our gifts to God, but that we should bring Him our lives as well. Just as the priest offers the host to God, so should we give ourselves to Him.

Preparing the Chalice

THE PRIEST first fills the chalice with wine. He then blesses water and adds a few drops of it to the wine, asking God that "by the mingling of this water and wine we may be made sharers in His divine nature who was pleased to share our human nature — Jesus Christ, Your Son, Our Lord."

The drops of water represent ourselves. The chalice of wine represents Christ.

Just as the water mixes with the wine and becomes one with it, so can we become one with Christ. Just as Christ came down from Heaven to share our human life, so can we share His divine life. If we give ourselves to Him, He will give Himself to us and bring us to His Father in Heaven. If we live only for His sake, we will become one with Him.

After the chalice has been filled the priest raises it and prays: "We offer to You, O Lord, the chalice of salvation and beg that by Your mercy it may ascend before Your divine majesty with a pleasing fragrance for our salvation and that of all the world." The words "pleasing fragrance" refer to the incense sacrifices of the Old Testament which were a symbol of perfect prayer.

The priest then bows low and asks that we who are "humble in spirit" and "contrite of heart" may be accepted with our gifts of bread and wine which are now on the altar.

This reminds us that the Mass is a truly spiritual worship. We must be sincere in giving ourselves to God.

The priest then makes the Sign of the Cross over our gifts and prays to the Holy Spirit: "Come, O Sanctifier, almighty and everlasting God, and bless this sacrifice prepared for Your holy Name."

The Lavabo

IN THE early Church, gifts of food and clothing, as well as bread and wine, were brought to the altar at the *Offertory.*

Because the priest usually received these gifts from the hands of the faithful, his own hands often became soiled and had to be washed before continuing the Mass. This is why the priest washes his hands while saying part of Psalm 25: "I will wash my hands in innocence."

He then says a prayer to the Holy Trinity, offering the Mass not only in honor of Christ's death, but of His Resurrection and Ascension as well.

The Secret

THE PRIEST now prays the oldest Offertory prayer of the Mass, the *Secret.*

After the gifts of bread and wine were brought to the altar, the priests set apart — "made secret" in Latin — enough of the bread and wine for Communion. A special prayer was said over "the things set apart" and was called the "*Secreta,*" or Secret.

In the course of time, other prayers were added to this old Offertory prayer.

The *Secret,* like the *Collect,* changes with each Mass. It usually asks God to receive our gifts of bread and wine and to give us His gift of Holy Communion in return.

Preface and Sanctus

THE PRIEST asks us to raise our minds to God, saying, *"Sursum corda*—Lift up your hearts." We answer that we are already thinking about God. *"Habemus ad Dominum*—We have lifted them to the Lord."

He then says, *"Gratias agamus Domino Deo nostro*—Let us give thanks to the Lord, our God." We reply, *"Dignum et justum est*—It is fitting and right [to thank Him]."

These words come from the Passover prayers used by Jesus at the Last Supper.

The priest then offers a prayer of thanksgiving called the *Preface,* which joins our worship with the worship of the angels in the *Sanctus* hymn.

You, therefore . . .

THE MOST solemn prayer of the Mass, the *Canon,* begins with the words *"Te igitur . . .* You, therefore, most merciful Father, we humbly beg and pray, through Jesus Christ Our Lord."

The priest asks God to accept and bless the bread and wine we have offered. He asks Him to protect the Church, the pope, our bishop and all bishops who believe and teach the Catholic faith.

He prays for the faithful who gather "around the altar" and mentions some of them by name. He also remembers the saints: the Virgin Mary, St. Paul, eleven of the apostles, and twelve early martyrs of Rome.

Consecrating Our Gifts

THE PRIEST now offers two prayers asking God to accept this sacrifice in the name of all His Church, both clergy and people.

"This oblation [sacrifice] of our ministry and of all Your family we therefore beg You to accept. Govern our days in Your peace, save us from eternal damnation, and number us in Your chosen flock, through Jesus Christ Our Lord. Amen."

The priest then says a prayer whose words are borrowed from old Roman law. He asks that our sacrifice may be "approved, ratified, reasonable, and acceptable" in God's sight.

The prayer goes on to ask that the bread and wine now on the altar may be changed, for our sake, into "the Body and Blood of Your beloved Son, Jesus Christ our Lord." Bowing low over the altar, the priest takes the bread into his hands and says: "The day before He suffered He took bread into His holy and worshipful hands, and raised His eyes to Heaven — to You, God, His almighty Father — gave thanks to You, blessed it, broke it, and gave it to His disciples, saying 'Take and eat of it, all of you,

FOR THIS IS MY BODY.' "

With these words the priest does what Christ did at the Last Supper when He changed bread into His body and wine into His blood. The bread is no more; only the appearance of bread remains, for the body of Christ alone is truly there.

Our gift to God has become God's gift to us, the body of His beloved Son, our Lord Jesus Christ.

Elevating the Host

THE PRIEST genuflects to adore Christ present in the host. He then raises the host for us to see and adore. This is done to remind us that Christ was raised on the cross.

When the bell rings, we should look up at the host and quietly say the words St. Thomas the Apostle used when he saw the risen Christ: "My Lord and my God!"

Consecrating the Wine

THE PRIEST says, "In the same way, after supper, He took this noble chalice in His holy and worshipful hands, then gave thanks to You, blessed it, and gave it to His disciples, saying, 'Take and drink of it, all of you,

FOR THIS IS THE CHALICE OF MY BLOOD
OF THE NEW AND ETERNAL TESTAMENT
— THE MYSTERY OF FAITH —
WHICH WILL BE SHED FOR YOU
AND FOR MANY TO FORGIVE SINS.' "

The words "Mystery of Faith" are believed to have originally been said aloud by a deacon to tell the people that the consecration was taking place — that Christ was coming.

Elevating the Chalice

THE PRIEST genuflects to adore Christ truly present in the chalice.

He then raises the chalice for us to see and adore.

When the bell rings, we should look up to the chalice and welcome our Savior with the same words we used to greet Him in the host: "My Lord and my God!"

"We offer . . ."

THE PRIEST first recalls our Savior's death, resurrection, and ascension. He then offers Christ's Body and Blood to God the Father: "We offer to Your most glorious Majesty . . . the holy bread of eternal life and the chalice of everlasting salvation."

He then asks that our sacrifice may please God as did the sacrifices of Abel, Abraham, and Melchizedek. Then, bowing low, he prays that the Body and Blood of Christ on our altar may "be carried by the hand of Your holy angel to Your altar on high. . . ." These words remind us that the Mass is the same perfect sacrifice Christ offered on Calvary.

"All Honor and Glory . . ."

THE PRIEST now asks God to remember all faithful Christians "who have gone before us with the sign of faith and sleep the sleep of peace."

The "sign of faith" is the sign of the cross given to all of us at Baptism — the same sign under which we live and die as Christians.

The priest then mentions some of our departed friends by name and asks that they, and "all who rest in Christ," may share the peace of Heaven and dwell in "a place of refreshment, of light, and peace."

He humbly prays for himself and his fellow clergy, saying, "And to us sinners [striking his breast] . . . give some share and fellowship with Your apostles and martyrs. . . ." He names two apostles, Matthias and Barnabas, then St. John the Baptist, St. Stephen, the first martyr, and other early martyrs especially venerated at Rome, and prays that we may "enter into their company."

All we have done and prayed for at this Mass is now given to God with the words "through Christ Our Lord."

The priest first praises our Savior as the Word of God through whom the Father creates and blesses "all good things." He then raises both host and chalice, saying, "Through Him and with Him and in Him all honor and glory are given to You, O God the Father almighty, in the unity of the Holy Spirit." Now the great prayer of the *Canon* is coming to an end. Like most of the Church's prayers, it is a prayer to God the Father offered through Christ His Son. This offering of a prayer "through Christ" is done because Our Lord promised that whatever we asked His Father "in My Name" would be done.

The Breaking of Bread

THE PRIEST has now done what Jesus did at the Last Supper when He said "This is My body. This is My blood." And God has changed our humble gifts into His only-begotten Son, Christ Our Lord.

We have offered this gift, this perfect victim, back to God, just as Christ offered Himself for us on Calvary. And God has received this offering, because we have made it in the name of His beloved Son.

Now we are to share the divine food God has given us, but before we do so we must pray to receive it worthily. We have no better prayer than the one Christ taught us, the *Our Father*. That is why the priest now says, "Taught by His saving precepts and strengthened by His divine command, we are bold to say: Our Father, who art in Heaven . . ."

After the *Our Father* comes the breaking of the bread. At the Last Supper, Christ broke the bread before He gave it to the Apostles. In the early Church, the breaking of the bread was one of the most solemn ceremonies in preparation for Holy Communion. Small hosts have taken the place of the large loaves, but the ceremony still remains.

The priest says a prayer for peace based on the last words of the *Our Father:* "but deliver us from evil."

"Deliver us, O Lord, from all evil, past, present, and coming. . . . Mercifully give peace in our days that by the help of Your mercy we may always be free from sin and safe from all trouble."

He then breaks a small piece from the host and drops it into the chalice. This is a sign that the Body and Blood of Christ are united, that He has risen from the dead.

"O Lamb of God . . ."

ST. JOHN the Baptist greeted Christ as the "Lamb of God." The priest now repeats his words, saying:

> "Lamb of God, who takes away the sins of the world, have mercy on us.
> "Lamb of God, who takes away the sins of the world, have mercy on us.
> "Lamb of God, who takes away the sins of the world, give us peace."

Until now, we have been praying to God the Father through His Son. In this prayer, we pray to Christ Himself, present in the Blessed Sacrament.

Prayers before Communion

THE PRIEST now says three prayers to prepare himself for Holy Communion.

The first begins, "Lord Jesus Christ, You told Your apostles: 'Peace I leave with you, My peace I give to you.' Do not look at my sins but at the faith of Your Church, and give her peace and unity according to Your will." The next asks, "Deliver me from all my sins and from every evil by Your most holy Body and Blood. Make me always keep Your commandments and never let me be separated from You."

The third prayer asks that this Holy Communion which we are about to receive may protect and heal us in both soul and body.

"Behold the Lamb . . ."

THE PRIEST holds up a small host and says: "Behold the Lamb of God. Behold Him who takes away the sins of the world!"

We say, three times:

"Lord, I am not worthy for You to come under my roof. Only say the word and my soul will be healed."

This is the moment we have waited for since the beginning of Mass. God is giving us His perfect Gift—Jesus Christ, His Son.

As the priest gives Communion to us, he says, "May the Body and Blood of Jesus Christ keep your soul for everlasting life."

The Communion Verse

THE PRIEST reverently cleanses the chalice and paten to prevent any part of Our Lord's Body and Blood from being lost. He prays that "what we have taken with our mouth we may receive with a pure mind." He also asks that "no stain of sin" may remain in us "who have been fed with this pure and holy Sacrament."

He then goes to the right side of the altar to read the *Communion Verse.* This is a verse taken from the long Psalm once sung as people came in procession to receive Our Lord in the Blessed Sacrament.

The *Communion Verse* is usually joyous and helps us to give special thanks to God for the gift of His Son.

The Postcommunion

AFTER THE priest reads the *Communion Verse,* he greets us with *"Dominus vobiscum,"* turns again to the altar, and reads the *Postcommunion.*

Like the *Collect* and the *Secret,* the *Postcommunion* changes with each Mass. It usually asks that what we have done at Mass may help us live holy lives on earth and bring us to eternal life in Heaven.

The *Postcommunion* often tells us that the Mass is really the beginning of our eternal life, that the Communion we have received is God's promise of heavenly joy and a proof of His great love for us.

Dismissal and Blessing

THE PRIEST greets us again with *"Dominus vobiscum,"* then says, *"Ite, missa est*—Go, it is the dismissal." We answer, *"Deo gratias*—Thanks be to God."

The Latin word for Mass, "missa," is believed to have come from these words.

The priest turns to the altar and prays that his celebration of the Mass has been pleasing to God: "May the service of my ministry be pleasing to you, O Holy Trinity..."

He then turns and blesses us, saying, "May almighty God bless you, Father, Son, and Holy Spirit."

The Last Gospel

Read in the Traditional Latin Mass

ONE OF the most beautiful passages in all Holy Scripture is the beginning of St. John's Gospel, read as the *Gospel* for the third Mass of Christmas. In the Middle Ages, this passage was much loved and was often used in blessings. This is probably why it is still read here as an additional blessing at the end of Mass.

The priest goes to the left side of the altar, called the Gospel side, and greets us with *"Dominus vobiscum."* He then announces the reading: "The beginning of the Holy Gospel according to John."

The reading tells of Christ's Divinity and His reign from all eternity with His Father: "In the beginning was the Word [Christ], and the Word was with God, and the Word was God.... All things were made through Him, and without Him was made nothing that has been made."

This is the same lesson the *Creed* taught us earlier in the Mass — that Christ is "God of God, Light of Light, true God of true God." When the priest reads the words, "And the Word Was Made Flesh and Dwelt Among Us," we genuflect with him in reverence for Christ's incarnation.

At the end of the reading we say, "Deo *gratias* — Thanks be to God!"

Then, if this is a low Mass, the priest kneels before the altar to lead us in the "prayers after Mass." These prayers ask God to protect the freedom of His Church and to defend us from Satan's power through St. Michael the Archangel, the heavenly warrior. They are always offered for Russia because it is the Church's prayer that the rule of godless men there may end and that Christianity may again flourish among the Russian people.

Sophia Institute

Sophia Institute is a nonprofit institution that seeks to nurture the spiritual, moral, and cultural life of souls and to spread the gospel of Christ in conformity with the authentic teachings of the Roman Catholic Church.

Sophia Institute Press fulfills this mission by offering translations, reprints, and new publications that afford readers a rich source of the enduring wisdom of mankind.

Sophia Institute also operates the popular online resource CatholicExchange.com. *Catholic Exchange* provides world news from a Catholic perspective as well as daily devotionals and articles that will help readers to grow in holiness and live a life consistent with the teachings of the Church.

In 2013, Sophia Institute launched Sophia Institute for Teachers to renew and rebuild Catholic culture through service to Catholic education. With the goal of nurturing the spiritual, moral, and cultural life of souls, and an abiding respect for the role and work of teachers, we strive to provide materials and programs that are at once enlightening to the mind and ennobling to the heart; faithful and complete, as well as useful and practical.

Sophia Institute gratefully recognizes the Solidarity Association for preserving and encouraging the growth of our apostolate over the course of many years. Without their generous and timely support, this book would not be in your hands.

www.SophiaInstitute.com
www.CatholicExchange.com
www.SophiaTeachers.org

Sophia Institute Press is a registered trademark of Sophia Institute.
Sophia Institute is a tax-exempt institution as defined by the
Internal Revenue Code, Section 501(c)(3). Tax ID 22-2548708.